Otra vez para
Roberto,
compañero
artístico
de Hugo

agosto de '95

COMPAÑEROS
AN ANTHOLOGY OF
WRITINGS
ABOUT
LATIN AMERICA

COMPAÑEROS

AN ANTHOLOGY OF WRITINGS ABOUT LATIN AMERICA

EDITED BY
HUGH HAZELTON
AND
GARY GEDDES

CORMORANT BOOKS

Published with the assistance of The Canada Council,
the Secretary of State for Multiculturalism, and the Ontario Arts Council.

Cover from an acrylic on canvas, entitled *Andino,* by Ana María Pavela,
courtesy of the artist.

Printed and bound in Canada for
Cormorant Books
RR 1, Dunvegan
Ontario, Canada
K0C 1J0

Canadian Cataloguing in Publication Data

Main entry under title:

Compañeros

Includes texts translated from Spanish and French.
ISBN 0-920953-37-9

    1. Latin America—Literary collections.
2. Canadian literature (English)—20th century.
3. Canadian literature (French)—Translations into
English. 4. Canadian literature (Spanish)—
Translations into English. 5. Canadian
literature (English)—Translations from French.
6. Canadian literature (English)—Translations
from Spanish. 7. Canadian literature—Spanish-
Candian authors. I. Hazelton, Hugh, 1946-
II. Geddes, Gary, 1940-

PS8237.L38C64 1990 C810.8.0328   C91-090006-X
PR9194.52.L38C64 1990

Table of Contents

V Brazil, Argentina, Uruguay

VI Chile

Introduction

Latin America is both a unity and a vast galaxy of different national and individual experiences: eighteen countries and one colony that speak Spanish, another nation and several colonies that speak French, and a single country, the largest, that speaks Portuguese. The area covered by these peoples includes one entire continent and a third of another, plus a sea of islands. Although climate and national character differ, Latin Americans share many patterns of historical and intellectual development. To the Canadian and *québécois* imaginations, Latin America has always represented the other and the self, the remote and culturally exotic together with the familiar face of the Americas.

Compañeros is a collection of poetry, short fiction, and descriptive writing about Latin America. The eighty-seven authors who are represented include English-Canadians, *québécois*, and Latin Americans who have immigrated to Canada. Half the work included has been translated from French and Spanish, most of it for the first time. Almost all of the pieces have been written in the last two decades, as Canada has emerged from its boreal isolation and has increasingly begun to view itself as part of the Americas. Latin America has had a strong appeal for English-Canadian writers ever since the works of Lowry and Birney in the 1940s and '50s, and *québécois* authors since the 1960s have often closely identified with their Latin counterparts to the south.

Simultaneously, the Hispanic world has discovered Canada. The political repression in Latin America during the 1970s and '80s has brought successive waves of exiles and immigrants to Canada, particularly from Chile and Central America, as well as Haiti, though virtually every country in the region now has a substantial immigrant population in Canada. Many of those who have come are writers and artists who have continued their work in the north and thus in turn have influenced Canadian thinking and perceptions of Latin America. A strong cultural exchange and emotional and intellectual bonding has taken place between the two spheres.

The present anthology begins its exploration of Latin America and its culture in Mexico and progresses through the Caribbean, Central America, the Andean nations, Brazil, and the Southern Cone. Texts by English-Canadian and *québécois* authors are interspersed with those of writers of fourteen other national origins who have set their work both in their own countries and in other parts of Central and South America. The resulting luxuriant diversity is veined with common themes that recur regardless of the author's nationality. Given the contemporary nature of the writing and the immediacy and commitment involved, many selections naturally reflect the political and social trauma that Latin America is currently undergoing.

The objective of the anthology, however, has been to represent as many different aspects as possible of Latin reality, from childhood in the countryside to adolescence in the city, from ancient Indian civilizations to villages along

12

the Amazon, from tropical sensuality to attitudes toward death. Latin Americans who now live in Canada and Quebec write from greatly varying points of view, while Canadian and *québécois* writers reveal what has drawn so many of them to Latin American culture. The result is not only a new Northern view of the South, a fresh exchange and intermingling of the cultures of the Americas outside the confines of U.S. domination, but also, and not surprisingly, a new view of the increasingly outward-looking sensibilities to be found north of the 49th parallel. Finally, this anthology is the work of authors from widely divergent backgrounds, all of them united in their common interest in and solidarity with Latin America, all of them *compañeros*.

* * *

It should be mentioned that *Compañeros* is offered as a modest, and by no means exhaustive, representation of what is being written about Latin America from within Quebec and the rest of Canada. As the anthology was nearing completion and limits of space had been surpassed, interesting new work was received from writers such as Daniel McBain (translator of *Cocori*), Stephen Henighan (*Other Americas*), Ramón Sepúlveda (Red Rock) , Manuel Betanzos Santos, Luciano P. Diaz, and many others. It is hoped that this gathering of materials will alert readers to the wealth of material available.

Compañeros is dedicated to Earle Birney, one of our imaginative pioneers to Latin America, whose very first poems of Mexico, Colombia, and Peru held up the hope of brotherhood and whose last letter to one of the editors, before his disabling illness struck, was concerned with a bilingual Spanish-English publication of his poems, translated mostly in Chile and illustrated by a Canadian visual artist living in Mexico.

We would like to express our gratitude to the Office of the Secretary of State for Multiculturalism for special assistance in the publishing of this material, and to the Ontario Arts Council for its enlightened funding of translation.

Thanks to the generosity of the contributors, the translators, the owners of copyright, and the publisher, Jan Geddes, proceeds from the sale of this book will be donated to an OXFAM PROJECT in Earle Birney's honour for Latin America.

Hugh Hazelton
Gary Geddes

The Glassblowers, 6 A. M.

Susan Glickman

Night draws its plough through the fields.
A fine mist; the breath
of a black horse, dreaming.
Under its eyelid, the moon.

This early no one wakes
but the glassblowers
secretive insects in their hive.
At the end of each sting
a dollop of luminous honey.

Mostly they are just boys,
lean shadows aping the maestros.
When nobody's looking they clown around
swapping greasy sombreros, goosing each other,
then lapse from play so quickly it seems
a mirage
the after-image of that childhood
they've long since left behind.

Muscles steaming with sweat
eyes glazed by smoke
how they dance round the furnace
transforming night's lead into gold!
Even while eating they circle the fire.
The ordinary sun cannot draw them
outside, where the black horse churns the furrows
and girls in flowering blouses
stroll to the dairy.

No magnet beyond this centre
and the girls know it
crowding the doorway for a glimpse
of ruddy flesh,
scattering at the first sight
of those burning, devoted eyes.

How Ali Cran Got His Name

George Szanto

THE CURANDERA SAYS if I am stung by a scorpion, kill him and cut in half his corpse, then with a mixture of lime juice and garlic stick down the head part on the wound and this will save my life. In fact in twenty minutes I will be cured. Maybe half an hour.

I can imagine my doctor back home, Bob Carson, who's done a bit of alternative medicine, going so far as to concede something like antivenin might really be present in the head. Or that maybe there is real curative power in the garlic-lime glue. But I also know how talk of magic potions and country cures leaves him uncomfortable and in about three minutes he'd make it clear that really the whole business was absurd: If you're ever stung, even just a nip, *instantly*, get yourself to a real doctor. Don't muck around.

Myself, I think the cure comes from revenge: one bite, one dead scorpion. But having so far avoided being stung I have no personal experience. Therefore I listen to all advice. So when the time comes—

Listening to tall tales is how I began to hear the stories of Alejandro Cruz Ocampo, known here as Ali Cran or Alicito by those who claim to be his friends. More people than I'd have thought possible say they're close to him. Before anybody put scorpions and Alejandro Cruz together for me and I learned how he got his name, I'd heard half a dozen mentions, bits of stories— because Ali Cran is a kind of reference point for the citizens of Michoácuaro. His name began to reach me from the edges of gossip or from recited memories.

For example, when Maria Cecilia at the beer depósito became pregnant, the story was mainly how Cecilia's mother would at last get a new baby in the house, the mother having been barren since Cecilia's sister Guadalupina, ten months younger than Cecilia herself, was born. Cecilia wouldn't say who the father was so people blamed Ali Cran and, to my fascination, that seemed appropriate. Similarly, when years back Sebastiano broke his leg and couldn't get his avocados picked and couldn't afford to hire, he woke one morning out of a sad pulque dream and found the trees bare and all the fruit piled below. He was so happy he got drunk again and the next day he found the avocados boxed also. The town agreed: Ali Cran. Or when Nisi Calderón's ancient truck was forced off the road into a ditch by a jeep, the old man, with a smashed arm and broken ankle, tried to get the police to find who had careened the jeep against him. The jefe de policia explained to Nisi the jeep was stolen. But Nisi said people had seen Ali Cran admiring it earlier in the evening. What proof was that, the jefe asked: and anyway there'd be no finding him—if it was him, well, ¡madrecita! by now he'd be deep into tierra caliente, the hot country to the south and west of us. Ali Cran seemed to be the source of both blessings and disasters.

It was Rubén Reyes Ponce who told me about Alejandro Cruz as a boy. We were sitting in the courtyard, Rubén and I, sharing the last quarter of a bottle of good dark tequila, Comemorativo. I had learned the hard way to keep my tequila bottles no more than a third full because whatever was in them when Rubén came by had to be finished before he left.

And no less than about twenty percent full: Late one morning, thinking I'd be really smart—I was at a piece of the novel that felt like it was moving well—I brought out a bottle with only a couple of sips left in it. Rubén made that gesture, thumb and index finger two centimeters apart held toward me, hand jagging back and forth half a dozen times, which means un poquito, just a tiny bit. Specifically, here, of time, just a few seconds . . . He turned and went. This is the gesture which has impressed on me completely that in the state of Michoacán the time-space continuum is a living and breathing reality. Rubén was back in five minutes with a full litre. But of the cheap clear stuff, the kind that's aged to its particular local perfection maybe five seconds before it's bottled. Naturally we had to finish what was before us.

That was the first time he told me about Ali Cran. The story, paid for with the drinking plus a full aftermath in the head and stomach and joints, cost me a day and a half's worth of writing hours.

It seems Rubén and Alejandro had been at the same school, Alejandro twelve, Rubén ten. Alejandro was a skinny kid, good at math but barely literate, lousy at soccer, always wearing clothes at least four of his older brothers had worked their way through at the elbows and knees. That wasn't particularly abnormal—most boys wore whatever their mothers could find for them, and few were exceptional in their schoolwork. Most prided themselves at being good at sports, though. What distinguished Alejandro was his interest in details, in colours, textures, plants and especiallly insects: ants, grasshoppers, wasps, even cockroaches—the three-inchers that come out in April and May, Rubén said; details, and a tendency to daydream. His reveries would be either active or passive. That is, he might be sitting at his desk in school or on the steps of the arcade of the plaza or by the fountain in the middle of it, and for fifteen minutes, half an hour even, he'd be connected only to his thoughts. Anybody looking at him would know his mind was in its own world. Where, nobody could guess; just, away. In class his teachers didn't bother him at these moments—at least one of the kids was keeping quiet. Who cared what was going on upstairs.

He would daydream actively, also. ("Daydream" here is Rubén's word. I'd call it concentration.) For example, there was the time Rubén saw Alejandro sitting on the crumbled curb in front of his house, watching the ground. And what was happening now? A centipede or a scorpion, dying slowly? No, a regiment of ants dragging a dead wasp to their nest. The wasp would have outweighed the fifteen or so ants maybe ten to one; undaunted, the soldiers pushed and pulled, making slow headway. Rubén had watched Alejandro with nearly as much fascination as Alejandro had ants. With less patience, though; breaking into Alejandro's world was necessary. So Rubén came up behind Alejandro and with a blade of grass pretended some bug was tickling the back of his friend's neck. No response. Rubén found a small pebble and dropped it down the back of Alejandro's shirt. Nothing. Finally he pulled open his fly and peed in the dust, spattering mud directly beside Alejandro, splashing the procession. The ants struggled on. Alejandro's concentration remained intact. Except, when the peeing stopped, Alejandro without shifting his eyes from the ants said "Go away." Rubén left in frustration, Alejandro's eyes followed the ants. Rubén wondered what would have happened if he'd peed on the wasp itself. Now he is much happier he didn't.

For his daydreaming and for his absent-mindedness a lot of the kids gave Alejandro Cruz a hard time. Once he came to school wearing a shirt that had belonged to his sister Camila. Before Camila it had been Arturo's. That made no difference. Camila's friend Silvia remembered the shirt because Camila had once unbuttoned it to show Silvia how her breasts were starting to grow from out of nowhere and now Silvia told everybody Alejandro was wearing a girl's shirt and there were probably breast marks on the inside. So, Rubén said, because the fool kid had that morning put on a one-time girl's shirt, probably while thinking about bees or silverfish, they all called him Alejandra for days.

The best joke was to snap Alejandro out of his reveries, bang, like that. He'd be shocked back to the daily world as if he'd fallen off a cliff and down into icy water. He wouldn't have any idea where he was, everybody laughing ready to burst because they'd been holding their giggles in till he plunged back to their world. This happened so often Alejandro learned to hide most of what he was feeling, he'd wait with faked calm till his burning red cheeks and neck went away and the pouring sweat started to clam into his shirt-back and he'd figured out how to hold in the tears this time. He didn't run anway anymore; though he still wanted to, as far as possible. Not home. Into tomorrow, if he only knew how.

One January around nine in the evening the full moon was high and its reflection off the still water in the big fountain down at the plaza was of a silver purer than any from the mines of Taxco or Guanajuato. Now and again a slight breeze would press down the top of the water as if enraptured with the moon. Alejandro knelt on the rim of the fountain and watched enchanted as the silver formed and melted, patterned and resmoothed. What was in his mind, Rubén said, was impossible to know. It mattered not at all who else, at Alejandro's side or over across the fountain's pool, might be glancing at the glimmering water; Alejandro and the moon were unquestionably separate from everyone else.

The culprit this time was a mean little kid, Nabór, a cousin of Alejandro's. Nabór remains to this day unequivocally nasty and, though in his late thirties, still a repulsive kid, Rubén tells me. It being a few nights after Christmas, Nabór had firecrackers. Not his; those had blasted the early mornings three days running. Forty-five minutes before the churches sent off their own into the heavens to wake the population for 4:00 A.M. mass, Nabór's explosions had driven two of Michoácuaro's earliest risers, the Vargas Martínez sisters, pious ladies who liked having time to wash before early mass, to complain to the Bishop about the sleep-shattering blasts. No, Nabór had stolen these firecrackers, little ones, from his younger brother Angel; Angel was the hoarder. Is even today, according to Rubén.

So, firecrackers in hand, Nabór, true to form, found his moment: the spellbound Alejandro, the silent evening, the argentine water. Coming up directly behind Alejandro, Nabór dropped a small jacaranda twig, a test-twig, between Alejandro's motionless shoulder blades. No reaction: moon and Alejandro in mutual admiration. Nabór took a match, lit the fuse and let it sputter. As the burn reached the first two crackers—one of those cheap strings of ten, five pairs of two—Nabór dropped it on Alejandro's back and leapt away. The first pair exploded nearly simultaneously. Alejandro remained kneeling. Suspended. Nabór stared, amazed, even an explosion hadn't— Then, with nearly the slowness of a leaf growing, Alejandro curved lightly forward. His face was halfway to the water as the second pair exploded, his forehead and hair touched the water with the third, and there was time for two more to go off before Alejandro's skinny body submerged head to knees in the fountain pool. The final crackers fizzled to wet silence.

Nabór laughed and laughed. Two other boys ran to pull Alejandro out. By this time the sopping kid was standing in the pool, dripping silvery water. The story was the buzz of the school for a week, really hilarious.

I broke in at the end of that tangent. "But what about Alejandro's name, Rubén."

Sure, that was the best part of Ali Cran's early life, Rubén was just getting to that, the next piece of the story. We'd been drinking for two hours. Rubén took a bite on his lime, dunked a finger in his tequila, stuck the finger in the salt, sucked off the finger, drank down the glass. I poured him another, wondering how much of all this I'd remember in the morning. He toasted the young Alejandro and we sipped.

All the kids and the teachers at the school were off to Cerro Madre, a good-size hill a few kilometres from Michoácuaro, for the annual picnic. It was early May, summer vacation around the corner, the rains would be here before long, the sun shining defiantly through the smoky haze of nearby burning cane fields. Everyone was feeling rambunctious. The teachers kept them in check.

Alejandro too was in a great mood. An uncle who'd gone north, his favourite uncle, Pedro, his mother's brother who mailed home a hundred dollars a month—which was her only income, though Alejandro didn't know this at the time—Tío Pedro had sent Alejandro a New York Yankees baseball cap. The Yankees were Pedro's team—Pedro worked, illegally like so many from Mexico, in New Jersey as a painter's assistant. The Yankees were doing fantastic that year and Pedro wanted to send his favourite nephew an early happy birthday present. Alejandro's birthday was in November but by then the season would already be over and the Yankees probably world champions, so

Pedro's early gift meant Alejandro could start cheering for the Yankees right away.

Well Alejandro was even worse at baseball than at soccer. When he had to play in school they always stuck him in right field, deep right if there were too many on each team and they could double-platoon the position. But he loved the cap. These days you can buy Mexican-made American baseball caps and tee shirts or whatever you want here. This cap, though, this was the real thing. It made Alejandro feel as if he belonged, not simply to the daily activities of his street or his school or Michoácuaro, but to a bigger world, one that really mattered. So on this day when he wanted to pretend he was as okay and as happy as all the others, planning their special games and secret walks and hunts, he wore his Yankees cap. He knew it was a good choice as soon as he got on the bus and started to get compliments—from some of the boys, even from a couple of the girls. He let two of them try it on, those who'd sometimes been nice to him, who'd talked about themselves to him, helped him with his verbs. The bus wound out of town, across the narrow valley the stream flowed through, and up Cerro Madre. The top was level, another volcanic cone, this one filled in over millions of years to leave a flat surface. Clumps of pine trees created special sitting places. A tiny spring burbled out of the ground there, the water not clean enough for drinking but great to stick your hot feet in. It flowed into the stream below.

The happiness was catching. Boys teased girls as they usually do at eleven, twelve, thirteen, feeling juices they don't know the meaning of but have to do something with. Girls giggled together about boys, knowing a bit more but for all that not having much more control over their feelings, let alone knowing how to deal with them. No one was unkind to Alejandro. He felt pretty good, though the initial enthusiasm with his cap had worn off. There were tortillas and gordos and enchilladas and soft drinks. Rubén and Arturo caught a scorpion and a centipede and put them in a glass bottle and tightened the top and after watching them fight ran with the bugs after two girls they liked, to frighten them. Despite the haze the sun got hot. Everything slowed down. Kids sat in little groups and gossiped; boys and boys, girls and girls, two small groups of boys and girls. And the teachers were at last off by themselves.

Nabór was bored. He tried to convince Silvia it'd be great fun to steal Alejandro's Yankees cap. Silvia didn't know what was so much fun about that. Nabór said it'd give them something to do. Silvia said it was too hot. Nabór said they wouldn't have to run very hard, Alejandro probably wouldn't even notice, he'd be watching some birds in a tree or some clouds or something. Silvia finally agreed. So they snuck up behind Alejandro, he was just on the outside of one group of boys, right at the edge of the shade. Nabór came up quietly from behind, grabbed the cap and stepped back, raising it high to show Silvia. Suddenly Alejandro was on his feet. "You—give—me—that—cap!"

"Come get it! Run and get it!" Nabór held it out, Alejandro lunged, Nabór pulled to the side, Alejandro's thrust missed, Nabór ran. As he passed Silvia he grabbed her hand with his free one and together, laughing so hard they nearly fell over themselves, they ran down into the valley where there were more trees to hide behind.

Alejandro waited while the blood drained from his face and the sweat soaked into his shirt. He clamped his fury inside. Only the cap was important. All else would come later. He stared downhill, saw no one. He willed himself: Find the cap.

He searched for more than half an hour. Finally he found them. They were behind some bushes beside the stream. He heard them before he saw them. They were groping at each other and panting. The cap was on the ground. He tried to be silent but they saw him before he reached it. They pulled apart. Nabór grabbed the cap and held it out: "You want it? Swim for it!" and threw it into the stream. Alejandro watched. It floated. Slowly water soaked in. Soon it would sink. He ran into the water, shoes, pants, everything. It was still ahead of him, caught in the current, turning slowly—then it disappeared. He got back on the bank, ran downstream of where it should be, splashed back in, through the water, fished about, saw something white—and found it! Caught along a submerged branch. The white was the cloth. But it was in bad shape. The cloth would dry but no way would it ever be really white again. The cardboard in the visor was sodden, probably ruined. He stared at it, his only real friend, squeezed it to his chest— Slowly he walked out of the water. He sat by a tree, dripping water. He held his cap to his face and cried into it. He leaned against the tree and lost himself, first to anguish and despair, soon to all the psychic exhaustion of his brief lifetime, at last to sleep.

Which was the way Nabór and Silvia found him. They hadn't bothered chasing him, they'd returned to their exploration of each other's bodies. Then the drives and urges had reached a very strange state, the feeling was familiar yet unknown, then suddenly it was gone. They were uncomfortable with each other. Neither understood, neither admitted ignorance. Neither wanted to go back up the hill to the others. They found some blackberries and ate them. They poked gingerly at two scorpions hiding in the cool crack of a rock. They threw stones at a family of finches.

Then they saw Alejandro. The baseball cap lying by his side gave Nabór the idea. Alejandro was, this time, deeply asleep. Nabór stole the cap a second time. He returned to the rock where they'd seen the scorpions. One was gone. Silvia banged the rock on the opposite side. The remaining scorpion, disturbed from its warm afternoon peace, panicked and rushed the other way, into the Yankees cap. It was a big fellow, over two inches long from the tip of its claws down to the dark brown stinger. Nabór held the edges of the folded cap firm. They ran back to Alejandro, hoping he was still asleep. He was. Quietly again Nabór crawled up to Alejandro and placed the cap on his chest, opened it, crawled back to Silvia. They watched breathless.

The scorpion, probably stunned, slowly meandered out of the hat. Scorpions like to choose their own dampness and this one was no exception. It seemed to look about proudly, as if thinking, Who could have dared do that to me? Perhaps at this moment it realized it was on something breathing.

Certainly at this moment Rubén, under orders from the school principal to look for the three missing students, came up behind Silvia and Nabór. They knew he was there, he started to speak. Nabór tapped his fingers to his lips, "Sshhh!" and Silvia giggled silently. They pointed. Rubén saw.

Alejandro was awake. His eyes were wide open. So was his mouth. He was trying to stare down to the bottom of his chin. There was a scorpion sitting there, tail wound tight over its head. Slowly it crawled, one tiny tickling leg, then another, another, up Alejandro's chin. It stopped for a moment, as if considering the possibilities of the face; where next to test this immediate landscape? It started the journey again. Its pincers reached Alejandro's lower lip. Nothing moved. Only Alejandro's eyeballs.

Rubén panicked. We must do something! Silvia and Nabór were choking back uncontrollable giggles, wiping away tears to see better. Rubén could do nothing. Alejandro! Only Alejandro could save himself. How? Instantly. But Rubén knew as well: if Alejandro moved to swat the thing the tail would lash out and the stinger would stab through the skin and into the flesh of the chin before the hand moved three inches. Frozen, Rubén watched.

Alejandro was stiller than time. Only the scorpion moved. Slow, like sweat. Inexorably forward. Its front part stood in fine brown contrast on the lower lip. Still it moved forward. The head and claws were hovering now above Alejandro's tongue—

Instantly it happened. Quicker than any eye. Only the result told. Alejandro's teeth snapped shut and bit the scorpion in two. The tail, arrested before its adrenalin could signal a strike, fell down the side of Alejandro's chin to the ground.

Rubén remembers he peed his pants.

Nabór and Silvia were so shocked they couldn't move. They lay there, their mouths open, as if waiting for scorpions of their own.

Alejandro got up slowly. He walked toward the three. With his soaking wet shoes he kicked Nabór in the head and then in the side and, when he rolled over, in the shin. Silvia was getting to her feet, she was off balance, Alejandro grabbed her by the wrist, bit her forearm, broke the skin, dragged her to the stream, threw her in.

Rubén, shaking, embarrassed, walked slowly to the tree to pick up Alejandro's cap. The tail of the scorpion lay on the ground, less than an inch long. Alejandro came over. Rubén handed him the cap. "What did you do with the head?"

"I swallowed it."

That story went around the school and stayed there. Even after Alejandro Cruz Ocampo graduated two years later it remained, handed down, as permanent as the passing generations. After the picnic on Cerro Madre they didn't call him Ali Cruz anymore; he had become Ali Cran. Alacrán is the Mexican word for scorpion.

Irapuato

Earle Birney

For reasons any
        brigadier
           could tell
this is a favourite
      nook
         for massacre
Toltex by Mixtex Mixtex by Aztex
Aztex by Spanishtex Spanishtex by Mexitex
by Mexitex   by Mexitex   by Texaco   by Pemex

So any farmer can see how the strawberries
are the biggest
        and the reddest
              in the whole damn continent
but why
      when arranged
            under the market flies
do they look like small clotting hearts?

Canuto: Blind Black Dog

Antonio D'Alfonso

¡Todo es noche! Cactus, palm
do not have the form of sight nor its sweep.
What to you seems shape of vision
is to me aura of smell, feel
of body, taste of black honey.

Night and day, outside and inside
maunder the same fundamental plaint.
Sound makes my tail wag, not light.
The hand that unlocks garden gates
brushes my back, guides like white cane.

Quiet roads, despite cans, boxes
I bump into, disclose music,
secrets I can sadly retrace—
alone the smell of bitch surpasses.
Gifted supreme sense of magic,

sightless, I have come to master
corners of activity curs
with eyes would never dare to face:
barefooted sex, pinched fire-eaters, friends
exploited to last spark of faith.

New visitors can pity me
seeing me stagger in the yard,
to them I never go. But they
who know eyes' true value, are aware
of daily visions, I stay near.

I was made to see without eyes,
to see the world unfold without eyes,
I do not complain. And those eyes
dazed in opaqueness of abuse,
eyes sealed in eclipse of truth,

eyes lost in factories' dimness,
eyes glued to dullness of duty,
those eyes that forget what to see,
eyes that forget what seeing is—
too faint to complain — how they haunt me!

from Adrénaline

Yolande Villemaire

It's funny that you should speak about Castaneda in your letter because I remember that the time I spent the whole day lying in a stuffy room near the frog pond, trying to remember everything that had happened, I remembered him too. Because I met him in Puerto Vallarta in Mexico in December, 1979. Bryan was busy writing a piece for the radio. It was called *The Tough Time Machine*. It made him brutal, violent, nasty. One night he bit me when I was sleeping. I couldn't stand it any longer. He said that I had punched him in the stomach but I didn't remember anything about it. We were marked for physical and mental violence that threw us endlessly against each other in the tumultuous vortex of Molino de Aguas, a very tropical town. It was just before the Soviet Union invaded Afghanistan. It was the beginning of the end. And, between us, it was war. We still loved each other, though. But Power had already made me its prey in the airspace over Concepción de Oro, 4,308 nautical miles from Buenos Aires, while Bryan was sleeping off the depths of a down from coke. At that time I still hadn't realized that he was hooked. Bryan was going to stick his head in the sand for a few years just when Mexico was really starting to get under my skin. I cried all the time. I wanted to tear him from his destiny. But I myself was falling prey to the shadow. So I cried at night on the beach, stretched out on the wet sand and listening to the glaucous murmur of the Pacific.

One evening, a little before Christmas, I decide to give the whole thing up. I leave Bryan to his Tough Time Machine, dry my tears, put on my mauve satin suit and go out to celebrate my new life in the Estrella de Oro, a restaurant and bar overlooking the sea. I even have a strolling photographer take a picture of me toasting myself with a margarita. It's funny: I've got a miniature black Tikal on my forehead in that photo. It's because of the poor quality of the film. But I've still got a black Tikal on my forehead. I celebrate my blood wedding and the dried black blood on my forehead reminds me of what's awaiting me.

I'm already in the thrall of the alcohol-god when a young blond man with extremely dark skin smiles up at me from the bottom of the spiral staircase that connects the mezzanine to the first story of the Estrella de Oro. I return his smile. He slowly climbs the staircase and then comes over to my table. He's tall, thin, dressed in white. His smile is strange because he's missing a few teeth. He speaks to me elemental English, and tells me that his name is José Luis Solis and that he would like to invite me to have a drink with him at the bar as soon as I finish my dinner. I accept. He smiles again and goes back downstairs. He's obviously Indian. Probably a mestizo. He looks like an Aztec.

But at the bar three-quarters of an hour later, I can't find him. There are a lot of people and noise. It smells like suntan oil, burnt skin, alcohol. I order my umpteenth margarita and finally find a quiet spot, a grey upholstered alcove in the back of the room. Across from me is a man in his thirties in a grey suit who seems totally boring. I turn my attention elsewhere in hopes of possibly catching a glimpse of José Luis Solis in the crowd that is squeezed onto the dance floor.

I absorb one margarita after another and my head begins to whirl in the odour of tequila and taste of lime, an alcoholic maelstrom that drowns me in memories of Mexico. I'm now on the eighteenth step of the Pyramid of the Magician at Uxmal and I'm afraid of falling head first into the green head of the Yucatan savannah. On the way to Tulum, a gigantic iguana crosses the road just two inches from my toes. A Mayan woman speaks to me for a long time in Mayan on the bus in Isla Mujeres. I smile and understand everything she says. But how can this be possible? I am looking at the temple of sacred writings at Chichén Itzá. It's late afternoon in December, 1976. A hot wind runs along the paths of the ruins and rustles the tall deep-green grass. Chac Mool roars, and rain falls heavily on the beach at Cancun. I'm afraid of the wind.

I open my eyes. The air-conditioning and ventilation system in the bar is blowing on my neck. I change places, and find myself sitting next to the grey man. He's wearing horn-rimmed glasses. I look at him more closely. He seems very serious. And then suddenly, like a fact that unexpectedly becomes totally obvious to my body at least, just below my navel, I have the feeling that this grey man with the horn-rims and serious look is Carlos Castaneda. Exhilarated by the alcohol, I quickly reveal my insight to him. He answers, in Spanish, that he doesn't speak English. I summon all my Spanish vocabulary and try to make him understand that he is Carlos Castaneda. He says no, his name is Miguel Ramón. I ask him if he knows who Carlos Castaneda is. He says no, he doesn't know him. He pretends to think that Carlos Castaneda is an Estrella de Oro regular. This Castaneda is tricky. All the same, I set about explaining to him that Carlos Castaneda is an American ethnologist who, while working on a thesis on the properties of medicinal plants, found himself being initiated into sorcery by Don Juan, a Yaqui Indian. I want to see how long the author will be able to stand someone summing up his work right in his face. I've gotten around to laborious explanations of what it means to be a warrior and some spicy anecdotes about Don Juan's impulsive personality when the young blond man with dark skin reappears. He asks me what I'd like. I tell him a margarita would be nice. He introduces himself to the man I'm speaking to, who politely replies that he is Miguel Ramón. I quickly point out to José Luis Solis that the man goes by the name of Miguel Ramón but that he's actually Carlos Castaneda; this seems to leave him completely cold. Then I also start telling him who Carlos Castaneda is. This time I add that I'm well aware that a warrior must erase his entire personal history, but that, come on, just between us, he might as well admit his real identity because I've already unmasked him. As I say this, I remember when I discovered that Djinny was really Réjean Ducharme. Which he still refuses to admit. But I know it's true. That's what counts.

Lost in my voluble explanations, I don't immediately realize that Carlos Castaneda has slipped away. It's only the next day, while describing the scene to Bryan, that I discover the oversight. Bryan asks me how I was able to recognize Castaneda: had I ever seen a photo of him? I have to admit I hadn't. How did I know it was him, then? Because it was him; I'd bet my life on it.

A few days later, I'm lying on José Luis Solis's bed in his little stone house in the mountains behind Puerto Vallarta, smoking a filter Gitane and looking at the ceiling through the pink mosquito net. It's sunny outside. I can hear the Beatles singing *Michelle, Ma Belle* on José Luis Solis's tape recorder. I tell him that it's funny to hear that in the jungle. José Luis laughs and says that it's not really the jungle, that there aren't any tigers except the *señor tigre* which happens to be him and begins to make love to me again.

Later I ask him where that strange covering on his bed comes from. It has the Egyptian god Ptah on it. It's as surprising to find that here as it is to hear the Beatles' *Michelle*. He says that it's from a French tourist that he met at the bar in the Camino Real two years before. He asks me if I want to take a shower.

There isn't any electricity or water in his house, so I ask him if there are showers in the jungle. He tells me to put on my bikini if I want to find out and then leads me barefoot down a tiny path that climbs up the mountainside. A half an hour later a large house appears at the end of the track. José Luis Solis is still holding my hand; I'm afraid of getting my feet bitten by exotic bugs. We go up a little stairway that leads to the house. I ask whose house it is. José Luis Solis says that friends of his live there. There's a smaller wooden house to the right. We get to the door. There's something painted on it: a drawing made of brightly-coloured circles. Around the outer circle is written *Asociación Internacional de Gurús*. I say, "What the heck is this?" and want to look closer, but José Luis pulls me away and says we shouldn't bother anyone: the guru is sick. Just then a rather small man with glasses appears out of nowhere and goes inside the little house. He even says "Buenos días," but I don't have time to answer: José Luis Solis leads me around to another stairway to the house. I've never been so curious in my life, but José Luis's eagerness is irresistible, and I can't help obeying him in spite of the mystery we've just left burning. There's an open-air shower on the terrace. There's even some shampoo. Sunlight and no one around. We wash our hair, laughing. Far below in the valley, Indian women are washing clothes in the river. I ask if it's the same river that we cross on a rope bridge when we go down to Puerto Vallarta. José says that it is, but it looks to me like it's at the ends of the earth.

We climb up on the roof to dry off. José Luis Solis takes out a joint of Acapulco Gold that he'd hidden in my shoes. We pass it back and forth. We're sitting a few feet from each other, side-by-side on the gently sloping sheetmetal roof. We're facing the river, a fine green thread that winds down through the deeper green of the valley. The horizon is walled in all around by mountains planted with palm trees. I turn my head and spot a pass between two mountains that gives me a view of the sun setting over the Pacific. It reminds me that I am in Puerto Vallarta. It reminds me of Bryan. It reminds me of *The Tough Time Machine* and Molino de Aguas. It reminds me of my hand being bitten in the dark and of the nights crying on the beach. It reminds me of the Estrella de Oro and of Carlos Castaneda who insists that his name is Miguel Ramón. It reminds me of the god Ptah on José Luis Solis's bedcover. It reminds me of the Beatles' *Michelle, Ma Belle* and of that little girl with braids whose name is Michelle and who wears a Wonder Woman bathing suit on the beach. She is five years old and showed me how to make a sand castle the day I got my first sunburn here. Then, while I'm watching the green serpent river flow toward the sea, I say, "No entiendo nada." And Don Juan answers, "Sí." Because I have the distinct feeling that it's him. It's him and it's not because it's also José Luis Solis and he hasn't even read any of Castaneda's books. And I begin to slide down the narrow rift of the river valley because the universe is open. I run through the seven sacred pools, natural ones formed by the stream. That's when I see her, the sticky monster rolling around in the last pool. I stop, stupefied. It's not that I'm afraid. It's worse. As if my whole will were condensed into a single tiny dot in my right eye and I were desperately trying to hang on to it while being overcome with curiosity. She emerges from the water, gigantic, covered with green scales, her hair black and shining. It's a frog-woman that looks like a dragon, a mythical beast that blinds me with her presence. I sit down at the end of the natural pool of black water. I tell her that I know who she is. That I want to learn everything from her.

Little by little, in the darkness, she regains her human form. It's a *nagual*-woman. She's wearing tight-fitting snakeskin pants, an emerald-green silk blouse, green shoes of crocodile skin, a close-waisted jacket made of phosphorescent lime-green imitation leather, and earrings shaped like green stars. She smooths back her jet-black hair, which is cut short and glistens with brilliantine. And she smiles. And what a smile! A smile of triumph, suave and diabolic at the same time. She gestures to me to follow her up a steep path that comes up over the ocean. We sit down facing the Pacific that rolls in its heavy warm rollers, stirring up memories of the Land of Mu that the *nagual*-woman tells me about for hours. I listen to her avidly, and yet the net of my memory isn't catching what she's telling me. But she says that she was waiting for me. That's clear. She says that I am a true earthwoman, rooted in the soil. That I have to learn to move through space if I want to see the hologram. She says that it's foolish of me to want to believe that Miguel Ramón is really Carlos Castaneda. She says that what's foolish is to believe that there is a reality. She says that there is no reality. None.

A feeling of cold invades my body as she is speaking to me. I want to run away. But my curiosity holds me back. I can't see where I could very well run to anyway because I don't know which reality I'm in. But the *nagual*-woman says there is no reality. She also says that, besides, Carlos Castaneda is an imbecile who got all of Don Juan's and her teachings backward. She says that he is beginning to remember what she taught him about the seven sacred pools of sexual pleasure, but that his guilt is keeping him deaf and dumb. I ask her what she thinks of feminism. She bursts out laughing. I'm a bit upset. She says that the important thing for a warrior-woman is not to hide the fact that she will never give up her sexual power. And to be on guard never to surrender it to anyone. The warrior-woman abandons herself totally to her body and to the body of the other when she makes love, she says. Like a salmon swimming upstream against the current of on icy stream, the warrior-woman sings her thoughts and lets her senses awaken her heart. Her soul opens from orgasm to orgasm, swimming up through the seven sacred pools of azure water to the luminous spring of the spirit.

She tells me especially not to make love with Miguel Ramón. That he would lead me from my path because he hasn't yet remembered his body. A warrior-woman should never give up her sexual power, she says, and to make love to Miguel Ramón would be to surrender my power to him. I tell her that I don't understand anything about what all this means. She roars with laughter and says that's fine, she didn't expect anything better of me.

She also says that it's time for me to break my ties to the *tonal*, which have become so strong that the *tonal* has hold of me like a leech and the *nagual* will never be able to wrench me free if I don't at least start slacking up a bit in my appetite for the *tonal*. She says that I must tear myself away from the alcohol-god, from nicotine, coffee, language. She says that the *nagual* is lying in wait for my body and that I should be constantly on guard because it could possess me at any minute. She says that we will see each other again soon.

On Christmas Eve, at a party given by friends of José Luis, I met Juan Flores, who told me, "Puerto Vallarta es el paraíso de la Nueva Atlántida." And I never saw Miguel Ramón again.

Merida

Daphne Marlatt

On the other side of the square, they are, we are, he is saying, on the side of the square we never sit on, morning, swallows the zócalo, filled with it, that light ease light pours, into at centre (hole), pole they are taking the xmas tree down, no more lights, daytime dead outline of what was, at night, a coloured fantasy, but the tinsel wreaths still swing, looping across paths that ray out from that spot their eyes are fixed on, still, he is right, we are, on the side we never sit on, & though morning swallows, in its light space freshening of day, all that night lets run, strange currents, vampire bats at the movie house, or the laughing seductive strays, giving way to the world, teenage derelicts at midnight play around the original derelict himself swept, even he swept out by morning, its shallows, leaving them all a little beached, the paltry litter of yesterday, light raying through the indian laurel, their old trunks' tatter whitewash adrift in peels the balloon man goes slowly by, trailing pinks & blues, through a trickle of hose, someone's watering, halfhearted, gone off for coffee, gone off into the morning scatter through the day, knowing, even the gardener knows, how one must splay out, simply, to be here & not—it's not the zócalo, it's not the morning swallowing, it's night, under the o so solid scatter of these pavingstones, dark clings, & she must not, step into that house again—

did you see him, she says (can you keep me here?) the shoeshine man on the other side of the square, we must have passed him, on our way here, though she had actually forgotten to look. No, he says, I didn't, but the blind man's there, & she could see him inching his way along the wall to change position, all day with his hand out, blind faith, not the scrawnier hand of the dwarf woman in the sidestreet who, humped in a doorway, massiveness of that flesh between her shoulders somehow packaging all that was absent from her legs, begged with a kind of bitter grimace (still knew how to curse, 'encountered on a journey to the west,' they said, 'old mannikins') who'd marked their journey in the dream even before they left, & now she is here it is something else, *her* journey not theirs, he, living out in the street, on the square, sees earth for what it is, a vast terrain, these people here, sloped on benches or walking, these women, these cabdrivers, passing the time of day, it pools, it shallows here, she wants to stay, play, insist, this is not west, but east they have moved to, the fact of it, we sit with our backs to the sea, we are facing south, all day lightens the air before us, we are facing into the yellow earth, toward the men of yellow corn, so the muralist had said in the building behind them, held in the palm of the bacab of the south (it is warm here, it is safe)—'así pintó el mayab eterno Fernando Castro Pacheco'

& she who must struggle to come up out of the dark, out of the west, they say is black or, coming from north, a white they do not know, of invisible bodies on visible streets, those cleaner colder roads we walk, spectral or absent, where no one lives behind the eyes that skim by: that is a kind of hell

she came up from, with owls, she came up out of the nine dark worlds of bolon tiku, & left, no not her father, lord of death, but mother—why does it change, why does the dream change it like that? He has taken his arm away from the back of the bench to light a match, his hand curved to protect the flame. I had a dream, she says, last night, so vivid I can't seem to leave it behind—Go on, he says. I was flying over a graveyard, at least I think I was flying, looking for a new coffin which was at the very end. It was out of line with the two beside it & I was supposed to straighten it but when I bent over to do that I realized I had to hang on to the middle one to give myself enough leverage & when I did my hand went through it was so rotten & I felt myself fall into the darkness of it. I was running through the dark to get home but when I got there the house was full of people, I could hear voices in the kitchen where I knew my mother was but twins of my cousin, I mean they were my cousin but twins, came into the hall to greet me, only I didn't want to see anyone so I turned to go & then I heard her voice from the kitchen call out 'I don't want to lose that one too!' I ran terrified, trying to get back here, it was as if I was separate from my body, it seemed to take an extraordinary effort to get back into myself, to get back beside you & wake up.

Even telling it, terror clouds the edges of her telling & yet, now she has told it it isn't like it was, the telling fixes it in a way that wasn't felt then, a map that doesn't quite fit the terrain she was running through, doesn't take him back to that terrain the dark inhabits but like the square they are sitting in, on the same bench in the mutual day, occupies them. Not that she had meant it to take over the day, obscuring bench, trees, the balloon man, but now she can't take it back & a little embarrassed waits for him to survey it, the cigarette flaring between his fingers like a small signal. She had expected him to laugh, to make some joke, placing it thus in a waking perspective she might also enter. She has wanted him to say, as she has said to her own child on his waking, it's only a dream. But this morning he is quiet, thinking, & then he looks at her: so you went to visit your mother, he says. She hadn't thought of it as voluntary, as a 'visit,' but as a descent, perhaps she had sought out? & was that her mother? Mothers live on the earth in the day, one ascends out of the dark to mother, that's what all the stories say—but then the stories, the old stories, are always told in soomebody else's language, & we don't really know. She's everybody's mother, he says, mother earth. She laughs, oh but who is that? she was definitely someone. You just met her he says.

& the falling begins, o the horror of falling into, earth, in that we are alone—she had wanted him to pave it over, into nothing more than leaf play on paving stone, a surface she or anyone might walk across—she hadn't wanted to be alone

... ¿hamaca? a voice says, only one hundred fifty pesos, special price for you, henequen, very

30

good, & the end of a pink doubleply hammock is tossed into her lap, thickly coiled end ring nestling in her skirt, look, he says, a boy no more than a boy, nodding at her briskly, I show you, & he fans it out for her, the hennequen slivering & filming between them & separating finally into a pink & white fan extending six feet across the stones between his hand & hers. Matrimonio, he says, for two, & nods at the man beside her. She looks at Yo who laughs, who is already, in the way he sits back, dissociating himself from this exchange (she hadn't asked for—& their talk, o what about their talk?) It is to her the boy has made his advance, and though they have turned away other salesmen, the square infested with them (always a quick resentment at their fixing them so obviously as 'marks') having agreed they would not spend what money they had on a hammock, still something about the way this boy hovers, not carrying on in the usual manner, not even accompanied by a mate (as, usually, they worked the square in pairs, these hamaca men) not, obviously, out to talk them into buying but in some way waiting as he hovers there, that makes her almost want to give in—but no, she says, we don't need a hammock. Good price, he insists, but as if on the fact of it, you get nowhere else. No, she says, gracias, as he loops it toward him, deftly taking it from her lap in the last fold. ¿Habla español? Un poco. From where you come? he asks, setting his bundle of hammocks on the stone beside their bench & sitting on it next to her. Canada. So glib, the answer to that question, but what might make sense across the divide he is trying to bridge—up north? beyond the United States? how far does his sense of north extend? She lets it rest & is surprised when he says, On-tahr-io? Of course, hamaca man. Another part of Canada, she says, the West Coast, on the sea, & points, roughly, to where she thinks the Pacific might be. He is taking a small notebook out of his back pocket, ¿y su marido? what, ¿perdón? hus-ban? he points, she hesitates (¿mi amigo? with his eyes set across the square, who is there already, butting his cigarette for a stroll, with camera, through sun & shadow, forms on benches, all that is out there she returns from, to this insistency) yes? What country? Canada too, & divining his curiosity adds, Japanese-Canadian. Ah! japonés, he scans Yo's retreating back & gestures at the book, you write for me, en inglés? Taking the stubby pencil, she sees as he flicks through searching for a space, that it is full of words & that the writing differs, some words printed in big letters, some written phrases, some Spanish, some English. I learning inglés, he looks up seriously, people write me & I learning the words—ésta, la señora de On-tahr-io, she write me. The words he is pointing to say, 'take the freeway' & below that 'North-south.' Freeway, he says, his finger under the word, stocky & vivid on the much-handled page, hand of a farmer, broad palmed, no hamaca salesman, hands that are used to making, & suddenly, as if from some dusk, his body comes forward under the pale blue shirt, sneakers, red billed baseball cap, a young man's insistence, quiet but humming there beside her, silent & waiting.

His eyes are on the page, as hers, & out of the force between them she asks the question, what are freeways? He audibly answers, she say me, in America, in Canada too, el camino, big trucks, much cars, go very fast very far. Of course, she thinks, & no, she thinks, you go very far here too. But how can she say that? what right has she? Me, I want to know it, he is saying, so I learning inglés. But why (perhaps he wants to see America like she wants to see Mexico?) He looks at her scornfully (no it is different) hamaca, he shrugs & gestures broadly across the square. Tixkokob my village, I live with my mother & father, my brothers, is small village, fifty kilómetros from Mérida. En la mañana las hamacas, he smacks the bundle he is sitting on, en la noche, las hamacas—I sell two maybe three, no good, ¿m'entiende? not much money.

It is so clear the way he sees it, lucid as a map, but she, doubting on the far side of it, sees him lost there, the freeway of his imagination snarled in immense complications he has no vision of. It isn't only size, or only speed what can she say? that the duplicity of map & terrain, that maps are something we are good at, countries in themselves, unreal, but perfectly believable, until one tries to set foot there & the land falls away—

Glancing around she catches sight of Yo at the heart of the zócalo facing one way & shooting down the path that leads to the eastern edge—'las lluvias olorosas' (was it promise? hope?) There is nothing she can say, he lives where he lives & will carry that with him in a way she can't foresee. And grinning sideways at her he says suddenly, first I see México, & she knows he means the capital, whence all roads lead, & which is just as far away. I learning inglés, you teach me? tapping at the book. Sí. Insistence will get him there. El inglés es difícil, ¿no? En mi escuela—¿cómo se dice? School? Sí, school, I learning Spanish— What do you speak at home? she guesses in the same instant, Mayan? Sí, maya. Now I help my family pero en mi escuela, they have teach to me the words, to write, ¿m'entiende? El español no es difícil, mira: el día, same ¿m'entiende? pero en inglés, este, ¿de? ¿como se deletrea de? ¿De? (from what?) oh! day, d-a-y, she spells it out for him. Sí sí, es difícil (This boy, who speaks Mayan, for whom Spanish is a second language, who is trying to teach himself English phonetically, is ready to take on North America—plunked beside her on his bundle of hammocks, 'hennequen, very good.')

Y este, he says, tapping the book, ¿qué es r-e-y-l? Reyl? He says something in Spanish, something she doesn't understand though she gathers it's a word picked up from dos americanos, & staring at it suddenly she gets it, rail! (of course, distance again) Sí sí, reyl, ¿que es reyl? It is what a train runs along, a railroad, do you know that word? Reyl ro? please. She writes it for him in his book, sounding it out, ra-il ro(a)-d, the a, this letter, doesn't have a sound, just o, ro-d. She thinks to tell him about the sign RR, that intersection of rail & road, which after all he will know (a disappearing car) but that might complicate it for him (he who is separate, who in his Mexican version of American clothes, in his Mayan skin, comes out of some village to the east, separate & solid). No, he insists, los americanos gave him the word & they did not say it was a train. What else could it be? rail? railing? something you hold onto? she enquires, looking around for one, sees Yo a few yards away, pointing the camera at them,

& calls, what could rail mean besides railroad & railing? Ranting & railing? he laughs, an impish laugh. That's too complicated. Oh well you know I don't know English (I can't drive, he said. The package bundled up & set aside, beside him on the seat there, & separate. Wait, he would set off into that strange terrain without it, & she must stop him. Or was it her? Wait—he did not speak, or he said, they knew how to depict expression certainly, & then their iron heads rose up, scowling or grinning, out of that earth, & it was her who had brought them there—what does it mean?) ¿Qué quiere decir?—reyl? (not even a photograph can rescue them) Rule? she says, Royal? (whose rule? how get at that?) No, no (he digs away, the little man with pickaxe) something else (it was 'the power of?')

Oígame, he tries again, reyl, REY—L. Oh! (the pronunciation)you mean REAL? Sí sí, his face breaks into that smile, & they are there, they have hit it. ¿Qué es *reel?* He calls it into question (& is this real? any of of it? their ground has fallen away & she is falling, how speak to that with her impoverished Spanish, his broken English?—help, it is instinct, she looks around for Yo & spots him in the centre of the square again (what is he doing?) shooting west, place of the sun's going, place of evil winds, hunger, death—this is her undertaking, this is what she must come up from. Real means actual, means, here (she slaps the bench), a thing, here (no dawning) verdad. ¿Verdad? ¿sí? (What is the Spanish & suddenly it dawns on her, but isn't it?) En espanõl, real, (rey-ál) ¿no? ¡Ah sí, sí auténtico! What? I mean ¿qué? Auténtico. Authentic! yes (he knows that word. Always it is pronunciation gets in the way, they have the same words, unrecognized, he asking her for the English she thought he hadn't known, already knowing the word she hadn't recognized. But what was the question then? What is real? (reyl, some Texan speech) Auténtico he said (in the author's own hand).

Astonished, she glances up, sees Yo still at the heart of the zócalo, turned now, towards them. She wonders is he taking them or taking what stretches all around them, they only points in the whole, sees, suddenly, him seeing herself grown small with this stranger, from whom, with whom a real conversation sprouts, between them, like the trees they sit under, live among. What is your name? She asks. Manuel. Will you write it? & taking the back of the dictionary she offers, he prints

MAnvel Jesus

that Spanish use of Christ's name, but why not? power name, she thinks, anyone might have, saviour, & connects, Manuel, Emmanuelle—wasn't it, god is with us? His hand continues to mark, abrupt strokes against the white:

$$P\acute{E}^{c}h \qquad PAT$$

so that they form a square— these two, names form a language she doesn't recognize, printed beneath those two of heaven. Pech, mi padre, Pat, mi madre, he explains, en inglés, you write only the name of the father, no? Pero, además, you are the child of your mother, ¿m'entiende?

ground, he is saying, his or anyone's. under heaven, earth. what she had wanted to overlook, that dark, that other self she has fought up through. he comes to the edge of, telling her how it lies, horizon, what they are bound by. But where do you live? she asks, ¿su dirección?

he writes,

$$DoNMiCiLio$$

house, but spell it, 'don,' gift, house

$$CoNoci\,do$$

known, he writes, is known (give up you know) this house you fight up through, at centre, dark, hole at the heart of the field, 'thup,' little one, where the world disappears, reaching up through the dark, through mother & up, this branching growth, gift—('in my father's house are many mansions')

When she looks from the words to his eyes they are cast down, busy under the shadow of the baseball cap with the page on which he continues to print

$$cALle\ 21$$
$$ACPSA\ 136$$
$$Tix\ Kokob$$
$$Yuc\ Mex$$

Mi dirección, he smiles, returning them to earth, where they sit on a bench, in the heart of, handing back the book (but wait)—¡Allá! ¡mi amigo! loitering several yards away, who calls, ¿cómo le va? with a nod at her as Manuel shrugs, & slipping the notebook into a back pocket, es un vendador muy bueno, mi amigo, standing up, tipping the baseball cap at her, adiós señora, hammocks slung over his shoulder, he joins his friend & fades back into the day.

Or their day *(El Mayab)* out in he square *(es la tierra)* the men with xmas tree lights have got them down & left, the others stay, much as they have done, slumped on benches or halfturned watching passersby. Sun falls silently all around them. From a sky advanced to noon the whitewashed trunks of indian laurel bear up masses of glossy leaves against—four corners light & shadowy, these trees make of themselves, among, light bearing down *(misteriosa y antigua)*, she sees Yo coming toward from across the square, she sees him walk, quick & almost light, almost disappearing into the ones he walks among, this man with whom she shares the day, whose face, alight with question, singular in that field that lights all ways—she takes her eyes from his, embarrassed by the distance— not them, they dark against its lighting—eyes slide back to, making of them in the way dark lights them, shining, showing forth what each one is, each of them in the night they also rise up from, *in which everything speaks* —well? he will say, did you learn any Mayan?—*into the .* . .*(silence)* .

Seven

George McWhirter

They doled out land like soup after the war. Like black
soup here in the Valley. Seven hectares for my man
was a colonel. Forty days we trekked from the North
to Mexico City. Seven hectares South of Cuautla,
they said. Four days more eating pure tortilla
through the Cerros at Tepoztlán. Seven to seven
we worked. Seven to seven by seven hectares,
that was the size of our marriage, he and I
side by side. As soon as the sun dunked
in the dirt, we pulled out our petate. As soon
as the colonel dunked in the dirt, I sold out
the hectares. Land is like love, it takes two
to work it. This is what I have to show:
this roof and that patch. Seven hectares
shrunk to nothing like the cheap handkerchief
I wore at our wedding. Love is a land for two
to work, I tell you. Seven to seven.
Open to the Cerro and to the sky.

Twenty-one

All day

mimicking the bee
a man milks
a maguey, his bottom up

between the spikes.

Through tequila and mescal
they pierce by proxy and in time;

through tequila and mescal
the mouth of Pablo Iribas,

an appliance dealer.

                              Long
                              laggard
                              lance
of a taste
                              the light
can splice
                              and root.
Oh lightning
summered in a row of cactus.
Oh Pablo Iribas,
the appliance dealer,
all day simmered in his shop
like the trajectory of his taste.

Across

the on/off
strip he strikes
out the TV set with his finger
and touches the last taper
of light
with his tongue.

Tequila, he states.
Sauza

for the stars,

bees that retreat
with their sharp taste

into the hive
of morning.

For Quetzalcoatl

or the one God

who returns and glorifies
with the *viva:*

let there be life
and light

all day.

Foreign Aid

Lionel Kearns

Relaxing all day in this tropical atmosphere
glass in hand, a mosquito net and fans at night
sweating a bit but never exerting yourself
you think how easy it would be to make it permanent

becoming a modern version of the old white planter
You've met a few of them, no pith helmets now but
they still observe the decencies, dressing for dinner
playing bridge at the Yacht Club, having cocktails

with our High Commissioner. Perhaps you could be
an oil-field specialist or missile tracking technician
British or American, even a Canadian might fit in
as bank manager or some kind of Foreign Aid expert

living on a small portion of your Canadian salary
with 4 servants and 3 cars and a house on the hill
with a sea breeze and white neighbours. So what if
your wife insists on flying to New York each month

and the cost of educating the children is ridiculous
at least you still enjoy fine liquor and imported food
and a view of the young maid servant on her knees
scrubbing the floor. She's a wonderful creature

strong, pretty and always cheerful. Yes she's asked you
to be god-father to her second child, and you are
so delighted you raise her wages to $40 a month. Oh
It's good to be good and still live the good life

And though your face grows redder each year
and your body gets flabbier and you lose your hair
and your paunch sticks out above your khaki shorts
at least the skin under your clothes seems to be

turning even whiter, and you joke about this
when you have guests visiting from home and you are
discussing interesting features of the local scene
the quaint behavior of the native population, their

innate laziness and lack of initiative, but they're
a happy lot generally. And finally, after years
of this pleasant life (and you're still an amiable
chap yourself) one night you are disturbed

by the air conditioner cutting out, and some
unrecognizable commotion, and you open your eyes
in time to meet death in the blackness
on the swift warm blade of a cutlass

The Daughter of the Marquis de Syria and Her Lover

Gilberto Flores Patiño

The quiet of the night. The clouds have gone. I see the moon. I hear the spring. Down there, El Chorro. I'm leaning on the porch railing. There are cedar trees. Two or three. They're growing across from the door to the temple. A neglected bush of false flax—the gold of pleasure—spreads entangled over a stone bench. I can see the tops of the trees in the park. The herons nest in the cedars over there. When they fly at night they look like comets; kites, we used to call them. They float, sway. They fly out of the moon. When the wind blows the moon crumbles and the herons come back on its dust. They screech from their nests in those cedars. They tell stories that come from far away, from other times. An old female speaks. She says that she left the moon long ago, on the first winds. That she lived there at the top of a white cedar, in the garden of a palace inhabited by elves that wove people's dreams. Ghosts and wondrous beings wandered through the garden. She says that the elves stopped working one night and all humanity began to go mad from lack of dreams. That night is with us still. The looms are silent. The skeins of thread for weaving dreams are rotting in their cellars. The thousand-year-old wizards who live on distant stars have stopped shearing the galaxies, and their distaffs lie abandoned. The elves no longer ask for thread. The galaxies are suffocating in their own heat. Many have died and wheel across the skies as black holes. The elves on the moon are asleep in the dreamless human night. The old heron says that she doesn't know if they'll ever awaken. She is tired. She stops speaking and closes her eyes. The wind blows on the moon. More herons arrive. White comets waver in the dark air.

I go down. There's a damp smell. The ochre-coloured light from the wall of the house over there envelops the burning lantern. From the gate, I've seen the jacarandas that grow in the garden of the courtyard. I go up to the gate and sit on the stone bench, which is covered with red cement. I can see the jacarandas. The wind is blowing. The ash trees are dripping. The clock strikes an hour that is long past. The spring. On those luminous mornings you could hear the water coming down through the pipes. Water of the Dogs. Izquinapán. Dog on the Water. A friar once came to live down there, way way way over there, far from here. He spread out over the fertile land and engendered a people. They say that once, when the elves still made dreams, another friar, from France this time, also showed up down there, because the first one had gone to Acámbaro. The Indians saw the Franciscan being guided by little dogs that stopped here to drink. They'd found the spring. A little jet of water, of water that ran down the hill. El Chorro. And the Indians came up here; they moved their village, which was later called Grande and then given a family name. San Miguel el Grande, San Miguel de Allende. I walk down the hill.

The light of the streetlamps washes over the paving stones. Flights of stairs. Arches. A clock on the little tower. The ceaseless murmur of water as it spurts from the fountain. Houses slip away down the slope. A woman is singing at the washing place by the river. Wet clothes spread across barbed wire. Gold of pleasure and jasmin spill over the wall of a house. I enter the park: the French Park for some, Juárez Park for others. Ash trees, coyol palms, elegant leaves, whisper of running water, nests of herons in the tops of the cedars, the reddish light of the streetlamps. The spout of the fountain is a heron holding its beak up high. It's the female that used to live in a white cedar many years ago. The fountain splashes. The heron's stories come burbling out of her beak. Once, long ago, a woman used to stroll through the park every night. She wore an orange dress and tangled shimmers of straw shone in her hair. Like a spirit, her languorous form slid through the veil of light from the lanterns. A murmur rose from her mouth. Her story. I was born over there, near the forest of evergreen oaks, in the home of the Marquis of Syria. I don't remember when my mother died. I've forgotten her face and voice, or if I ever actually saw or heard her. The woman who became my nanny told me stories from her village. Like the one about that rain god who falls in love with a woman made of flowers who is snatched away from him by the sorcerer of darkened mirrors. The sorrowing god searches the world for her, spreading spring behind his cry. And the story of the lying magician, who comes out to trick warriors at the end of summer. He touches the leaves of the trees so that they lose their colour. Then he tells the warriors that these leaves make the best arrowheads and asks them to listen to the metallic sound of the forest. He blows and blows, fluting his mouth. The warriors stretch out their hands and the leaves crumble in their fingers. Then the magician bursts out laughing and fades away, after days and days of trickery. And they would tell me the story of the man who is always cold. He appears every year, looking for the warmth of his body. He left it in a sack, on the edge of the woods, because he needed tips for his arrows and the lying magician was up to his usual mischief. When he left the forest, the bag was empty. The wind had taken the heat of his body to warm the summer months, and he never finds any way to get it back, because he doesn't want to kill the young flowers that come out to meet him as he goes by, nor the tender green of the trees. In the house of the Marquis of Syria, I fell in love with a young man who arrived one day from Spain with paints and brushes and began painting my portrait. I don't know why, but he was never able to finish it from the outside, so he began to work from inside the painting itself. They say that my father, the marquis, killed him. Ah, the things that people imagine! That the marquis found us in bed together. That they locked me in my room with seven keys and that no one ever saw me again. That at night, when the wind blows through the evergreen forest, you can hear the painter's voice calling my name. They say he is searching for me. That I also cry out to him. But none of this is true. Because I know where he is and I call to him softly to come out of the portrait. One day I felt my body becoming light. I floated. I could pass through furniture and walls. I left my room without opening the door. I came into the living room. There was a coffin in the centre of the room. Candles. People crying. I saw my father and my nanny weeping. I spoke to them, but they didn't answer. I wanted to touch my nanny, but my hands passed through her flesh without hurting her. I left the house and went into the forest, flying over the evergreen oaks. My body was so light. Then my body abandoned me, or I left it; I don't know which. I saw it down there, far away. It looked like a tree. It was a tree. But not an oak, no. It was a tree with softer wood. The fountain stops; water no longer bubbles out. The old heron flaps and returns to the top of her cedar. The dust of the moon floats through the trees in the park. The wind blows.

from Violation of the Virgins

Hugh Garner

Joe slowed the car to a crawl at times as they passed small groups of hurrying people. The laughing, shouting people waved at them. Before reaching the village, Georgina looked away as she found herself staring at a couple of drunken men urinating through the railings of a bridge. On the other side, Joe had to blow his horn repeatedly to clear the road of five or six boys wearing Western shirts and Levi's and waving wide sombreros from the backs of burros.

"They're *muy machos* today," Joe said, laughing. "They're going to show off as bull fighters, but against cows and calves."

"Where did all the people come from?" she asked him in amazement.

He shrugged. "Some of them probably began heading this way yesterday."

On the outskirts of the village she noticed a jostling crowd of men trying to push their way into a wooden building that boasted a fresh-painted green-and-pink sign reading LA COMPAÑERITA. "It's a *pulquería*, a beer joint," Joe said. "The little Companion." She had begun to wonder if it was something worse.

The narrow dirt road changed into a potholed paved street lined with houses and here and there an open-fronted store garlanded with hanging fruit. In the middle of the village stood a couple of adobe buildings fronted with shuttered stores, a wooden shed with a gas pump in front of it and an open bazaar full of trinkets. An unpainted three-story building could have been either a hotel or the municipal office building. Beyond this were two or three wildly-painted 'dobe tenements and small individual houses set back from the street in front yards bordered with cacti or flowering trees.

The sidewalks, paved here and there between long stretches of hard-tamped earth, were filled to spilling with a dancing, staggering, shoving, jostling, patting, goosing, pinching mob of people, children, youths and the middle-aged. They sang, shouted, strummed guitars, laughed, banged bongos and beer bottles, made rude remarks, waved, screamed, and tripped each other as they were led, pushed or carried through the village street. Small boys dashed into the street and dared Joe to run over them, taunting him with laughing cries and skinny upraised arms. Girls in couples, threesomes and quartets, arms linked, bounded from the sidewalks to escape tormentors and the importuning overtures of boys and young men.

The crowd's clothing was as motley as the crowd itself, stiff formal suits, T-shirts and dungarees, store-bought dresses and blouses of all patterns, in every colour of the rainbow. A small boy in knee pants and bow-tied shirt was led by a young woman in a swishing dirndl dress and dancing pumps.

There were girls in skirts and halters, a very few in slacks and pedal-pushers, young men with shirts unbuttoned to their navels and pants skintight against their thighs, middle-aged campesinos in farm clothes, serapes, mestizo women in bright flowering dresses, a couple of soldiers in olive drab, girls in bandanas, boys in beanie caps, blondes and redheads out of a bottle, old men in Stetson hats, young women in mantillas, and a moustached young man in a beret and a camouflaged jungle uniform. The jet-black hair of most of the girls and women was piled up like haystacks, held with sequined combs, in buns, over the eye, long and straight to below the shoulders and burnt and frizzled into a golliwog style. The men sported crew cuts, town and country haircuts, bald heads (a few), grey hair, pepper-and-salt mixtures, and here and there a head that was completely white.

The crowd carried handbags, munched on tacos and enchiladas, pushed baby buggies, carried babies in their arms or against their sides, held fireworks, spilled ice-cream bars, and drank beer or pulque from bottles. Men, women and boys carried bottles of tequila, newspaper-wrapped tamales, the green, white, red tricolor of Mexico, balloons, walking sticks, feather ticklers, horns, fighting cocks, shoes hung around necks, handkerchiefs, rags, boxes of Kleenex, folded canvas chairs or stools, and small children. The men were smoking brown cigarillos, Havana cigars, and cigarettes. Georgina spied one unbelievable little man wearing a battered black top hat, a T-shirt bearing the word "Cheerios," ice-cream flannels, and carrying a small screeching monkey. Hanging on to his arm was a girl wearing a blue-checked housecoat and a long green feather boa.

The noise was a psychedelic accompaniment to the forward move-ment of the crowd, languid, loud, screeching, jabbering, halting, piercing, laughing, sobbing, slobbering—beyond description. As the car moved slowly through the throngs of people, horn blaring, Georgina smelled the smell of the crowd and found it had the odor of spicy spaghetti and meatballs, cheap pomade and perfume, tobacco, leather, cloth, strong soap, unwashed bodies, alcohol, gunpowder, face powder, humanity, spilled cola drinks, flowers, beer and a fleeting smell of burnt sugar.

"My goodness!" she exclaimed in Joe's ear. "It's fantastic. It must be like this in Bombay!"

"Coney Island," he shouted back.

She shook her head. "No. Shanghai."

"Never been there. Manila on VJ Night."

"Dante's Inferno."

"The crowd at a Madrid-Barcelona football game."

"What's the population of this place?"

"What?"

"How many people live in Nueva Carmelita?"

"Three, four hundred most times."

"How many in Mexico, the whole country of Mexico?"

"Over forty million."

44

She screamed in his ear, "They're all here today!"
He nodded and laughed.
She groped under the seat and pulled out the wine bottle and took a long drink. Joe roared with laughter as the wine spilled over her chin and bodice as he swerved to avoid running down a little dog wearing a clown hat.

* * * * *

"What are those grey heavy balloons on sticks?" she asked, pointing to some being carried by adults and children alike.
"Balloons. The balloons of the poor. Goats' bladders."
"What!"
"The bladders of dead goats."
She laughed hysterically. "What next!"
He said slowly, "*Maestrita canadiense, ¿quieres una gota de tequila?*"
"*Yo no hablar—*"
"I said, 'Little teacher, do you want a drop of tequila?'"
"After the wine! No thanks."
"Let's get out of the car then, and we'll walk to the fiesta grounds before they run out of pulque."
"What's that?"
"The local beer—home brew—local to all Mexico."
"Don't want any."
"You're not a baby. Even a baby doesn't turn down its mother's milk."
When she began walking she found she was inclined to stagger, and was grateful to him for gripping her elbow and leading her into the press of the pushing crowd. She was shoved, pinched, tripped, jostled, patted and elbowed. It was like being inside a hot, sweaty, crazy kaleidoscope, and she kicked back, pushed, elbowed, laughed and screamed as Joe steered her into the crowd's vortex. A bleary drunk stared at her and breathed his breath into her face as he exclaimed, "*¡Qué mona!*"
When she could she asked Joe what it meant.
"It means your're a cutie, a dish."
"It'd better."
The fiesta grounds were almost as crowded as the narrow streets, and stretched away in three directions. Beyond a banner over the entrance were two lines of stalls punctuated by standing and sitting pedlars with carts, trays and counters. The stalls sold fruit, food, souvenirs and remnant piecegoods; the pedlars old semi-precious stones, paintings, blankets, leatherwork and pottery. Beyond them, here and there in the crowd, were small combos and hippy music groups, sometimes centred around a marimba, twanging guitars and singing hillbilly or flamenco songs, adding to the din.
They stopped and watched a long queue of small children waiting

their turn on a hand-cranked carousel, and a line-up of youths and girls having their pictures taken with a box camera by a photographer who was wearing a peaked cap and black smock. Small groups crowded around upended kegs and bought milky drinks, gulping them from the pedlar's tin cups or from their own glasses and containers. A little man waving a flag staggered through the crowd wheezing, "¡Viva Mexico!" A young man in a white shirt and jodhpurs raised a shotgun to his shoulders and pointing it into the air fired a noisy sound.

Small boys, and some not so small, sent strings of firecrackers she had once called niggerchasers under the feet of women and girls. Floats, decorated with papier-mâché or painted scenes, stood where they had been unhitched from their tractors or teams of horses and mules, garishly advertising commercial products, villages, places of interest or historical events. Joe pointed out to her the most important one, which he said had carried several costumed boys and alleged virgins from the local school. Its centrepiece was a painted scene of sixteenth-century Spanish soldiers dragging young Indian girls by the hair from the doors of their village houses.

Scattered everywhere were the ubiquitous pushcarts that looked like narrow soft-drink coolers on wheels, and from them hoarse enterprising young men sold tortillas, frijoles, bottled beer and soggy ice-cream bars. Nearly everyone was either eating or drinking or both, and those who were not or could not, were screaming, laughing or harshly uttering greetings, slogans, scatological invitations or good-natured advice.

A gnarled old grandmother sat on a flimsy box in an ankle-length black skirt and reined in several half-naked toddlers connected to her with long rope umbilical cords, rasping out importunings and imprecations with all the charm of an ancient macaw.

Georgina felf her buttock being pinched for the umpteenth time, and an old man's voice in ear shouted, "¡Qué chula!" She tugged at Joe's arm, but he only said, "He called you a doll."

"This is bedlam!" she shouted at him.

He shook his head. "It's people, it's humanity, it's life, it's Mexico."

He led her to a group clustered around one of the upended kegs and had the seller fill his wine bottle with the sour-smelling milky pulque. When he handed the bottle to Georgina she backed off, shaking her head.

"Take a drink," he said, as if ordering a child to eat her spinach.

"No!" she shouted, aware that people were looking at her, and aware too that Joe was capable of walking away from her right there.

"You're turning down our hospitality, Gringuita," he laughed to hide his anger, pushing the bottle at her.

"It'll make me sick. I don't like the smell of it."

"Hold your nose then."

She looked around her at the solemn faces of the crowd, unable to find one of them whose owner was on her side. Brashly, she tore the bottle from his hand and tipped it, swallowing a long draught of the tepid stuff. She was unwilling to admit that it tasted better than it smelled.

"See," he smiled at her, thankful that she had not allowed herself to shame him. He too took a long drink, while she stared in hypnotized fascination at his bobbing Adam's apple above the black mat of hair that ended in a straight shaven line within the V of his open collar. He placed an arm around her shoulders and led her away.

They watched a troupe of Indian girls and men in flat-hatted ancient costumes dance a shuffling step to the atonal percusssion music of a native band.

"The *danza tzental,*" Joe said.

Pushing themselves through a deep crowd that surrounded a new board fence they watched the amateur antics of would-be bullfighters who goaded cows and calves with their makeshift muletas, only to be knocked sprawling or chased up the fences of the tiny ring. In another place Georgina had to pull her escort away from some noisy bloody cockfights over which cigar-chewing men screamed their bets and passed paper money from hand to hand. From a boy whose pushcart was decorated with a painted photo of Cantinflas, Joe bought some tortillas, handing her one from their newspaper wrapping. She folded it and ate it as she'd seen others do.

* * * * *

The crowds seemed to thicken rather than diminish as the afternoon lengthened, but the noise no longer bothered her and she had learned to skip through openings in a wall of bodies, afraid to let Joe out of her sight as he led the way. Once he handed her an enchilada, which resembled a Cornish pastry, but when she bit into it and swallowed, liquid fire seared her tongue and throat. She welcomed a long fire-dousing drink of the pulque that Joe handed her in his wine bottle. She dropped the remainder of the food surreptitiously as she skipped behind him through the crowd.

* * * * *

A grey-haired little man whose chocolate face was lined like a relief map and whose shoulders were bent beneath the heavy skin bag he was carrying on his back with a strap, appeared from behind the lines of cars. He was hoarsely crying something Georgina couldn't understand. He glanced between the parked vehicles, stepped out of sight, then came back and shouted happily, "José!"

Joe jumped to his feet and rushed to the old man and hugged him in an abrazo. Then they pulled apart and looked each other over, exchanging excited words. Georgina smiled at them with the happy tolerance of a wife or sweetheart watching her man meeting an unknown figure out of his past. The little old man returned her smile, and Joe said something in which she caught the word *turista.* Joe led the old man back to the truck and said, "This my very old friend Paco Carapán." Georgina looked into the old man's face and smiled.

"Señorita Marks."

" *'Tardes, señorita.*"

"Paco is from my village," Joe said. "He's our local moonshiner." He took some change from his pocket and handed it to Paco. His friend pulled the heavy skin bag from under his arm while Joe crouched in front of him. The old man tilted the bag so that a long stream of clear liquid squirted into Joe's open mouth. Paco tipped the forward end of the skin bag into the air, cutting off the stream. Joe stood up and shook his head while Paco twisted a heavy elastic band around the nipple on the bag.

When he got his breath Joe said to Georgina, "Paco makes the best tequila in Hidalgo. Would you like to try some?"

The old man looked from Joe to Georgina and back again.

"*¡Mucho hombre!*" he said admiringly. Georgina smiled and nodded in agreement.

from En México

Louis Dudek

1

In waves of weariness,
allergy to foods,
climatic migraine—
such poetry as there was:
of the rudiments of living
in their tropical stir,
storms, and the building trade.

A roar of sea, in constant surrender
to sun and rain,
and palm trees opening genital limbs.

By shores where Cortés landed.

In a world of strangeness
all thoughts run together,
then come singly
lke those bell-birds of Vera Cruz.

Beside the ditch the boy was defecating,
as the train passed by he covered his face with his hands.

They live in hovels,
on the harsh crude maguey
that yields string and needle,
paper and twine,
and the hot drink tequila:
beside them the sad dark Mexican,
or a small brown boy with a donkey,
and a woman shielding her mouth with black.

Eat the cactus, own many dogs.

Do the arts matter?
Only as tourist faddle,
              as the rich man's pride.
From a beginning of adobe huts
and jungle kraals . . .

We have been in the place where hurricanes begin
with hot sidereal spin
taking their rise from the turbulence of the water.
And the dusty horizon
is a dream of distance,
of silence,
then a sudden roar—
among the ruins of blood-hungry gods.

The Cortésian enterprise
turned a continent into a tornado
that rose from this silver spout:
now the jewelry of the cheap stores!

Cortés died old and poor
who was the young Alexander.

As language, it is to be read as language—
the Virgin of Guadalupe,
              and a brown Mexican mother
leaving the church with her child.
They say 'we all suffer
and therefore pray'.
They say 'we suffer
and Christ, through love,
can release from suffering'—
through love, formed of the love of the mother,
not out of males and females
                in their joy.
Guadalupe
      on the road to Teotihuacán.

Here where they killed for the god
        with knives of obsidian,
and the Spaniards "massacred ten thousand"
and the Spaniards "massacred four thousand"
              building crosses.

Yet for us it's only a process
                that a pill can control . . .

We are near to the earth-shaping waves
and the gargoyles of gods,
by the empty palace of Hoon
on the beach at Mocambo.

2

It is most quiet
where it is most violent.
That's why we appear so good.

In a tropical cemetery
hardly a grave is to be seen,
so much is overgrown.

And where Cortés with his men
        (their pockets full of booty)
waded in blood, they've drained the lake
and streetcars glide
where he shook the Indian by the arm and cried:
"You have destroyed the most beautiful city in the world—
                Tenochtitlán!"

He opened the continent
                like a cornucopia.
Now the jungle has an oceanic luxury:
boys by a heap of papaya
(above them, the cornfields,
                maguey rows, cactus)
and thatched native huts
with little children in the puddles.
Rain, out of a solitary cloud,
then sun, more sun—
building pyramids of green
and *las flores*
in the Huastecan jungle,
the pre-Aztec world.

On dry-weather roads,
we were speaking of—what?
                The birth of galaxies,
the reproduction of moon-struck snails.
Imagination
                under the beta rays!

How to discover the elements
and to define the natural
and then the skill-won form;
how to reconcile these

with the real conditions
of living, which are universal carnage
in a jungle of fertility—
under the aspect of new knowledge
not of old mythology.

Given the conditions,
energy is there,
    water and sun
    making the jungle.

Then walled haciendas
with all the animals under one roof.
And the temple
    of Quetzalcoatl.

Cortés and Moctezuma
    two primitive faiths
pitted against each other,
weaving the continental horn.

So Mejicano, mestizo,
have got religion up to the gills,
conferred on them by the Spaniards
(to give enslavement a proper face).

As language. . . Silence is also a language.
When there is no order in heaven
we make what we make
by luck, or strength,
or the composition of desire.
Power grows
    like vegetation,
and there are no preferences under heaven.

I do not know why a leaf should be of less worth
    than a Vatican,
or why builders care.
The mathematical stones recite their logic
of cruelty and despair—
we arose to gratify some searchless reason
shaping the empty air.

But men have stood on a great eminence
over nature's smoke

when the idea ignited the desire
and desire spoke.

(Even if the idea was wrong, as Teotihuacán
was made to be perfectly functional
as a sacrificial altar.)

How the temple came out of the heart of cruelty,
and out of the jungle the singing birds!

3

Religion,
       always used
to put a safe stamp on terror.
First the enemy one hates
          is "sacrificed"
then one's own kind—
to contain fear, out of ignorance.
In our time weakness, insecurity, mental pain.

They say no more, as language
              (art, or faith)
than any other language;
speak as leaves do,
as dogs sniffing,
as the mating glow-worm sending a call.

And may be wrong.
We make advances
          toward "humility."

Religion is an open question.

I thought, seeing the layered stones—
how wonderful
       the pursuit of knowledge!
When on the lettered rock-face
appeared a skull and bones.

Optimism is foolish. Life can only be
tragic, no matter what its success.

But the universe does not wait
for me to judge it, nor is death itself
a cause for condemnation.

Knowledge is neither necessary nor possible
to justify the turning
of that huge design.

That turns in the mind, for love.

That it should come into being out of nothing
                    (grass . . . bird . . . machine and metal),
that they should come into being.
Man come to shape out of smoking matter,
        out of male secretion in the womb, take form.
All things, all bodies,
        that they should come out of nothing,
rise, as projectiles out of rock,
with spicules, eyes, limbs,
with ornaments, accoutrements, skills,
amid an abundance of flora and fauna,
and each to itself all—
in a jungle, devouring graves!

We have passed through the earth's middle
and emerged as we are.
Climbing mountains, living in valleys,
can we miss the end of living?
(Since we have looked death in the face.)
To be is the palm of creation,
and all that we are is seed from a pod.

You may hate the jungle,
its inimical insects, flies,
and the chaos of growing
everything at once;
but we return for fertility
to its moist limbs and vaginal leaves.

They grow over each other, overgrow,
and the whole thing, by elimination,
is also an order that exists.
Hence the necessary magnificence of all reality.
(Where an artist is only a pipsqueak
in a forest of mocking birds.)

So praise the glory of the green jungle
with all its terrible thunders;
praise death and generation
and the embracement of lovers under all skies.
Praise frost and thaw, and the congealing of elements,
or their prismatic flow; praise the disposition of ferns,
and the erection of great trees.
Praise hovels and giant domes
and the ant's most secular mound.
Between cathedral spires
and the plum tree's pleasantness
there is no distinction. Praise these.

Anythings we shape in fire,
as anything that grows, by living . . .
There are degrees of beauty.
But as to what makes one flower
more to be prized than another—
we can define the elements, their order,
and what they do in the eye, or mind,
but the shaping hands are undivined.

There is the stubborn, obedient donkey.
And equanimity, as the cow had it
when the busy bus went by.
And thatched cottages, roofs on four sticks,
under which they live
in the mango groves.

(Not to imagine
that we understand anything.
The universe turns
                    me, not I it.)

Imagination makes
the organ cactus,
the autocar,
and a poem with six feet in every line.

And there is intelligance
of the kind that can choose
and of the kind that cannot choose:
the short range of the individual
and the long range of the species
(evolving by generation

in the moment when we breed,
or answering the immediate need)—
on different time-clocks, yet the same,
a groping fallible mind.

All the green blanketing the hills,
the braided streams,
and the brown sands bleaching;
horses with heads akimbo,
small lambs that leap,
children with huge eyes,
and lovers shy in their look:
        praise these to the bewildering heavens,
knowing no other tongue but praise.

And death also is in the process.
Our bus killed a calf on the road as we passed.
It looked at us coming
then turned into our path as we swerved.
Just a thud, and we kept on going.
(Earlier, we nearly killed a mother and child.)
Not an uneventful voyage.
Those who survive
will have enjoyed the ride.

Perhaps we die
in order to make room for others.
Why should one gang
hold the charabanc of existence for ever?
But what doesn't exist is no matter.
Out of all that death, the real emerges.

Under the shading palms, in the evening hour,
like all creatures who have come to no grief,
like all shoots who have come to flower,
we enjoy the languid air.
There is no travail here,
no passion, pang, or impulse of despair.
The breeze cools the temples with a summer's swell,
and under the tropic starlight all is well.

from Under the Volcano

Malcolm Lowry

It was stiflingly hot in the sunken deserted road. Yvonne gave a nervous cry
and turned on her heel; Hugh caught her arm.
'Don't mind me. It's just that I can't stand the sight of blood, damn
it.'
She was climbing back into the *camión* as Hugh came up with the
Consul and two passengers.
The *pelado* was swaying gently over the recumbent man who was
dressed in the usual loose white garments of the Indian.
There was not, however, much blood in sight, save on one side of his
hat.
But the man was certainly not sleeping peacefully. His chest heaved
like a spent swimmer's, his stomach contracted and dilated rapidly, one fist
clenched and unclenched in the dust...
Hugh and the Consul stood helplessly, each, he thought, waiting for
the other to remove the Indian's hat, to expose the wound each felt must be
there, checked from such action by a common reluctance, perhaps an obscure
courtesy. For each know the other was also thinking it would be better still
should one of the passengers, even the *pelado*, examine the man.
As nobody made any move at all Hugh grew impatient. He shifted
from foot to foot. He looked at the Consul expectantly: he'd been in this
country long enough to know what should be done, moreover he was the one
among them most nearly representing authority. Yet the Consul seemed lost
in reflection. Suddenly Hugh stepped forward impulsively and bent over the
Indian—one of the passengers plucked his sleeve.
'Har you throw your cigarette?'
'Throw it away.' The Consul woke up. 'Forest fires.'
'Si, they have prohibidated it.'
Hugh stamped his cigarette out and was about to bend over the man
once more when the passenger again plucked his sleeve:
'No, no,' he said, tapping his nose, 'they har prohibidated that,
también.'
'You can't touch him—it's the law,' said the Consul sharply, who
looked now as though he would like to get as far from this scene as possible,
if necessary even by means of the Indian's horse. 'For his protection. Actually
it's a sensible law. Otherwise you might become an accessory after the fact.'
The Indian's breathing sounded like the sea dragging itself down a
stone beach.
A single bird flew, high.
'But the man may be dy - ' Hugh muttered to Geoffrey.

'God, I feel terrible,' the Consul replied, though it was a fact he was about to take some action, when the *pelado* anticipated him: he went down on one knee and, quick as lightning, whipped off the Indian's hat.

They all peered over, seeing the cruel wound on the side of his head, where the blood had almost coagulated, the flushed moustachioed face turned aside, and before they stood back Hugh caught a glimpse of a sum of money, four or five silver pesos and a handful of centavos, that had been placed neatly under the loose collar to the man's blouse, which partly concealed it. The *pelado* replaced the hat and, straightening himself, made a hopeless gesture with hands now blotched with half-dried blood.

How long had he been here, lying in the road?

Hugh gazed after the *pelado* on his way back to the *camión*, and then, once more, at the Indian, whose life, as they talked, seemed gasping away from them all. '*¡Diantre! ¿Dónde buscamos un médico?*' he asked stupidly.

This time from the *camión*, the *pelado* made again that gesture of hopelessness, which was also like a gesture of sympathy: what could they do, he appeared trying to convey to them through the window, how could they have known, when they got out, that they could do nothing?

'Move his hat farther down though so that he can get some air,' the Consul said, in a voice that betrayed a trembling tongue; Hugh did this and, so swiftly he did not have time to see the money again, also placed the Consul's handkerchief over the wound, leaving it held in place by the balanced *sombrero*.

The driver now came for a look, tall, in his white shirt sleeves, and soiled whipcord breeches like bellows, inside high-laced, dirty boots. With his bare tousled head, laughing dissipated intelligent face, shambling yet athletic gait, there was something lonely and likeable about this man whom Hugh had seen twice before walking by himself in the town.

Instinctively you trusted him. Yet here, his indifference seemed remarkable; still, he had the responsibliity of the bus, and what could he do, with his pigeons?

From somewhere above the clouds a lone plane let down a single sheaf of sound.

—'*Pobrecito.*'

—'*Chingar.*'

Hugh was aware that gradually these remarks had been taken up as a kind of refrain around him—for their presence, together with the *camión* having stopped at all, had ratified approach at least to the extent that another male passenger, and two peasants hitherto unnoticed, and who knew nothing, had joined the group about the stricken man whom nobody touched again—a quiet rustling of futility, a rustling of whispers, in which the dust, the heat, the bus itself with its load of immobile old women and doomed poultry, might have been conspiring, whole only these two words, the one of compassion, the other of obscene contempt, were audible above the Indian's breathing.

The driver, having returned to his *camión*, evidently satisfied all was as it should be save he had stopped on the wrong side of the road, now began to blow his horn, yet far from this producing the desired effect, the rustling punctuated by a heckling accompaniment of indifferent blasts, turned into a general argument.

Was it robbery, attempted murder, or both? The Indian had probably ridden from market, where he'd sold his wares, with much more than that four or five pesos hidden by the hat, with *mucho dinero*, so that a good way to avoid suspicion of theft was to leave a little of the money, as had been done. Perhaps it wasn't robbery at all, he had only been thrown from his horse? Posseebly. Imposseebly.

Sí, hombre, but hadn't the police been called? But clearly somebody was already going for help. *Chingar*. One of them now should go for help, for the police. An ambulance—the Cruz Roja—where was the nearest phone?

But it was absurd to suppose the police were not on their way. How could the chingados be on their way when half of them were on strike? No it was only a quarter of them that were on strike. They would be on their way, all right though. A taxi? *No, hombre*, there was a strike there too. —But was there any truth, someone chimed in, in the rumour that the Servicio de Ambulancia had been suspended? It was not a red, but a green cross anyhow, and their business began only when they were informed. Get Dr. Figueroa. *Un hombre noble.* But there was no phone. Oh, there was a phone once, in Tomalín, but it had decomposed. No, Dr. Figueroa had a nice new phone. Pedro, the son of Pepe, whose mother-in-law was Josefina, who also knew, it was said, Vincente González, had carried it through the streets himself.

* * * * *

The Consul went to see to Yvonne; the other passengers, shielding their faces against the dust, climbed on board the bus which had continued to the detour where, stalled, it waited still as death, as a hearse. Hugh ran to the Indian. His breathing sounded fainter, and yet more laboured. An uncontrollable desire to see his face again seized Hugh and he stooped over him. Simultaneously the Indian's right hand raised itself in a blind groping gesture, the hat was partially pushed away, a voice muttered or groaned one word:

'*Compañero.*'

Trotsky Collecting Rare Cacti

David Lawson

Partisan Review became the centre of . . . .
'literary Trotsyism' . . . . The editors invited
Trotsky to contribute.
—Isaac Deutscher, *The Prophet Outcast*

His white hair torn by the wind
up there amongst the boulders,
wearing heavy gloves, of course,
and a blue French peasant jacket
he did not quite look the part
of a Commissar of War, though still
there was strength and a determination
set this time to another purpose.

Dark years of exile in places
he would not have chosen
had led to a 1936-37 crossing
on a petrol tanker, the *Ruth*
from Norway to Tampico, to the spacious
haven of Diego Rivera's Blue House—
a two-year paradise—almost enough
to atone for all that had gone wrong.

And yes, he was a sought-for
contributor to American journals
from this place in the sun. A falling-
out with Rivera led hm nearby
in Coyoacán to "the little
fortress" at 45 avenida Viena
where he raised rabbits and chickens
in the months before being murdered.

Also, in the meantime, with wife Natalya
and others, the expeditions to far places
like Tamazunchale in search of cacti—
cereus, mamillaria, opuntia, viznagas.
And so it was fitting, in sunny exile,
thus to become a connoisseur
amongst the boulders, wearing heavy gloves
and a blue French peasant jacket.

The Two Hearts of Frida Kahlo

Fraser Sutherland

I was 13 when I saw him painting murals
in the school auditorium. He looked exactly like
a big bull-frog. So this was the famous Diego!
I soaped his stairway but he didn't slip:
he planted his feet like bricks.

                      And his girlfriends—
when he wasn't painting it was someone's arms;
I used to break up embraces by whispering
that his wife was on her way.
                    "Holy Shit, Diego, here comes Lupe!"
All the time I wanted to have his child
but something got in the way.

I was studying for medical school when
a streetcar collision skewered me
sent a steel rod
through my body. I wanted to die quickly,
instead I lay for a year in the hospital,
strapped to a board, encased in a plaster cast,
a human junkyard: wrecked spine, leg, foot, pelvis fractured
in three places.
             I began to paint.

When I could walk I took my work to Diego,
"Look at these and no bullshit."
                  "Not bad, little girl,"
he said and I invited him out to my home in Coyoacán.
Sundays he'd take a cab out, other days
I'd watch him cover walls with the proletariat.
Sometimes he'd paint me.
                  "You have a dog-face."
"And you," I said, "have the face of a frog!"
I was 18, he 43: he married me.
Lupe came to the wedding party, flung up my skirt
and screamed,
             "You see these two sticks?
These are the legs Diego has instead of mine!"
                Then she stomped out.

Diego and his fat belly were everywhere.
I had a fat belly too but not from
refried beans. They hauled us off to Detroit
so Diego could do something with the mastodon
they called the Institute of Art. I trailed around
with him to the factories until the night
I started to bleed. They rushed me to the hospital,
I remember the ceiling of the surgery, so many colours
the loveliest thing I ever saw.
                                        I lost my child.

I painted again, there was nothing else to do:
2,000 children and they all looked like me.
And there's a bed, and a skeleton, and a snail
and various funny items at the ends of cords, and
vines on the bedspread, and a little girl
with a death mask.

I should have been an Aztec princess asking for
a flayed heart as an offering
but born in this bloody century
I could only dress the part—
brilliant wool in braided hair,
gems carved with gods, swirling skirts.
On my face scarlet and mascara.

In the 30s our friends were always getting shot
or clubbed on the head by the pig police.
We fought that donkey Rockefeller
who had Diego's mural ground to powder.
We came back to Mexico and fought
each other because Diego was always screwing around
yet I couldn't love him for what he wasn't
and no matter how I cried and fought and took
revenge I felt our hearts were one.
                                        He divorced me in 1938,

threw a party to celebrate but I got on with my
"Two Hearts."
                        One gets her blood from a portrait of Diego
held by Frida #1. The other heart
has her artery ruptured, ah, poor Frida #2
who tries to staunch the flow with forceps.
One lives in memory and hope, the other's dead.
Two years later Diego sent for me from San Francisco.

The idea was to get treated for osteomyelitis:
he married me again.

The body was going to pieces: for my show in '53
they had to take me in an ambulance.
I waved to the fans from a wheelchair and that year
they did their 14th operation in 16 years.
                                        Gangrene.
The bastards cut my leg off at the knee.

Now my clown politician husband was trying for the nth time
to get the Communist Party to take him back. It
wasn't bad enough that Trotsky got an icepick in the skull
but Diego tried to borrow the pen Leon had given me
so he could sign for re-admission. Sweet Jesus,
life is one big joke.

I was doped up all the time. Mother of mothers,
the pain. On my 44th birthday I dressed up,
held court to *amigos, amigas*.
Less than a week later, at 3 a.m. . . . .

They draped my coffin with a red flag.

from Aesthetic of Death

Claude Beausoleil

> *¿Qué me importa la muerte si no me importa
> la vida?*
> —Octavio Paz

for Maurice Roche

The sugar skull immediately challenges anyone already familiar with Jorge Luis Borges, the Argentine writer fond of culture and metamorphoses. A text will follow from it, a private place where facts transform the circulating intuition. Death in Mexican civilization manifests itself in multiple forms. Philosophically Death transforms itself into the everyday. For the poet and essayist Octavio Paz, "The dead do not exist; only Death, our mother, exists." Using this mask as a foil, words are shiny bits of paper, fictional possibilities. These sugar skulls are overdone. The gilding is excess. The intimate becomes public. So much for the facts. In the shop window. Books. Signs speaking to the nothingness and the projects in all of us. Mother of forms, as Paz writes, Death invents its beams. It does not disperse, it brings together. On a sunny afternoon on the Avenida Madero, México, D.F.

The bookstore has a decided effect. Its window like a certain eye. Tracks. Stakes. There is no dust on these fresh sweets, recently made for this festival of the Day of the Dead. The look of the place clarifies things. I advance only in shadow, like a story, because the exact moment of capture has something imaginary about it. I watch and hesitate, not knowing how to situate the allegory. I speak to the bookseller. I don't resist, not even in my perfunctory Spanish.

Everything is up in the air. This moment. This unexpected representation of Death. Impressions juxtapose themselves. Illusion. Reality. Other clients. The humid sidewalk. Shop window of skulls, pastel expectations. Thought that wanders. What can be done in the face of Death when it's presented with so much peace and colour? Breathe it away. Impossible. Borges. An answer to these questions. This ruse of creating a work to foretell digressions. The bookseller informs me. All these skulls, these books, these offerings. I'll be back. Words always come back.

* * * * *

The avenue has resumed its morning rhythm. The haze of the great city rises from the jostling sidewalks. There is a quiet melody in all this din. A memory drifts along the shop windows in which the sugar skulls of these world-famous writers have been arranged. Writing on this subject is like

64

following a ritual. Writing on Death is a survival described in each book. Writing. Essays. Fiction. From the order of things to the savour of research. Death sets out its doubts here in a bookstore where all the signs remind me of the fragility of the present.

Death. Is it the foundation of universal art? Add quotations from Mexican essays on the subject. Iconography. Poems. Fragments of sentences that have fallen here onto the page of the voyage when the trip back is already besieged by words, entranced by a half-seen mystery. Footsteps. Silence. Rusty cars. *Mexico City Blues.* I hear the murmur of a text—Kerouac—fragmented by its own story. Jazz. Differently. Transposed confusion. Profusion too. Dreams. And then time arises, pre-Columbian. The idea of Death filtering the disorder of a city consigned to its own disproportion.

* * * * *

Every endeavour is a free fight with Death. A lost battle to which words provide silent testimony.

I imagine Death in the form of that woman in a feather boa strolling about between the serial white of the trees in Alameda Park. She is haughty, familiar. Her hat casts a shadow over her jaw. Obvious and magical. Beautiful clinging vine. The painting by Diego Rivera takes up a motif with a popular resonance. To be inhabited by Death. To open it up avenues from a calculated centre in which all segments receive its slow step. To note the work's brush-strokes and overall effect. A daily prayer. Pleasures. The tiny details of an implacable unity. The fresco was in the lounge of the Hotel Prado that was heavily damaged during the earthquake of September, 1985. They tell me that it survived. Missing from the disaster because it was the disaster. White behind the barricades blocking the main entry to this attractive hotel visited at random in July, 1983. Rivera survived. Death is elsewhere. Facing the void it rejects. Facing the era of the painting that various notes have minutely described. The work as an offering to the inconstancy of fate on an afternoon, over there, directly across, in this park with avenues as rigid as its white corsage. He wanted to initiate us into the hideous secret.

* * * * *

Through this slice of life I gain access to other visions underscoring what the call of the ancestors can reveal about the future and its signs. Zócalo of colonial memories, dumping-ground of Indian millenia, anthropology of a violent, open torrent of superimpositions on the profusion of horizons polluted by vestiges of stone images. Life uses itself up in its own exploration. Through the streets of one city that hides another, blocking out the leading edge of the roar, I advance sentence by sentence, dazzled, without a thread to follow, farther away than what I can glimpse of the pathetic heights of the Torre Latinoamericana. Monuments. Destruction. Parks. Intersections. Cathedral of stupor with a baroque temperament. Fallen warrior. Superhuman race. Chance. Naming. An imaginary painting.

Thought in this spectacle is the shadow of an arcade. Scraping off the facts, the tracks are obvious. Life is an assault; its tissues breathe the passing time.

* * * * *

A dancer. Aztec costume. In the immense plaza. Seeing a belief there in spite of all the trinkets. Time is deaf; the city looks at itself heavily.

Nagual. Philosophy. Cult. Vision. A notion of Time as a preface to Death. A welcoming attitude. Ruse. Death triumphs. They know it. They jeer at it. Death knows it. Its mask imagines an anxiety that has been tamed by the people's fiesta of candles and offerings that use the altar to trap masquerading fears.

* * * * *

The Art of Death is a dimension of everyday existence. The sacred is a dimension of the truth. Monumental frescoes open perspective. University. Palacio de Bellas Artes. Siqueiros Polyforum. Other sites of the phenomenal. Reinvented churches. The sacred transforms Death into a less blinding ceremony. Plastic flowers. Tortillas. Cigarettes. Details of a joy that resembles life, fleeting representation of a white history with a whitewashed face. Caricatures by Posada. Frescoes by Rivera. Let the outrageousness of Death walk among these bodies! Flesh inverted from the silence contained in this end reinvested with belief and emotion. Bone. Cavity. Skulls of sugar. In this store window filled with books that shine even as they disappear. A remembered phrase that becomes white again like the ineluctable description of a destiny fulfilled.

* * * * *

Death as hope, the only thing that can give peace to humanity, is a theme of Mesoamerican poetry. Perceived as the supreme enigma, Death can be liberation, lightness, or fatalism. Death dialogue. Death of pain that has flown. Death of love that has broken free.

El rostro de la muerte. The title of the major exhibition in the National Museum of Anthropology. The face of Death viewed from every angle, placed on the line of Time. Ancient figurines and objects of today. Adoration of Death. The unfailing obsession rediscovered in Nahuatl poetry. Transcendence and the idea of warriors reincarnated as richly-feathered birds. Appeal of the signs of the crossing. "Todos se van," says the poem. Everyone leaves and we follow them beyond appearances, into renewed infinity. Death in this museum room laughs at culture. We can't control something that surpasses us everywhere. Naming the objects that participate in the veneration of Death is like trying to conjure away the irrefutable.

An essay on Death mandated by impressions felt while living here. Mexico is this possibility that opens reflection on the most serious questions of life. Death on the page of Time.

* * * * *

A pre-Columbian poem translated into Spanish; the questioning of Death is central:

"Sólo venimos a soñar, sólo venimos a dormir
no es verdad, no es verdad
que venimos a vivir en la tierra."

Here the language sings of the unreality of our time on earth. These words use melody to say that it's all a dream, we're sleeping, nothing is, nothing is true; we haven't come to live on earth, we pass through it as spectres. From the most ancient Mexico to the Mexico of the present, Death has always haunted reason and concepts of reality. The return to Death, place of fecund mutations. This version of human life differs greatly from other Western attitudes toward the phenomenon of physical death. In spite of the effect of the Catholic Church, Mexican civilization is fiercely anchored in a deification of Death as the original chaos to which our return is inscribed in cosmic law.

* * * * *

Death reveals itself in more than one place. I watch television in my hotel room; the set is too large for the room's dimensions, which barely leave enough space for my suitcases between the bathroom and the door. People's fiesta. Learned speeches. The two levels of the country are clear to me. Professorial analyses of the place of Death in pre-Columbian civilizations. Scenes from Veracruz, where a village is getting ready for the Day of the Dead. Images of the past. The present actively redistributes traditional habits. A lunch on the television screen. They are chatting about death. Skeletons for laughs. Altars filmed all over Mexico. Advertisements. Video. Bones clatter between ads for flights to Nueva York, Montreal, or Madrid.

* * * * *

Carlos Fuentes articulates the dynamic of his characters against the challenge of confrontation with the obsession of Death as the only legitimate stakes. Death is the blindingly attractive precipice in his novels. In 1914, in the middle of the Mexican Revolution, an elderly American embodies the final demands of the challenge. *The Old Gringo* is the trajectory of this man who wants to die, offered to memory, thus cleansing himself of the horrors and pettiness of his life and his community. General Arroyo is the agonizing symbol of a Mexico filled with suffering and of the absolute that the mirage of revolution has not been able to soften. All are there under the burning sun in order to invoke Death. Symbol and apotheosis. Grandeur of the Mexican landscape. A narrative blown apart in the quest for meaning, *The Old Gringo* has come to die, beyond words, fantasies, and lands *(Terra nostra)*. He has come for the experience of Death, which holds all secrets between its shores. Through him and Harriet Winslow, who came to Mexico for Life but has found the more fascinating gulf of Death, the United States collapses into another dimension, another America, immemorial and vast, that flows through the jungles and high plateaus from the Río Bravo to Tierra del Fuego. Another version of a continent that refuses to accept the portion of historic consciousness that seems to be solely English, while Spanish, the Indian languages, Portuguese and French also determine its living contours. Ancient Indian America covered with memory and Death. Mexico rises in the song of Carlos Fuentes and gives its excessiveness to the beauty of Death.

* * * * *

Conquered by Spain, Mexico will only live through its Death. The fall of Tenochtitlán. Epidemics. Famine. Death prowls the colony. Firearms. A new world. Death is resistance. In his text, *Criticism of the Pyramid*, Octavio Paz speaks of the Museum of Anthropology as the glorification of the past, presenting succeeding civilizations as witnesses to Death, the supposed essence of Mexico. A place of tragic imagination, the Museum shows culture as a force that transforms guilt (memory and destiny) into power (death and the present). Here modern Mexico regains its glory and projects its future onto the achievements of the past that are exalted in the present (the architecture of the Museum itself, and thus its verifiable signs). The apotheoses of Death become intermingled within this vast Museo Nacional de Antropología. Obscure and white, the representation of Death gives its consent. Stripped. Buried and offered to the paradox that revives it and makes it seem capable of explaining everything. Death. Death. Death. Mistress of sovereign Time.

* * * * *

José Guadalupe Posada. His engravings insist on reproducing Death. It takes up all the critical space. Social art. Grating art. Skeletons of civil servants, soldiers, employers, return the mocking laughter of a consciousness that knows what is awaiting them. Whether behind desks, holding rifles, or smoking cigars, Posada's skeletons are literal caricatures of a corrupt world composed of nothing but stupidity and exploitation. Death smoulders in these drawings. When unmasked, it becomes vitriolic. Evil demon of power. Ghost of a society ground to bits by its defects. An acidic and entertaining satirist, working in this people's art form, Posada displays Death as both yoke and thread, an image that reiterates its support for the social body. Irony shows the abuses of politics and makes Death bustle about in the form of strident bones.

* * * * *

The great night of Death. The city and its monuments. Everything ruins pride. Human questioning. The murmur of the congested streets becomes clearer. The city's downtown, where bodies become entangled, saturated with the certainty of Death. Art is the final mask.

* * * * *

Some Indians are playing flutes. A child beats a small skin drum. Death is on the look-out, crouching in the entry to a store with garish lighting. Music. Death. Small sound of things. The Present. Flight. In an unhurried song, Death and its shadow, Life.

Mexico is a mixture of stricken peoples.

In his essay, "The Bow and the Lyre," Octavio Paz writes, "Between birth and death, poetry opens up a possibility for us that is neither the eternal life of religion nor the eternal death of philosophy, but a living that implies and contains a dying." Death as cyclical referent allows a merging of the time before and the time after Life that makes sense. This concept sets the tone for a whole range of cultural characteristics.

* * * * *

All that the Christian religion has poured into the Mexican imagination has become intermixed with ancient customs. Thus Good Friday goes off on a sacrificial tangent. From the theatre to that excitation that Antonin Artaud wrote was everywhere in Mexico and which made concrete effects possible in art. The Stations of the Cross. A whip on a naked back. Thorns. Simulated blows. A Christ in the flesh who relives the suffering of the crucifixion. The death of Christ. Death of Time. Realistic re-enactments of the Passion are organized every year all over the country. Death opens its wounds to a Christian memory amplified by contact with the world that reinvests it with complex and effervescent values. The blood of Christ still runs from the hyper-realist statues that abound in Mexico. Death the Extravagant decorates the imagination with plaster figures with nails through their feet. The village of Ixtapalapa, in the suburbs of Mexico City, has had a ritual celebration of the Death of Christ since 1743. Crowds gather there to wait in awe. Death climbs the hill. Mexico City lights up. Death using Christian symbols spliced by analogy onto Aztec sacrifices.

To use writing to evoke the Avenue of the Dead that links the Pyramids of the Moon and the Sun in Teotihuacán.

* * * * *

In front of the bookstore window on Avenida Madero, people observe the magic of the words surrounding Death. Pride. Humility. Fragile sweat of human labour placing lines before the Void that the Aesthetic of Death freely translates. There is logic in the passion to understand. Mexico that Death has left at the edge of earthquakes and wandering souls. Lyric Mexico with its eternal furies. Paz, writing about reading Borges, who died in Geneva after having lived and deceived so much. Transparent time. History of literature. History of the infinite. Books recover the dream of existence. This text on Death derives from the sugared skull of Jorge Luis Borges, Argentine writer, whose language is an architecture of paths that fork, noticed at random on an October afternoon on the eve of the Day of the Dead, in the window of a bookstore on the Avenida Madero, México, D.F.

from Passage mexicain

Joël Pourbaix

from "The Surface Erodes"

Yes, the tourists, black glasses, perspiration and cold smiles, the archeological site become commonplace. Plundering, haggling, restaurants, imitations, *what's left*? I imagine the niche where the objects sleep, those vases broken and placed in the tomb. May nothing ever disturb the life of things, their intimate wish to disappear.

* * * * * *

The pyramid of the sun at Teotihuacán, to climb it because it's there? It is not there, it *appears*, amalgam of dried bricks and mud; to guess where the tunnel is, the cavities, the four chambers hollowed out in the shape of a clover. A place of retreat and the retreat of place.

* * * * * *

The absence of the corpse. Necklace, breast plate, diadem, bracelets, rings, pearls, and especially the jade mask, a strange serenity, its look. It stares at an event that doesn't belong to me. The absence of the corpse—

* * * * * *

Two visitors are taking pictures of each other on top of the great pyramid at Cobá, disrupting my meditation—And a burst of laughter. The profound tranquillity of the place in the face of the horde of images. The buildings of Cobá: the material manifestation of obliteration.

* * * * * *

from "Rituals"

Solstices and equinoxes rub together against the walls to record the trajectories, angles, the beginning and end of time. The Observatory hangs by a thread from generation to generation, hum of the motionless eye. I gather in this instant; Venus rises.

* * * * * *

The cave. End of a stick moving forward, hand clenched, I place my words on the humid sand——Returning outside, the words sink down into the darkness behind me; I hear the long sigh of the earth.

* * * * * *

The ropes covered with thorn do not pierce my tongue, instruments abandoned, ritual inactive; no one asks for either my birth or my death. Then I'll take the blood and the ashes; a mask will float softly on my face.

* * * * * *

No god, no sovereign. Just the strangeness of the summit, vague pain, sitting and not knowing what to do. This entire emptiness lying flat in my lap.

* * * * * *

from "The Innocence of Place"

The cliffs swallow space, cleft in the sky that closes up again: Cave of Silence, Cave of Man. I am searching, to reach the innocence of the place, Río Grijalva, thin untangled thread of the weft of the world.

* * * * * *

The lianas, the roots, mahogany, palms, sapodilla, hevea, bread-fruit trees, vanilla plants, ceiba. The sacred tree, the tree of life at the centre of the world, ceiba, where are you? Running down, wandering, slowly fading, the slope and the mud.

* * * * * *

I will forget the worn and venerated names, and entrust myself to the copper skin of the earth. These steps that reformulate my existence.

* * * * * *

A crossroads on the way to Comitán, 5 A.M., thinking I've surprised reality, thinking that it's waiting for me. Then understanding the basic indifference of places.

* * * * * *

72

from "At the Edge of the Pacific"

The worn-out repetitions of the waves, this din of collapse, unending lament of thought—Luckily there's a black dog on the beach; his presence keeps me facing the immensity.

* * * * * *

The undecidable light, a buried sun begins to stir, a dance in the depths of things, loops, swirls, the opening, the loosened ring; there's the apparition, Tlahuitzcalpantecuhtli! For the first time I imagine dawn outside of myself.

* * * * * *

from "Visions in Mexico City"

Embroidered cloth, video cassettes, painted animal masks, the smell of leather, shouting loud-speakers, sizzling corn and slices of cactus, onyx, opals, amber, turquoise: nothing gets worn out by being shown. A gilded statue of La Soledad sleeps beneath the shop window.

* * * * * *

A form stretched out on the sidewalk, putrid stench, all has been overturned, Tezcatlipoca! He won't stop staring at me—I stop in the Zócalo, Palacio Nacional. A man is slowly rubbing the bronze balls that decorate the balcony; they will shine for the next President. But I can't get rid of that stench.

* * * * * *

Hollow, ill-fated days. A widower, no calendar will come to my aid; each of my gestures affirms its own rigorous uselessness. I am Xolotl, excluded, the fallen warrior, impersonal gaze on the flood along the boulevards. I leave the window, blood running from my nose, carbon, sulphur, ozone, and manage to read a few Aztec texts, poems colliding with the body's dust.

* * * * * *

For hours now, tequila at the back of dark room, I lose myself, again, for the first time, that mestizo half-smile; Tlazolteotl offers me her words. I keep uttering my clumsy sentences, for hours now, as if our words saved me from annihilation and upheld the entire universe; what's the difference? Tlazolteotl offers me her lips, the evidence naked as a touch—She gets up, her head held high and proud, her red and black skirt; she goes toward the white doorway over there, outside. I sit motionless before an empty glass—This is why fate must not be ignored.

* * * * * *

from "Epilogue"

Oaxaca, Hotel Pasaje, the languor of the lizard on the wall of the white room. I am made of silence; I have no memories, no nostalgia. The trace of what I experience is completely different.

from Le pays saint

Luc Racine

green dawn of the Americas
warm source of beginnings
here are the word and human song
before the arrival of he who was believed to be a herald
the quetzal bird the European exterminators the wild animals
(the catastrophe the catastrophe the white plague of Ecab)
here is what they said and how their life was spent
in this land of Anahuac at the edge of empire:

O never die never disappear
  remain there where there is no death
   but the great dawn
    never perish never be the one who leaves
    that suns devour and burn
     the great need the great sorrow
      and the singing tears of our hearts
       as though we were walking in flowering gardens
        impatient to leave this earth
       where for a single moment
        we live in harmony with one another

an tochan tinemi
ye nican in tlalticpac
zan ihui zan achic
zan tictotlanehuico

it's only a fragile necklace of herbs
  that scatter in our hands
   sad garlands that rise on the wind
    like a prayer at leaving
     for each of us to the other is only
      an offering devoured by the suns

may the flowers never fade
  the red birds become drunk with sun
   battered by the autumn rains
    no one will remain
     there where quetzal feathers now lie scattered
     where the great paintings crumble
      everything swept away like emeralds
      in this cold

we will barely have known each other
during our short stay on this earth
in this orange sleep
we are scarcely alive and our bodies are withering
faster than the winter prairies
this futile sojourn our names forgotten
on lips of coral or jade
no one will live here any longer
the words of this time so short
the faces that we recognize
the beautiful bodies of April warmth
and this May of white gold perfume
poured over our desire

once again
songs reverberate in this mountainous season
everything that we can't take with us
is given us for a single day
the turquoise green of the quiet mountains
we are hatched in purple hands
we speak to each other and it's a dream on earth
and then we already begin to disappear
nothing is left of the flowers of the song of friendship
jade explodes gold is torn to pieces
muddy snow where cries of anguish and waiting love
no longer have meaning

listen then my friends to these dreamed words
in which every spring gives us new life
as if knowing we'd been faithful to each other
farewell to the songs of May the fresh leaves of April
and to the proud gestures written in red
on purple mountains

four years
the sacred fire has burned
there at Teotihuacán
the sun stops the fourth sun
the hour had come for night to begin
the animals the gods had thrown themselves into the sacrificial fire
that arrow of sunlit flame

the gods met in Teotihuacán
to discuss who should live on the motionless earth
it was then that the quetzal god
descended to the kingdom of the dead
to rob the sacred bones from the lord of the underworld
so that humans would be born as an offering to the clay gods

but on the rainy earth
the gods grew worried about the people's food
the quetzal god went out to the fields as a swarm of red ants
that carried wild grain to the slopes of the Tamoanchan Mountains
on the lips of those who read the destiny of the gods
on the earth transformed by the April rains

humans gambled away their corn
for smooth quetzal feathers and green jade
thus it was that snow first appeared
and the sun's intense heat
burst open beneath the gentle stones

four years went by
before the tender sprouts of corn and the people's joy
were reborn from the rains
in a green palace far away

you remember I'm sure you do
I know child that you're not happy
we no longer have the same expectations at the ruins of Teotihuacán
in the evening when the Mexican sun the fibrous sun sets
and covers the celestial ruins
Teotihuacán Oaxaca Monte Albán
children still sell not marijuana no not marijuana to the tourists
but the sacred statuettes of the New World figures with elongated heads
and the beautiful faces the holy figurines found at Teotihuacán
where the pyramids are red fires under the sun
the sacred pyramids of sacrifice and red blood
in the setting of Teotihuacán
when the quetzal bird sacrifices itself to the gods of the West
its face white lime in the declining sun that flares over Teotihuacán
in the suns of the Creation
in Yucatan in Peru in Tierra del Fuego and always
the skies close again and blaze
jade skies over the city of the gods
over Teotihuacán the days of Mexico the colossal buildings

it's not the same anguish the same dream the same green fury
in the defeated cities the iodoform smells the ulcerous children
the pregnant women who sway against whitewashed walls
the old men who refuse to die
the deceitful shelters for guests in this bygone Paris
the wound of the inflamed rose the eyelids
the sleep of no one
on the Avenida de los Insurgentes an adolescent runs
wasted breath to the south of the city hammered by the rainy season
a teenager approaches his hands open to touch the ruins
it's a scattered world where so many loved ones no longer live

II   Caribbean and North East Coast

The Only Tourist in Havana Turns His Thoughts Homeward

Leonard Cohen

Come, my brothers,
let us govern Canada,
let us find our serious heads,
let us dump asbestos on the White House,
let us make the French talk English,
    not only here but everywhere,
let us torture the Senate individually
    until they confess,
let us purge the New Party,
let us encourage the dark races
    so they'll be lenient
    when they take over,
let us make the CBC talk English,
let us all lean in one direction
    and float down
    to the coast of Florida,
let us have tourism,
let us flirt with the enemy,
let us smelt pig-iron in our back yards,
let us sell snow
    to under-developed nations,
(Is it true one of our national leaders
    was a Roman Catholic?)
let us terrorize Alaska,
let us unite
    Church and State,
let us not take it lying down,
let us have two Governor Generals
    at the same time,
let us have another official language,
let us determine what it will be,
let us give a Canada Council Fellowship
    to the most original suggestion,
let us teach sex in the home
    to parents,
let us threaten to join the U.S.A.
    and pull out at the last moment,
my brothers, come

our serious heads are waiting for us somewhere
  like Gladstone bags abandoned
  after a *coup d' état*,
let us put them on very quickly,
let us maintain a stony silence
  on the St. Lawrence Seaway.

from Mother Solitude

Emile Ollivier

On the morning of the visit of the King of Kings, Desilomme had been hard at work since dawn, using his bare knee as an anvil. At his side, Agnès poured the coffee whose aroma did little to dispel the putrid odour of tan-soaked waters exposed to the dusty air. When Eva Maria came in sight on Rue de l'Hôpital, she was followed by two urchins with distended bellies beating out a wedding march on goatskins stretched over wooden hoops to which little bells had been attached. Little by little, the noise had drawn a crowd of idlers, so that by the time they reached the section of the street where the shoemakers were installed, an entire cortège was following in Eva Maria's wake.

"This can't go on," muttered Desilomme, shaking his head. "There are places for such people. The Public Health Department should step in, it makes no sense, she shouldn't be allowed to strut about in front of us like this, We have a right to our peace and quiet."

For a moment, Agnès forgot her coffee pot to watch Eva Maria approach on the opposite side of the street. "Yes, Father," she said, "it makes no sense." These remarks did not reach the ears of Eva Maria, who continued to move serenely in their direction. "Of course, she doesn't make any noise," conceded Agnès. "She's inclined to be quiet. But have you noticed how she's decked out this morning, Father? Imagine, getting herself up like that!"

"What a country! What a government!" muttered Desilomme, whose thoughts seemed to have taken an unexpected turn.

"But what sin can she possibly be atoning for!" wondered Agnès.

Desilomme set aside his hammer and leather. He took a few steps into the street to work the stiffness out of his legs, then abruptly raised his arms to the sky. "Where is God?" he cried. *"Where is God?"* And when his question received no answer, he returned to his seat and plunked himself down, placing his elbow on his knee and resting his chin in the open palm of his hand. Eva Maria had arrived within hearing now, prompting him to lower his voice: "If a member of my family were afflicted with such an illness (and he made a quick sign of the cross and tapped the wood at the end of the table) I . . . I don't know what I'd do. Ah! my daughter, let this serve as an example to you. You see here the results of love, the madness of love. No, no, it's not possible! What has become of the authorities? Ah! This city! This country!"

Eva Maria was before him now. Desilomme would later recount that when he looked Eva Maria Morelli in the eye that day, he had the impression he had been brought face-to-face with the void in all its terrifying dimensions, that he had made contact with the beyond, confronted with a pale fire whose blinding glow could only be that of hell. When he returned the young woman's look, he felt as if he were gazing into the eyes of a terrible Gorgon that gazed back at him from the farther side of a mirror. Like a man under a spell, he stood contemplating that visage of the dark underworld, that lost soul that seemed to have gone astray from some Luciferian revel.

The young woman's bare, bronzed shoulders palpitated perceptibly beneath the open stitches of an ornate lace shawl covered with a number of opaque, little flowers. Cut from a single bolt of white fabric, her dress, gathered loosely at the waist, covered her body from breast to heel, the hem of the skirt repeating the same lacy motif of the shawl. The delicacy of this lacework attested to the fact that it had been wrought by an uncommonly skilful hand, one that must have spent many a sleepless night bent over it. But the most curious aspect of the dress was an enormous collage that covered the entire circumference of the skirt which ballooned gracefully over a crinoline. A curious composition, it consisted of a number of magazine cut-outs interspersed with real objects. Images of skyscrapers, billboards, operating-rooms, debris from airplanes that had exploded in mid-air, human limbs, dismembered corpses, scaffolds, gibbets, guillotines, children's toys, antique automobiles, tanks and armoured cars were juxtaposed with household gadgets, disembowelled cockroaches, pumice stones, acacia needles, empty eggshells, thimbles, forks, knives and other eating utensils, hunks of bloody meat, dried cod fillets, and an assortment of pincers, lancets, cloves and caraway seeds. In short, a grotesque collage of the most baroque images coupled with the most outlandish objects known to man. On the bosom of the dress, the young woman had drawn a single, swollen, distended breast devoured by a chancre and endowed with a mutilated nipple. The entire animal, vegetable and mineral kingdoms seemed to have taken up residence on Eva Maria's person that day, brought together in a moment of bizarre apocalyptic union.

Thus adorned, she moved down the street.

She moved down the street with a steady, deliberate step, like a bride approaching an imaginary altar, advancing to the rhythms of her two youthful drummers. In the crook of her left arm, she clutched a spray of flowers that had the metallic look of artificial blooms, like those often seen on the better sepulchres in the city cemeteries. Composed of roses, carnations, lilacs and white jasmins, the bouquet was held together by a single long ribbon, from the end of which hung a picture of a gaping uterus expelling blood-spattered fetuses; one of these had a single leg, one was deprived of sex organs, one seemed to be suffering from water on the brain.

Thus adorned, she moved down the street.

When the cortège reached Rue des Miracles, it encountered another, larger cortège. Without a moment's hesitation, Eva Maria dropped to her knees and approached the limousine of the King of Kings. This unrehearsed scene took the organizers of the parade completely by surprise. The procession came to an abrupt halt. Beneath the stunned gazes of the guards assigned to protect the visitor, Eva Maria moved up to the King of Kings and graciously offered him her spray of flowers. The latter grimaced, hesitated a fraction of a second, then extended a hand to receive the bouquet. As he did so, the young woman threw back her head and directed a stream of spittle straight in his face. Then she turned and ran, breaking her way through the crowd. The stunned, silent onlookers gazed in horror as the members of the security service, emerging from their stupor, took off after her. Meanwhile, the little brown man was busy wiping away the saliva that had spattered his face. Clearly, he didn't understand what had happened to him. And who could understand? Two streets farther on, the security guards caught up with Eva Maria. She was slapped, cursed, kicked, struck repeatedly with the butts of their revolvers. She made no attempt to defend herself. Agnès would later recount that Eva Maria had smiled throughout the entire ordeal. Through the barred window of the van into which the police had hurled her, she gazed out at the crowd, a broad grin wreathing her bloody face.

Never again was that face to be seen wandering the city streets, that troubled face with its multiple lines of woe, that singular face that had always been seen in profile no matter what angle it was viewed from, that irascible face uttering an always mute but always audible, strangely intolerable cry.

News of Eva Maria's gesture quickly spread through the country. Almost overnight, The Bride, as she came to be called, acquired the stature of a legend. Children, hastily deserting their playgrounds on moonlit evenings, claimed to have seen her shadow looming up on the horizon. Gossip columnists reported that expectant mothers had aborted their fetuses at the mere sight of her; while others, dreaming of her during their pregnancy, had given birth to monsters. And there was the story of the woman who had been stricken with amenorrhea (or was it menorrhagia?), when, out walking one day in the street, she had sensed a presence on her heels and had whirled about to find herself face-to-face with The Bride, a ghostly white figure strolling calmly in her direction. And then there was the case of Jacinthe Estinval, a lovely, languorous, nubile, young woman, whose menstruations had permanently dried up when, caught one day in the street by the onset of her period and wanting at all costs to avoid the sarcastic looks of a group of rejected suitors lounging about a lamp-post, she had skirted a long wall, her dress clamped tightly between her thighs, only to be brought face-to-face with The Bride at the corner of Ruelle Piquant, just opposite the Paramount Cinema. Jacinthe Estinval had regained consciousness in the ambulance that had carried her to the hospital, all its sirens wailing. She had been confined to her bed for a month, a subject of controversy for the team of cardiologists, psychiatrists and gynaecologists assigned to her case. In the light of all these events, it is not surprising that the mere mention of The Bride's name was often enough to knock sense into the most rebellious teenager, to silence the most cheeky virgin, to tame the most dissolute lass. Even bearded women and those who were beyond the child-bearing age encountered her in their dreams, a powdered, barefoot figure dancing down the city streets. The Bride had come to inhabit the collective unconscious of an entire people.

Green Melody

Eucilda Jorge Morel

He was an elderly black man, quite tall, whose presence immediately inspired respect. He wore loose-fitting *guayaberas,* like many Cubans his age; his black shoes were always well-shined, and he liked to sport a green cap and dark glasses, which set him apart a bit. He told us his full name, but whenever we spoke of him at family gatherings, we always called him by the nickname we'd given him, "Green Melody."

He was a mason, and always used to puff on huge cigars while he worked. At times he would suddenly stop smoking and begin singing as loud as he could. He especially liked the song, "With You in the Distance," by Désar Portillo de la Luz, which was quite popular at the time, except that he would always change the line, "There is no beautiful melody," to "There is no green melody."

One afternoon the woman of the house stood watching him as he worked. He stopped smoking abruptly and said. "You know, *señora,* no political system is perfect. There are a lot of good and bad things about capitalism. There are struggles between the various levels of the middle class and the poor, who are terribly hard-up and slowly starve to death. That's the way it is: the exploiters and the exploited. Everything's based on money. Ah, but there's one good thing about it: you're free to travel anywhere you want, even to India, if you feel like it."

"Hold on a minute!"

"No, there's no question about it. I know what you're going to tell me. And I also know what I'm talking about. I'm black, and I've been through other times. I've been able to study and live with dignity and freedom."

There was an embarrassed silence. The old man became very serious. Neither of them spoke. Then he turned and went back to work, and at the same time began to sing, "There is no green melody / In which I don't think of you / And I'd never want to hear one . . ."

A little later he came down from his scaffolding, put on his *guayabera,* changed his shoes, and got his hat.

"*Señora,* I'm going out to get some cigarettes," he said, and quickly went downstairs.

He was back in fifteen minutes. His eyes shone; everything indicated that he'd just had a stiff shot of rum. He climbed back up on his scaffold and began to plaster the roof; a moment later his strong voice held forth again, "Beyond your eyes / Beyond the sun and stars / Far away at your side / There is no green melody . . ."

The following day he came earlier. He worked hard all morning, alternating between smoking cigars and cigarettes and crooning his favourite song, along with several more.

At noon he put on his good clothes and said that he was going home for lunch, but that he would be back as soon as possible.

He returned around two in the afternoon and continued working and singing. He went through the complete repertoire of his youth, including "Tropical Sidewalk" and "I've Got a Little House," but he always came back to his favourite song, which he'd sing with even greater gusto: "THERE IS NO GREEN MELODY . . ."

"*Señora,* come here a minute. You see? Now the ceiling's going to be nice and solid. Why don't you paint the room, too?"

"Yes, I should."

"A pale green would go well here, I think; yes, a light green."

"That's true; it's a soothing colour."

"I'm also a painter. I can do it for you if you want."

"OK, we'll talk it over later."

"*Señora,* as I was saying yesterday," he said emphatically, "no political system is perfect. You see, now we're socialists. But so what? It's true that we've got a lot more schools, but kids today have more knowledge but not much upbringing. That's obvious. There are clinics and hospitals, but there are also more sick people. And do you know why? Because there's nothing to eat, *señora.* You can't live on eggs and mackerel. You can't travel even if you want to. And if you do leave, you can never come back. Do you know what that's called, *señora?*"

"Give me a minute, and I'll tell you."

"No, no. You're going to want to make me feel like an idiot by saying that we're all equal and everything else. But look, the best thing would be to have a Third System."

"What?"

"A Third System: one that would take the best from both the others. That's what I believe, but I'm old now, and when I say things like this, people think I'm out of my mind."

He relit his cigar and began smoking; then he went back to work. The woman of the house left the room quietly.

A little later she heard his powerful voice booming out, though with a touch of melancholy this time, "There is no green melody . . ."

The Marriage of the Prostitute in Puerto Rican Folklore

Rafael Barreto-Rivera

the lights we saw were not
the lights of houses on a distant mountainside
at night
but, in another country,
they were the lights of light-haired girls
enjoying ice cream
or sitting on a wall in short skirts
    at the return of spring

    Impossible to listen after this
        If there were honesty, he said
and the moon shone in a peculiar way
over our low-lying shining heads
    In silence we smoked our ration
        the canal shacks on stilts
above the stench of the city

    The songs of the whores
audible, audible,

Lights shone on the smelly water
like cosmetics
So I said, why don't you stay
    and he wiggled his loins like a fan
over the edge of the bridge
buildings rose and fell like bottles
the city, fluid
radiance of the city, women
El Fanguito,
La Perla,
Los Bravos de Boston,
El Condado,
    soul slum

For sale, she said
    the best meat of the island

        In the ripples of my brain
smell of her loins appeared

fish-like
the heat rose and the humidity
I felt as if I had no arms
and tried to feel my way like hands
across the nightime

    (she said
        Feel!
       Taste before trying!)

until I realized
there were no victims rending anything
near the ends of sleep

Where do you live? she said
I said on the cliffs of Guajataca

Now, she said
        You coming with me?
Negroes were weeping, reclining
on the balconies
    Under the bridge the water
flowed like semen

      And the city, island city, wavered,
moved with the wind under African clouds
In Canada, I said, we swam in the Pre-Cambrian
Shield, Lake of Bays,
in the glacial, ancestral bone of the earth
Lily pads were seen to grow
The lotus flourished

and I told her of the dark brown hunter
whose audience threw coins upon the wharf
when he came out, victorious
He was death's tangible, frangible self
with ribs like scimitars
and a bronze stomach
One day, his body greased for battle,
he plunged into the harbor, naked,
with a sharp knife,
San Juan's fastest
        under water

and the harbor bled as of a small wound
and the shark's fin surfaced
cutting red waters
silent as the sea-depths whence it came
into the harbor noon like solid fire

I'd rather talk of Canada, I said
                whoosh   whoosh
                    the cars whooshed by
No one knows of the place down here,
                she said

        Speak to us of sex
        so we can understand you

at which point
I spoke of nothing, trembled
my beard, full growth of two months,
three days, five hours,
                she stroked
said
        Pubic hair in public places

vanished

I went to bed with my pants down

                River of silver, river
out of my skin you surface, silver;
river of silver, river

Y nada más

Rafael Barreto-Rivera

The flesh is soft
like a ghost.
  Rain gone.
Out of the huge frying pan
in the sky
  falls light like grease
  And I would weep, *caballeros,*
for the total lack of pity
that I feel

El Canto

Micheline Lévesque

it's at noon that the sun becomes most aggressive and i walk toward the shouts that speak to me from far away already i see the cone-shaped roof of that building they call the *gallera*. i hear the cocks crowing with fear on sunday it's well known here on this hot and golden earth two bodies on the sand take aim at the head and the eyes. i stare at the trembling of their armed feet that look like sculptures made of flesh that confront each other in the midst of their cries and money bets are placed on each attack shouting. these small warm bodies have been placed on the earth near each other so they'll exchange blows then blows more blows remind me that i also am no longer in anyone's arms. i don't know when the fight begins but the moment I'm left alone on the ground like them i feel my body trembling voice rising in the animals' blood. i wanted to forget that voice and it's not possible like on the sand i am the trajectory of blood runs down all the stairs and sidewalks the small creatures are dying in front of me. the sand has changed the colour of their flesh life slowly congeals in their heads hang softly at the ends of their bodies the voice has ceased in the cocks' eyes will never crow again. i try to efface my small body that is sculpted under the open sky of the *gallera* i cried out and no one heard me the blows fell on the steps and sidewalks in red tears. it's because of the crowing of sunday that my head no longer carries me toward the sun becomes so aggressive at this time of day precisely my voice rises alone till the end of the blows. then it becomes lost like a silence over the sculptures of flesh form two small piles of colours in the sun it looks like a deep gash opening the inside of something. i look through the gash and there is the *gallera* in all its bodily nakedness in multicoloured silence after the crowing little by little my vision clouds over.

afterward i dreamt that the shock was great in my body the shock was great but this time unarmed during the night a war ended in an deathgrip.

i warn you: the ending of the dream i hesitate to tell you

it's better to tell about that sunday of war trophies no one knows when it began i've cried all my tears have followed the same trajectory as the blood. tears always come after the crowing there's no longer any sound coming from the open gash in the ground my vision enters something and i am lifeless to talk about it. that is the end of the story of the cockfights in a *gallera* that i want to tell like a film love story that would flow in the cold blood of words written on steps and sidewalks. but with this dream during the night times change the end of the cockfights of the story tells something else progressively transforms the great shock inside. it is difficult to speak of a war that ends in a deathgrip in my dream my lips hesitate to free the throat to sing of the interior of something.

i admit that the cocks on sunday are like the movies

the screen lights up i take a seat then later i get up to leave the room but the dream's deathgrip has no screen and everything happens in the theatre of the body. it's therefore impossible to get up and grab the body says a lot about it in its words the deathgrip or embrace seems so naked in no one's arms. dreams are not forsaken so easily in the arms of everyone could walk on my sky uncovered with so many stars as far as you can see. i will not give away anything more to you for the moment i prefer to listen to the sequence of the *gallera* lights come on and go out in my head controls the unfolding of images. but it is getting more and more mixed up as the film goes on the insane deathgrip embrace in the night spreads over the warm and golden earth two cocks stand disarmed who cannot tear the life from one another by the blood flows.

i am disclosing a little you see

my stars one by one cling to this night despite the fear of being disarmed before you i still don't trust wars between words. i don't know how long fear has pushed me out alone into the arena with the gash opening the interior of something that is congealed in silence. sometimes you have to go so far in the blood to reassure the naked voice at the bottom of the gash hesitates to make itself heard between my lips yes between desire and fear i search how to describe the dream's end.

i am trying to crow: there

the first glimmer of sunday spreads across the steps and sidewalks my whole body timidly closes its eyes so it can better grip embrace the movement in the throat.

it's a small clear voice that wavers on the fresh morning air.

from Rupture de ban: Paroles d'exil et d'amour

Jacques Lanctôt

how many times have I looked around for fate i'm now seven or eight years older than that october when an english-speaking pilot in olive drab told us to fasten your seat belts while aircraft mechanics and sympathizers waved to us one last time a V with their fingers and i my eyes wet already feeling the emigrant's solitude invade me on board an old yukon that had been on a runway for several days suddenly flying toward premature exile in the heart of the caribbean where i thought i'd find guevara and fanon leila khaled and roberto santucho since then i've been a chilean and basque argentine and breton irishman and puerto rican very little french but always crazily left in the eyes of the status quo always crazily in love in my perverse cell on the banks of the seine or elsewhere on your valley hillsides where my flayed eyes have rested from their restless shadow

Hombre

Al Purdy

— Met briefly in Havana
among the million Cubans waiting
Fidel's speech on May Day 1964
under a million merciless suns
He came around and shook hands
with the foreign visitors
a guy who looked like a service station attendant
in his olive drab fatigues and beret
but with the beard and black cigar
the resemblance ended
— the Argentine doctor and freedom fighter
Che Guevara
And I remember thinking the North Vietnamese Ladies
looked especially flower-like beside him
I remember his grip particularly
firm but perfunctory
half politician and half revolutionary
for he had many hands to shake that day

Later he disappeared from Cuba
and there were rumours of quarrels
between himself and Castro
and U. S. newspapers asked nervously
"Where is Che Guevara?"
Then Havana Radio reported Guevara
had joined guerrillas in "a South American country"
but the U.S. expressed some small doubt
about the reliability of Havana Radio
while I thought of him—shaking hands

Back home in Canada I remembered Guevara
along with structural details of Cuban girls
the Grand Hotel at Camagüey with roosters
yammering into my early morning sleep
an all-night walk in Havana streets with a friend
a mad jeep-ride over the Sierra Maestras
where sea-raiders attacked a coastal sugar mill
and Playa Girón which is the "Bay of Pigs"
where the dead men have stopped caring

and alligators hiss in the late afternoon
Again May Day in Havana 1964
with a red blaze of flowers and banners
and Castro talking solemnly to his nation
a million people holding hands and singing
strange to think of this in Canada
And I remember Che Guevara
a man who made dreams something
he could hold in his hands both hands
saying "Hiya" or whatever they say in Spanish
to the flower-like Vietnamese ladies
cigar tilted into his own trademark
of the day when rebels swarmed out
of Oriente Province down from the mountains

"Where is Che Guevara?" is answered:
deep in Bolivian jungles leading his guerrillas
from cave to cave with scarlet cockatoos screaming
the Internationale around his shoulders
smoking a black cigar and wearing a beret
(like a student in Paris on a Guggenheim)
his men crawling under hundred-foot trees
where giant snakes mate in masses of roots
and men with infected wounds moan for water
while Guevara leads his men into an ambush
and out again just like in the movies
but the good guy loses and the bad guys always win
and the band plays the Star-Spangled Banner
Well it is over
Guevara is dead now and whether the world
is any closer to freedom because
of Che's enormous dream is not to be known
the bearded Argentine doctor who translated
that dream to a handshake among Bolivian peasants
and gave himself away free to those who wanted him
his total self and didn't keep any
I remember the news reports from Bolivia
how he was wounded   captured   executed   cremated
but first they cut off his fingers
for fingerprint identification later
in case questions should be asked
and I remember his quick hard handshake
in Havana among the tiny Vietnamese ladies
and seem to hold ghostlike in my own hand
five bloody fingers
of Che Guevara

Two Girls with Umbrellas

Colin Browne

Pleated
Blue skirts,
Chemises from
The People's Republic.
Cars. Fresh yellow cross-
Walk stripes. Rain. Pleats blue as
Sky's face fluted. A stink of dunked
Fried chicken tits in the hot evening.
Wet trucks. White shirts gleaming. Black
Hair drawn taut above each round collar, spilling
Through red elastics over olive-lovely necks, tumbling
Down each miniature back. And, secret beneath each white
Collar, tiny whirlpools and confusions of coiled black hair. My
Wandering tongue. Oh don't say you know. I'm not writing this for
You. Stand away. Over there. Please do not imagine you can interrupt.
Me, perhaps, it is possible. But to them I am you to me. A screen. They
Have passed. In perfect, starched shirts. The corners of East Pender and
Templeton. Look! Their shirts ascend, like gleaming paper dolls, solar wings
In movie space, lifting free of two girls with umbrellas. Soaring independently.
Mark, on their starched, sealed pockets (no one has slipped so much as a finger
Tip in), the exquisite, celestial embroidery. The intricate tintinnabulation of their
Windy frictions, an inference of tiny animals at the door. Small powders dust me. Ashes.
The petals glitter beyond high gulls. I walk home carefully. With skill, undress. Hang
My garments in the cellar over battery plates. Find the small paintbrush I selected
Last year for tomatoes. Begin at lapels, licking each fibre apse. I burn my ties.
In space the shirts have become marshmallows. Specks I find lodged in pockets,
Wedged in cuffs w/ old cigar debris, in buttonholing, between the teeth of my
Fly. Some basements are smouldering yet, acridly. I chuck suit and brush
Into jewelled embers. The particles I empty into an erect orange poppy.
Its black eye, or mouth, squinting. Who killed Celia Sánchez? Not,
Consular gossip has it, natural causes. The question bites its tail.
Twenty-three years since rumour carved its possibility into the
Spine of the Sierra Maestra, after she, Bob Taber, and a
Cameraman slit their way into Palma Mocha for the first
T.V. newsreels, after pricking up on her red toes
To pin a star on the unfamiliar beret of the new
Major, *el gaucho de voz dura*, who cares? Will
You tune in to the blacklit formal inter-
Section of her limbs, the droop her eye-
Lids made, catch perhaps a golden
Smile of breast peeking in
Perfect languor through
The tropicana shirt
Front? Tell me,
Had she been
drinking?

Mira
Allá, allá
Can you see
The utilitarian
Bed, a simple tiled
Floor? You are probably
The only Canadian wondering
About these things, the sole
Canadian to wonder about these
Things in this century. Do you feel
Relieved? If so, it may be because you
Are not thinking about your own recently
Over-rated history. I do not want to know, especially,
What you are feeling. Humour me. Raúl, I hear *Sr.* Bear
Hugs you, not your noisy brother. Forgive my sentimentality.
Was it a pistol? Was it even ballistic? Oh Celia, was living ever
As sweet as in your jungle hideaway, your lips ever as shiny with
Sweet juices? A cool January night, wind mauling palm fronds against
Louvred blue shutters, rain perhaps, sirens in the wet streets. She who
Was truer than your loyal Sierras, your lone link, Fidel, with the faithless
World, your *áncora*, was she wearing slippers? Ah *hermanos*, I am standing on
The slick corners of East Pender and Templeton streets, looking at small lumps of wet,
Green grass on the mown boulevard, two girls with umbrellas turning onto Hastings with
Their mother, certain of what my marks nag and rattle, and the poem is dying. Euthanasia.
Melodrama. The river is muddy tonight and runs like spit. The smooth-bellied stones
Rollick, but look chucked-down pell-mell where we spied faces and eggy, peristaltic
Shrines. Those were the days! Victory followed victory! *¡Venceremos!* But the
Segundo Frente never rests. You'll hear the spring trigger slam of your own
Back door. Clink of buckles when your head is altered. And on the sudden
Far side, among old smoke, arm chairs, and crumpled epaulettes, your
Own terrible brother. Aiming back. He is waiting. Two girls with
Umbrellas walk between you. They break from their mother's
Fingers. It begins to rain. Raúl, we are getting old. Yes,
Brother, and your poems are growing longer. Raúl, the
River is muddy. Do you remember when the rocks
Spelled out magic names? They will again,
Hermano. Celia Sánchez, the poem is
Dying! I smell bamboo. Girls, your
Shirts have fled! I had so much
Desire. *Hermano*, I heard my
Name on your lips. Brother
Commence firing, until
The river clarifies.
Every gesture its
Own betrayal.

Tomtom Vaccine

Hédi Bouraoui

"No poblem in Haiti"
And the bitter smile fades without the slightest conviction
A smile stuffed with endless stories
A smile that hides and reveals a whole world and way of life

"No poblem in Haiti"
Refrain in a tragedy, sung by an ancient chorus
commenting on destiny
"Noooo poblem in Haiti" and the fiery sun
fills the stomachs
A greenish dream of the tropics—Cancer to inject
like the rays
That tan the pale livid skin
of the overfed
"You don't die from hunger" say the imperialists
"You die from eating too much, from
obesity"—
While the bus driver wipes his forehead
with a faded handkerchief I hear him repeat
"Nooo poblem" a tragicomic chant
That takes the place of religion   Everything is taken lightly
the only way to avoid suicide

You have to see the envious looks on
their gawking faces
The arms hanging loosely idle barely moving
without work   content just to assassinate
the tourists with their eyes to envy and hate them in secret
until the right moment comes to extract
a few cents from their avarice to feed the starving
swarms
"No poblem" —everybody can become a guide
Not with Virgil and the concentric
circles of the *Divine Comedy* but in a
reality more surreal than hell itself Guides who
glue themselves to you no matter what who lick you
like flies on a sugarcube
A bargain to show off to their less-fortunate
neighbours who can only show
the whites of their teeth

"No poblem in Haiti" and the empty gourds
seem to dance on heads full of anguish and
worry   A harmony of fate that bestows
its paradoxes wildly, without
squabbling
The same avenue must be taken in times of
peace or war.
It's when stomachs are empty that
art flourishes
Eyes eat the gaudy paintings on
the unsprung dilapidated Tap-Taps. Bright
African colours.   Imagination is not
limited in form. The only snag
The words inscribed on the front of the truck
a religious "Psalm 59"   "God Saves"
Another way of reining in the revolution
Discontent expressed in
smoky backfires   A first-class pollution
of asphyxiating fuel oil and no one seems
to realize or care about it!

The infernal din of unending traffic sets
the rhythm of life despite potholes and
detours, the dust and its visible fall,
the risky sewers dampening the
road with a nauseating smell
A single sentence to describe the tragedy of all
these lives—what a farce!
Drawn to the great city of Port-au-Prince the people have
realized the miracle of granting everyone two
inches of land thus giving them the possibility of becoming
buyers and sellers

The charm and subtlety of bargaining. An art
wholly unknown to foreigners who loathe
human contact, who fear
touching the Other. Bargaining is the only way
to penetrate one another with emotions, touch,
intellect—to quench the thirst for others at the
very source of humanity—to struggle against and overcome
inflation—to create protective bonds
for the future—to find oneself amid
a mob of alternatives—to assert the non-
financial self   the vital self—A
humane bargain accessible to all   A fusion that

allows you to find yourself among your brothers and sisters
Statues taking shape within the intractable
stones.

If hunger ruptures stomachs, there's still a bit of canvas
To paint to colour to avenge yourself on
the tendrils that perforate
The world transformed into myriad glistening
paintings
Fresh art exhibited on all the street corners   Not to
mention the sculptures of ancient gestures that sell
for 50 cents each. It only took
a week to conjure them up from
nightmarish shadows!
       But even though they're sweating on the plains
       the air is nice and fresh and you can
       sprawl on the hill the observation post
       that helps you control these hard-working ants.
       Sharing is everything
Slavery continues   let's begin the revolution

from Black Orchid

Anthony Phelps

Black Orchid
a little just a little
an instant of city on the uneven pavement
a promise of beach
and your eyes block my horizon
shield my dream from reality
so that it grows grass root and vine
moss-covered *mapou*

A little just a little
and each time I go farther
into the other side of the mirage and the sheathed sound of bells
searching your eyes for the new face of evening
and the adventure renews the footsteps of the century
your eyes take on the form of the world
become the humus of all wonders

A little just a little Black Orchid
brought on the water mill of your hair
when I step by the night to jettison my words
like a dry pod its song of clear noon
like a flame its dance of fleeting tongue
And we again besiege our virgin sexes

Black Orchid
melting sun of my miracle
slipping between the why and how
our locomotive
has long shunted us toward northern basilisks
reducing our thirsty dawns
Caravan of two shakings of wonderment
before these ancient sites or future steel
we have walked through cities of temptation
sterile streets antiseptic
where robots without perspective
busily repeating the same gestures
with a semblance of equality
have lost all memory of the food of dreams
and of difference

Black Orchid my ingot of water
today our paths have crossed again
in a common vision of sea and space
have brought us toward this zone of spices
my first place
where my studious reflection sends me back to games of hopscotch
Without the stage of a slope to the other
in the tenderness of numbered friendship
here we are at the geographic level
of Caribbean diversity

Caribbean
green sea of Mayan jungle
grey sea of ruins
Caribbean god with a downcast head

Caribbean of high paganism
dam shattered without a trumpet
fragility of coral blades
and of ferns like a bishop's crozier
Survival of the testimony of the sea
the man with the red hiccup
anger still bent
beneath the memory of the flattened sand

Caribbean
O baldaquin of sex
annatto sex of pagan gods
solar womb
bloody womb
forced open by new words gluttonous for vowels
titillations of the uvula
and harsh scratchings of the throat
O Arabic and Muslim noises
in the clamour of the conquest

Caribbean
black sea of submarine jungle
sea of ebony
Caribbean of the King-with-a-bullet-in-his-heart
of the trapped Emperor and Republican
Caribbean of the discarded Visionary

Under the ebony canopy of corn and wheat
O slow and long and painful transformation

O long and slow and difficult acceptance
Caribbean place of all invention
where the negro space turns its cheek
and returns the slaps with lightning bolts
imposing a new dimension onto History

Caribbean of my generous fever
flower of water and islands
uncut silver jewels and fresh sweets
I tear myself apart childhood of shells
beauty intervening between adventure and page

Sun-wrinkled skin and vigilant ears
an iguana I slide
along this life that makes its noise of creation
On leave of ecstasy and courtesy of the heart
lungs unballasted and ventricle not misfiring
I am reconciled with the breath of market sellers
and the rhythm of donkeys
Women with fingernails like tortoises
scratch honey from my wasteland
and a weather vane I turn upon myself
drawing ships
in the bones of my Mother whose words were stifled
Mother of the generous heart
mother braided and shrunken by suffering

O sorcerer voyage full of ocean rites
Again I swim at the level of my scents
perfumes of khuskhus flowers and roots
frangipani jasmin and boxwood
for what is memory without a past

The song of the Victim sings its honey
beyond the obsidian
In the skin of struggle and leather of life
the song of the Victim
sings its song louder than the whip's octave
Red and Black
O time deflected from its source
O memory ensnared

(Giver of pieces of clear conscience
freeze your gesture as you reach in your pocket
no one gets farther than a coin

Keep your alms
you who come in arrogance

With bare feet calloused hands and rebuilt backs
we stammering humans reach
the promising shores of the twenty-first century)

O sorcerer voyage full of ocean rites
Waiting for a new dictation
like a poacher sniffing
the fresh tracks of lithe voiceless girls
I pour my voice of agile lead
Overhang of grey stones
cutting the prism like a prow
Dreams of words as round as granaries
my phrases lose their rust
under the sun of chrysanthemums
and I bet my surprises against the springing branches

Rain of purple petals
said released from maturity
seventy times seven times
the open-sesame uncovers the same nudity
the Sea
my palimpsest
Papyrus Sea
O text spattered with the blood of death
of exile and of forbidden games

Black Orchid
with two people's hands we piece back like amulets
what is left of our games
tiny fragments of parties
scraps of joy splinters of dances
fertilized by the bees of your summer
the hummingbirds of my autumn
and in the surge of liberty
we blend with the roll of History
to finally find the port
where we can sink our anchor and our seed

Lenin Park, Havana

Cyril Dabydeen

My camera flashes upon the variegated faces
Amidst the general activity
Of building, establishing—
How eager they are, these hands, bodies—
Nine—, ten— and eleven-year-olds
Bustling about without weariness—
Only a restrained air of the carnival
Of the young
This summer

I will speak.
"Hola," in bare Spanish
Eager to find out how the socialist man
Or woman can transform a state;
In command's way, they seem not to mind—
Innocence has its own currency, as I watch
A young girl driving a tractor,
A boy milling rice; another, refining sugar

Will they ever starve, as they pay tribute
To José Marti, Fidel Castro, or whoever else
Will be then?
Or will some stalwart spirit
Among them, given to brooding—
Later high on culture, insist on the right
To be free beyond bread?

Doubtful as I am, I banter, smile,
My camera snaps again, left and right—
Black hair bordering beautiful
Dark and brown faces—I love you all!
A hybrid breed chockful of Latin air—
Among you, perhaps, are eager dancers,
Singers, poets—how elegantly you proclaim
An island in the pulsation of your bodies,
In the greater exaltation of spirit yet to come
Far beyond Castro or Marti

from Una comedia no muy divina

Edith Velásquez

The third daughter was named Mara. She was a slender girl with markedly Indian features, smooth clear brown skin, and rebellious black hair that hung down to her waist. She was the only one in the family who knew how to read fluently; the others could only stumble through their letters. She owed her skill in reading to a European who had penetrated deep into the jungle and had actually lived in the town, where he had carried out a meticulous study of the area's geography, with a view to using it as a base for a guerrilla war that he planned in order to liberate the country and guarantee the ascendance of the indigenous and Afro-Venezuelan masses in a social order that had been invented in Europe. He was a man gripped by the romantic passions of previous centuries and firmly believed that his life would become meaningful only if he were able to redeem his own race from the barbarities that some of its members had committed against that whole peaceful and ingenuous continent. It was thus that, in taking the initiative of improving the life of the people of this marginal village and in helping those who had undergone sacrifices and endured mockery, he had appeared one day, accompanied by twenty well-disciplined Indians, each of whom carried twenty-five kilos of books on his shoulders, among which were especially visible volumes on political science, philosophy, the social sciences, and world literature in various languages, especially the works of the Latin-American Romantics, which he strongly recommended that Mara read, particularly since they were the first books that had been published in the Spanish-speaking republics immediately after the wars of independence. Through them, he said, he would be able to reveal to Mara the prelude to the whole political mechanism that had been woven around the continent on which they lived.

The men who carried the books resented the daunting task that had been imposed on them and conspired against their leader. One night, during a full moon, they stripped off the red plaid cotton shirts that were used for hunting moose in Canada and that the man had insisted they wear so that no disoriented hunter who happened upon them in the jungle would shoot them, stripped off their corduroy shorts and Italian sandals, tied together strings of the fine silk handerchiefs that the man had insisted they wear on their heads in order to keep the sweat out of their eyes, and made them into loincloths. They then ran away without harming the man at all and made their way through the darkened jungle by the light of the moon. The man, whose name turned out to be Regismundo, was therefore left with no other choice than to stay on in the village and teach everyone who wanted to learn how to read and write. Mara had been the one who showed the greatest interest, and he consequently gave her detailed explanations of how the first state had been formed and how civilized people throughout the centuries had tried to achieve the perfect republic but were never completely able to do so, because such would-be republics always ended up as economic parasites of countries that were considered underdeveloped. He also pointed out how backward their own country actually was. Mara didn't fully understand everything he was trying to tell her, because she was only fourteen years old and had never been outside the village, and thus lacked any kind of point of comparison. Yet she respected his desires to the letter when, with infinite patience and sensitivity, he at last asked her to read all the books that his men had brought, without overlooking the tiniest morsel of knowledge, emphasizing the fact that the greatest power of humanity resides in knowledge that can be stored in the archives of the organ that sets humans apart from animals—the brain—and that the best method for learning the humanities was memorization, but that before committing a particular passage to memory, she had to completely understand what she had read, and he insisted on recommending that she first thoroughly acquaint herself with *The Discourse of Method*, by René Descartes, in order to learn how to organize her ideas in a logical and orderly way, and that if she did so, she would easily be able, by using the infallible method of repetition, to memorize all the important citations which those works contained. He also reminded her that, due to her age, she had ample time for the task, and that every minute invested in memorizing an excerpt from those books was a minute more toward a positive future both for her and her country, which would eventually, he was sure, be well-administered, and that Plato, in his *Republic,* spoke of the individual qualities that he projected for the citizens of his perfect republic, and that those qualities were prudence, valour, justice, duty, and knowing how to assume one's obligations, and that the same book declared that reason should be the governing principle of the human mind, for only reason had the wisdom and ability to put prudence into practice and to subordinate all irrational passion. He further advised that *The Will to Power,* by Friedrich Nietzsche, would certainly help her reflect on the values that had been inculcated upon the Americas in order to weaken them, and that Machiavelli's *The Prince* counselled following an amalgam of immoral conduct in order to conquer other lands and that the philosophical belief that the end justified the means was a politcal tactic that had been used all over the Americas right from the moment of their discovery. Mara, without having the least idea of the true value of the man's sermons, yet impelled by the spirit of curiosity, devoted herself with enthusiasm to the study of his books. Regismundo himself later went off with a troop of government soldiers whom he had told about his efforts to civilize the Indians. He had promised Mara that he would come back for her, but it was subsequently learned that the troops had shot him one night when all of them were drinking rum and he had given a short speech on the Socratic teachings that instructed warriors to obstain from imbibing alcohol, since drunkenness was a confused condition of the mind that endangered the state's security, and he had added that moreover what the country truly needed was the resurrection of Karl Marx. The soldiers associated the name of Marx with the political philosophy that they most hated, and they executed him on the spot. Mara found out what had happened from several men who had witnessed the shooting, and she immediately immersed herself in her studies with even greater determination and laboured even more fervently at understanding the complex explanations that Regismundo had tried to teach her, praying for him occasionally and carefully poring over the works that he had instructed her to read. She would lie in a hammock hung between two leafy *cotoperí* trees that grew on the patio of her house. There she would wander through all those works of Plato, Aristotle, Descartes, Kant, Rousseau, Marx, Nietzsche, Schopenhauer, Voltaire, along with a poem by Rubén Darío dedicated to Roosevelt, writings of José Martí and Simón Bolívar, and others. Without being able to make a single comment to anyone about what she was reading, she would eventually became lost in thought. No one in the village had shown much of a desire to understand the historical, social, political, and philosophical revelations which the books contained. Instead, they entertained themselves with *Aesop's Fables*, *The Thousand and One Nights*, *Khalila and Dimna*, *Platero and I*, Bocaccio's *Decameron*, and a single remaining page from a lost essay which stated in an allegorical way that the most racist person in the Americas was a man whose last name was partly effaced and of which only the final "-iento" was still legible. The page in question had been written by an unknown author named Sideal Velma. Nobody worried about trying to find any meanings other than the literal ones in these books. When Mara was tired of lying down, she would embark on silent walks through the village and would sometimes enter the jungle. There she would lose herself for days. The family didn't worry about her, since Doña Concepción and Mara's grandmother had both always prayed whenever they could and firmly believed that nothing bad could happen to anyone as long as they availed themselves of the weapon of prayer. Without exact knowledge of any specific religion, they would instinctively join their hands and commend themselves to the care of the moon when it shone in all its splendour and to the planet Venus, which they came to identify as being the most beautiful star of the firmament. In this way, they would pray for the protection of the village. One particular event really made them understand the importance of their prayers: it was when Mara's grandmother was able to escape from a rattlesnake that had crawled up onto the patio. The reptile had used its rattle to announce its arrival, and she, with one foot inside the door and the other outside, had recited her prayers in order to protect herself.

Mara spent days in the forest by herself, living off wild fruit. She had found the value of prayer and had a blind faith in her grandmother's recommendations. She had discovered that prayer gave great mental peace, and she used it like a drug whenever she went out of the house. She felt the need to submerge herself in the solitude of the forest, to breathe in the aroma of the humid earth that mingled with the scent of dense vegetation. She delighted in the enigmatic and harmonious melody of virgin nature. It was a sound that vibrated to an underlying rhythm that made her concentrate on the dynamism of time and lose contact with what humans know as the Present. She discovered that the actual now didn't in fact exist, and that time was a continuous process of change from past to future. She went into ecstasy while contemplating the solar light that could be glimpsed through the foliage as it caressed the tender leaves and petals of the orchids, and was fascinated by the wild song of primitive flowering nature. She liked to feel the heat that emanated from the womb of the earth and to enter into intimate contact with her surroundings. It was a custom that she had learned from her grandmother, who had assured her that if she concentrated on her inner strength while communing with nature, she would one day be able to pierce the veil of sensory reality and discover true life. Her mother often found her in the house with her eyes closed, detached from household events, and therefore gave her the freedom to search out her own places of spiritual peace, so that she could practise the simple, spontaneous and rudimentarily metaphysical understanding that her grandmother had passed on to her. Doña Concepción had always had the impression that her daughter was exceptional, because she had heard her crying within her womb a week before she was born.

The hours would go by and Mara, leaning back against one of the leafy trees, would hear jaguars roaring in the distance without the slightest quaver of fear; instead, she concentrated on the names of those men whom Regismundo had mentioned as being the ones who had forged the first governments of the world. She couldn't relate anyone to anything in her readings, nor could she really see the need for books like The Republic, in which Plato imposed strict ideas that had to be respected by all citizens. She didn't understand how the state had been able to condemn Socrates to death for having corrupted the youth of Athens, nor why he had accepted such a verdict when any reasonable person would have realized that it was unjust. She also couldn't understand why Machiavelli had felt compelled to write The Prince in order to advise such a cynical course of conduct, and she was intrigued by the meaning of the wild attitude toward life that Nietzsche wished to propagate.

Mara lowered her eyes. All those writings seemed the product of unhinged minds. There wasn't any need whatsoever to engender such practices. The society in which she lived was an idyllic one, and she couldn't see any reason why the rest of the world couldn't be exactly like her village. The people who lived in other parts of the world certainly had to be just as intelligent as those who lived here; they too had to have learned how to live in peace and harmony, happy in the simple act of existence. She closed her eyes completely, letting herself be hypnotized by the tropical sounds, and went into a deep sleep.

III Guatemala, El Salvador, Honduras, and Nicaragua

Hunting for Tropical Plants in the Golfo

Rosemary Sullivan

Dawn shakes the trees awake
and reddens the river to attention
between ink-blue mountains
emitting their darkness like smoke.

We set off in the quiet waters,
hats in our hands, listening
to the wind advancing down the lake,
buffing the water to a soft skin
for the pelicans to scavenge.
Río Dulce — sweet river smelling of watermelons.

The jungle is alive with light,
ramón trees turn hands as we pass,
palmleaved pinwheels spin.
The lianas are deadly *fer-de-lance*
webbing a dark warning.

All day we hunted bromelias,
gaudy pink parasites
that lit the jungle with flares.
We climbed for hours
ripping bromelias from branches.

Flaming suns plunged to our boats
and we were a cargo of flowers
lacing through green waters,
the suns breaking
about our burning shoulders.

from Time Among The Maya

Ronald Wright

9:00 A.M. No one at customs is the slightest bit interested in my luggage. The immigration officer demands five quetzals for a tourist card which states explicitly in English, "The cost of this document is one quetzal." Everyone is charged five quetzals, whether he needs a visa, has a visa, or does not need a visa. The difference is a compulsory tip; if you refuse to pay it the answer is, "Go back to Belize."

Transport to Flores or Tikal? There will be a *camioneta* at ten, eleven, or eleven-thirty, depending on whom I want to believe. I walk across the long concrete bridge from the border post to the town of Melchor de Mencos, named after the latter-day conquistador who took King Can Ek of the Itzá in chains to Guatemala City. Like all frontier towns, it's a dismal place: a few hardware stores, brothels, and bars; a filling station, a flyblown market, an army base down the road. Tiny Guatemalan soldiers, little Indian boys in their teens, are lounging against walls and fidgeting under the weight of their Galil rifles. Someone is playing Christmas reggae from Radio Belize:

> We wish you a natty Christmas
> Natty Christmas, natty Christmas,
> Natty dreadlock Christmas....

11:00 A.M. Guatemalan Spanish is very different from Mexican: the *camioneta* is not a light truck or van, as I expected, but a bus. Until now bus travel has been painless but this is a return to the cramped, foul-smelling, and mechanically suspect contraptions of the Andes. There's a huge pile of luggage on the roof; a hundred people got off when it arrived; another hundred are getting on. I am swept aboard with the rest and have little time to choose a seat that (a) has padding, (b) is not on top of a wheel (no legroom), and (c) is not smeared by the droppings of animals and babies, vomit, or the remains of a meal.

We have to wait an hour while the driver has his lunch, meets his girlfriend, disappears with her for a leisurely dalliance, and then returns to fill the fuel tank, a leaking radiator, and a couple of slowly leaking tires. During this time the temperature inside the bus becomes unbearable, but no one dares get out for fear of losing his seat. I look on the bright side: if so many people are traveling they presumably estimate the risk of attack from army or insurgents to be low.

Before leaving home I read several books on the recent history of Guatemala. The statistics had a numbing and intimidating effect: 440 villages destroyed; a million displaced persons; 200,000 refugees in other countries; 100,000 political murders since the CIA ended ten years of democracy in 1954.

Guatemala has acquired the mythic status of a nightmare country, a Lebanon or Uganda. Sitting in your back garden with a book and a beer, you ask yourself: How can anyone live there? How do countries like that go on? And the answer seems to be that chaos has become normality: violence feeds on itself; one corpse nourishes another. Human beings have an endless capacity for optimism, a boundless faith that the worst is over, that terrible things happen only to strangers, that the villages destroyed are always tiny and far away.

Guatemala is a country where things are easily hidden, especially the truth. It is cloaked with forest, concealed by clouds, mists, and the smoke of volcanoes; culturally and geographically as convoluted as a brain. The land is repeatedly flooded, buried, burned, and racked by earthquakes. Perhaps such an environment exerts a baleful influence on culture. Perhaps the cycle of violence set in motion by the conquistador Pedro de Alvarado, is periodically given a tweak by the shudders of the Maya earth-monster. One reads that Guatemala is a social pressure cooker with the lid weighted down by repression: the stability of such a vessel is not improved by shaking the stove. There's a symmetry to history and geology. The recent guerrilla conflict gained momentum after the 1976 earthquake exposed and exacerbated government corruption and the misery of the poor.

1:00 P.M. About five miles out of Melchor, the bus slaloms through a large puddle and stops in front of a pole barrier across the road. An armed corporal sticks his head in the door: everyone has to get out to "*documentarse*"—present documents. "Men on the right, women on the left."

Fresh air. When I see fellow passengers waiting nervously to present their papers, I regret my misanthropic thoughts as I sweated in the bus. There's a young woman in a neat gray skirt and white sweater who appears to be a nurse. Three Indian women are travelling with two tiny babies; their beautiful clothes—the multicoloured handwoven *traje*, or traditional dress, of some highland Maya group— are faded and in patches, the threadbare plumage of captive birds. They seem frightened, especially of the soldiers. Displaced persons most likely, and I shrink from imagining what might have forced them from a mist-shrouded mountain village to this raw frontier where the badge of their identity is not only a discomfort in the heat but an invitation for further persecution.

"*!Hombres al otro lado!*" the corporal shouts; I have to join the other men already lining up with their backs pressed to the side of the bus. Thick peasant fingers produce scraps of yellowed paper bearing stamps, seals, and poorly developed photographs. The soldiers look closely at the photographs and then at the fingers' owners. Occasionally they squint at the writing, and once I see, as Lucy said I might, a document without a photograph being read upside down. Meanwhile other soldiers are going over the bus, looking under seats, prodding bags in the overhead racks, handing down bundles from the roof.

The corporal shouts something. One by one we are taken to the front of the line and made to face the bus, legs apart, hands spread high on the windows. A soldier puts his foot between my feet to trip me if I make a move; another points a rifle at my back. The intrusive intimacy of hands patting under the arms, down the inside leg, around the ankles for concealed knives: a subtle violation that Guatemalans must expect every time they go out. The soldier opens my small bag and takes things out one at a time. Forewarned, I'm carrying no camping or hiking equipment, and no khaki or dark green clothing, nothing that might be useful to guerrillas. I'm worried about my books and papers, but these attract no interest. The soldier lingers over a telephoto lens. Ah! Here's something suspicious—a sachet of white crystals, mysteriously sealed like a tea bag. Gringo drugs? Some newfangled explosive?

"Special crystals," I say quietly. "To keep the lens dry in damp weather." He glances at his corporal; the corporal nods. I'm in the clear.

With few exceptions the seating or standing arrangements on the bus remain as before. I begin to notice the old-fashioned good manners that I remember as characteristic of almost all Guatemalans. Where are the killers, the torturers, the experts in mutilation? They seem to belong to another country, one that existed in the recent past but is now miraculously purged, like Germany after the last world war. I am here at an exceptional time, the interval between the first and second stages of elections for the presidency in a much-touted but not altogether convincing "return to democracy." The country is swarming with foreign journalists. Hard-line generals and death squads are keeping out of sight.

The pole across the road is lifted, and we are waved through, between a wooden watchtower and a sandbagged machine-gun nest. Not far beyond the tower there's a billboard with a naïve painting of a Guatemalan soldier in camouflage fatigues. The soldier is shouting: "If I advance, follow me; if I delay, hurry me; if I retreat, kill me!" An inscription below him boasts: ¡AQUI SE FORJAN LOS MEJORES COMBATIENTES DE AMERICA!—HERE ARE FORGED THE BEST FIGHTERS IN AMERICA! I have just begun to wonder whether this is intended for Belizean visitors or rebellious citizens when I see the back of the sign, which directs its message to those coming from the Guatemalan interior. It shows a gorilla head in the King Kong tradition, or maybe Planet of the Apes. Maniacal eyes burn ferociously; the gaping mouth is dripping with blood and armed with sharp fangs; and lest anyone fail to get the pun (not quite as homophonous as it is in English) the creature wears a Che Guevara cap. Above it is the single word ¡ATREVETE!—roughly, MAKE MY DAY!

Nearby there's yet another sign: a huge death's-head with a knife between its teeth, and two words: INFIERNO KAIBIL—KAIBIL HELL. This is a camp of the Kaibiles, or "Tigers"—crack counterinsurgency troops modelled on the Green Berets. A witness of Kaibil training reported the following responsorial chant:

¿Qué come un Kaibil?	What does a Kaibil eat?
¡CARNE!	FLESH
¿Qué clase de carne?	What kind of flesh?
¡HUMANA!	HUMAN!
¿Qué clase de carne humana?	What kind of human flesh?
¡COMUNISTA!	COMMUNIST!
¿Qué bebe un Kaibil?	What does a Kaibil drink?
¡SANGRE!	BLOOD!
¿Qué clase de sangre?	What kind of blood?
¡HUMANA!	HUMAN!
¿Qué clase de sangre humana?	What kind of human blood?
¡COMUNISTA!	COMMUNIST!

Just a gruesome training song, or something more? There are several reports, mainly from 1982 and before, when the war was at its bloodiest, that the Kaibiles actually practised cannibalism. Deserters from Huehuetenango army base in the western highlands reported that they were made to drink the blood of torture victims as an initiation rite. A survivor of the July 1982 massacre at the village of San Francisco said he saw a soldier cut out the heart of a warm corpse and put it to his mouth. (He could not bring himself to watch what happened next.) At Todos Santos, a community of Mam Maya, a peasant claimed that an officer ate a human liver raw in front of the assembled soldiers and townsfolk.

* * * * *

10:00 A.M. The Canadian embassy occupies the upper stories of an office building in fashionable Zone 9. You walk past a security guard and board an elevator that stops at no other floors. At the top there are two more guards and a heavy steel door unlocked from within by a buzzer. You have to shout your business into an intercom, and when you get as far as the booth occupied by a very pretty but very junior Guatemalan employee, two inches of laminated plate glass make conversation difficult. (Secretaries are *always* very pretty in Latin America: lots of nail polish and mascara, frilly see-through tops, and silly shoes.)

"*Sí, señorita*: W-R-I-G-H-T." (The mantra is second nature by now.) I'm hoping to find a message from David, a journalist friend who's supposed to be flying down from Canada. We're planning to meet in a few days' time and rent a vehicle for a trip through the highlands. David is as reckless as I'm cautious. Last time he was in Guatemala he narrowly escaped with his life after trying to contact the guerrillas.

"*No hay nada, señor.*"

Just like David to be late and like me to be early. I ask if there's someone senior I could speak to. But the letter of introduction I sent from Canada is nowhere to be found; the person I wrote to has been reassigned to a desk in Ottawa; all the senior staff are out of the country—in Honduras to observe "democratic" elections favoured by the United States. I read something recently about the Honduran campaigns: one candidate showered the republic with leaflets claiming that his opponent was a sodomite riddled with AIDS. The Americans were embarrassed when it came out that the leaflets were dropped from a U.S. Marines helicopter.

Eventually I'm granted an interview with the only Canadian left in the place. Myron Blatherwycke has a pale complexion, white wavy hair, and the see-no-evil eyes of a career diplomat.

"I wonder if you could fill me in on the situation in the countryside—where I should go, and where I shouldn't?"

"Where have you been so far?"

"I just flew up from the Petén."

"If you'd come to me first, I would have told you not to go there."

"What about the highlands?"

"The government has recently had great success in pacifying many areas. Antigua is okay, and I gather tourists are returning to Panajachel and Chichicastenango. You should go there, everyone does, it's beautiful. However, I'd advise you not to travel anywhere after dark."

"I was thinking about northern Quiché and Huehuetenango."

"Those are two areas I would strongly advise you not to go to. I can't stop you, but I would ask you not to."

I have some other questions—about Canada's policy toward Guatemalan refugees. In March 1984, the Canadian government imposed a visa restriction on all Guatemalans, making it difficult for them to enter Canada on their own initiative. At the same time the Canadian embassy here began "processing" refugees internally. Surely this exposed them to scrutiny from informers watching foreign embassies?

"What about these guards outside the door," I ask, "are they embassy employees or members of a private security firm?"

"They're officers of the Guatemalan police. Why?"

"If I feel intimidated by them—and I do—what's it like for the refugees who try to seek asylum here?"

Mr. Blatherwycke opens a packet of Marlboros, taps out two, and offers me one. He leans forward and lowers his voice: "I can assure you that Canada is quietly helping hundreds of political refugees get out of Guatemala. But for the obvious reasons we don't want that spread around."

I tell him about a Guatemalan woman I met in Toronto. Before escaping Guatemala, she and her husband had been organizing homeless people like themselves to settle as squatters in the capital's wastelands and garbage dumps. One day they saw three men loading a machine gun on the bank behind their shack. They grabbed their two babies and ran. Somehow they got as far as the embassy's steel door, but were roughly turned away by the guards. Luckily for them a Mexican diplomat happened to arrive, and he personally ushered them through. They were given a special permit to enter

Canada—but what if the Mexican had not been there?

"Well," says Mr. Blatherwycke, a weary smile tugging at his cheek, "we could argue individual cases all day." His cigarette is at an end; and so, clearly, is my interview. "Guards or no guards we get about seventy people a day coming in here."

"I didn't see a soul in the waiting room."

"You hit a slow day."

(Months later, I discover that 382 Guatemalan refugees received visas and permits to enter Canada in 1985. Even if all came through this embassy, it would amount to an average of only one and a half successful applications per working day.)

I leave a note for David with the girl in the glass case. Then out through the steel door and past the raptorial gaze of the guards. Mr. Blatherwycke is right about one thing: Embassies in Guatemala have good reason for elaborate security. They remember what happened on January 31, 1980, when a group of Quiché and Ixil Maya and some student supporters staged a peaceful sit-in at the Spanish embassy.

For months the Indians had been fruitlessly petitioning the government to halt army atrocities in northern Quiché Department. In August a deputation had visited the national congress to protest the kidnapping of seven village leaders, only to be told that the Guatemalan parliament was "no place for *indios*." Some of the deputation were arrested on the spot and beaten up; others returned to northern Quiché, where they were greeted by the corpses of the seven missing men.

At about 11:00 A.M. on the morning of January 31, the Indians entered the Spanish embassy (which they chose because Spanish priests in the villages had been sympathetic to their plight). They presented the ambassador with a letter:

We ... direct ourselves to you because we know you are honourable people who will tell the truth about the criminal repression suffered by the peasants of Guatemala... To a long history of kidnappings, torture, assassinations, theft, rapes, and burning of buildings and crops, the National Army has added the massacre at Chajul.... We have come to the capital to denounce this injustice....

The ambassador contacted the authorities and asked them to keep well away because the protest showed no signs of turning violent, but by 2:00 P.M. hundreds of police had gathered outside. They broke down the doors with axes, undeterred by the ambassador's shouts that they were violating international law. Guns were fired; a bomb or Molotov cocktail set the building alight. Thirty-nine people were shot or burnt to death. Only the ambassador and one Indian survived. Next day the Indian was kidnapped from his hospital bed; his mutilated body appeared later at the university campus, a favourite death squad dumping ground. Spain broke off diplomatic relations with Guatemala. No one was ever charged in the affair.

Later. Houses in the upper-class neighbourhoods of Guatemala City are elegantly barred. Wrought-iron grilles, sheets of steel with brass knobs, and bars welded in diamond patterns confront the sidewalk or lurk behind riots of magnolia and bougainvillea: the defenses of the rich against the society they have made.

Servants, some of them Indian women in the mysteriously intricate costumes of their villages, are watering lawns. Other Indians pad along the sidewalk trying to sell potted plants and homemade brooms. A hopeful face looks up from beneath a tumpline across the forehead and a cascade of vegetation carried on a back bent almost parallel with the ground. There is a brief exchange between vendor and servant through a barred gate a responsorial chant in the shushes and clicks of a highland Maya tongue that sounds like two cooks chopping celery. Then the face bends again to the sidewalk, and the mobile garden glides away on feet so burdened that they spread beneath their load like camel hoofs on sand.

You can tell a lot about a country from its cars. Motor vehicles will one day prove as useful to archaeologists as potsherds and inscriptions. Their rapidly changing styles make them superb chronological markers. But they are more than that: they reflect the social pyramid; and when you add some statistics as to who owns what kind of car, you have a steel allegory of the human world. In social democratic countries cars tend to be small and cheap: proletarian Fiats, egalitarian Volkswagens. In most of Africa there are two kinds of car—decrepit Japanese taxis for the hoi polloi, and smart Mercedes-Benzes belonging to those government men known as the "Wabenzi" tribe. In Guatemala, as in Africa, most of the people have no cars. You must climb the pyramid at least as far as the lower middle class to discover the most archaic and feeble members of the mechanical race—American pickup trucks and finned dragons from the 1950s. A step or two higher up come Toyotas and Datsuns, so patched, welded, and improvised that in North America a scrap dealer would demand money to tow them away.

In Guatemala, where about 2 percent of the landowners own 70 percent of the land, the mechanical oligarchy of Range-Rovers, BMWs, and Mercedes-Benzes is exclusive. These are cars you don't see in Mexico or most other Latin American republics that have a rational import policy and a tax structure aimed at luxury goods. The telling thing about Guatemalan wheeled fauna is that there are so few species between the vermin and the exotica. If you are rich, you're filthy rich; if you're not, well, a '58 Chevy or a '66 Datsun is as close as you'll get to wheels. The fincas, which cannot afford to pay their peons more than about $1.20 a day, support flamboyant jeeps equipped with magnesium wheels, balloon tires, roll bars, extra lamps, and bucket seats in the truck box, filled with giggling señoritas. Urban businesses—coffee and cotton brokerage firms, soft-drink bottling plants, arms suppliers—nurture Cadillacs and luxury German sedans with smoked bulletproof windows, as dark as the faces behind them are pale. The army officers who make all this possible seem to have rather adolescent tastes: Blazers and Broncos with chromium rams and prancing horses. Similar vehicles, devoid of ornaments and license plates, prowl the streets at night, looking for *subversivos* to "disappear." (A Guatemalan I know claims that *disappear* was first used as a transitive verb in his country.)

Guatemala

Lionel Kearns

She says the Indians hear radio programs
broadcast in their own peculiar languages
by the Christian missionary stations
and he observes that in the capital
they speak Spanish and learn English

She talks about the beauty of the ruins
but he notices the elegance of policemen
whose polished cartridges glitter
like jewellery in their bullet belts

She says there is much land available
and he remembers that government troops
routinely clear remote areas of guerrillas
and their families then build in roads
and offer it for sale to North Americans

Our economy is growing stronger she says
but he is growing aware of men
who sell their souls to buy women who
sell their bodies to feed their children

She says there are many volcanoes
some are quiet and some are active
and next year there will be more

Two Paintings of Lily Pads

Jan Conn

One, green on black, stark, precise.
It's midnight on the pond
or the painter emerging
from three days of alcohol
about to be overwhelmed by a hint of pink,
a bud, a woman's sex freeze-framed.

Opposite, pastels immersed
in soap-bubbled light, vague impressions,
the light much as it is now,
late afternoon, diffuse,
so the lily pads are merely
projections of themselves,
underdeveloped negatives.

After dusk, the gravel causeway to Flores
an egret's wing balanced on black water.
The lake's membrane pulled tight
except at the edges, where it riffles—

letting go the trapped gas,
the intricate lives of micro-organisms.
Lily pads undulate,
landing pads for minute spaceships,
origin of these bizarre frogs,
in pairs, like handcuffs,
found nowhere but this lake.

We read about their delicate
nervous system, their mating habits,
a pornography of speckled, iridescent skin.
Their music swells the lavender sky,
breaking in on the painter's sleep.
He rolls over, cursing.
He would like to shoot
the frogs' pale bellies,
watch them splatter the lake.

He would also shoot the moon
for coming into his room uninvited
and making the woman's skin
glow like pearls, like the unprotected
side of a fish.

He pushes his penis into her
to shut out the raucous frogs,
their uninhibited couplings.

Elegy for Otto Rene Castillo

Naomi Thiers

Otto Rene Castillo as a Guatemalan poet who lived in exile much of his life because of his political activities. The last time he returned to Guatemala in 1967 he was tortured and burned at the stake by the Guatemalan army. Tecun Uman was a Guatemalan Indian leader also burned at the stake. The italicized words in this poem are from the writings of Otto Rene Castillo.

> *And the poets of vigorous swords...*
> *will know how to love life*
> *where it rises*
> *with its flaming face...*
> *because life*
> *is the highest poetry.*

In Río Hondo, in Zacapa
they caught you, Castillo.
They tied your mestizo bones
to a stake in the equatorial
sun. I was ten
when they lit your hair and flamed
what was left of your face.

> *The eyes of my bones*
> *will be lost in a wind*
> *of ash.*

You pressed into my mouth
the bitter earth of Guatemala,
your german wife's hair, and your longing
for corn and clay gods, I eager
to hear you read

> *Tomorrow, for my joy chiming*
> *in the walls,*
> *the bride will hold her most beautiful bell.*

But there was not even a stone for you in Zacapa.
Your blood did not even seed the earth,
only a scar of ashes trailed across scorched gardens.

There was no last poem in your torture.
Peasants saw smoke rising from the mountain
and went on harvesting hunger with machetes.

Little by little we turn
ashen from our skin to our souls.

You knew,
every second of your exile and return,
the exact heat of the grave they had waiting for you

now I am
the skeleton
of a house on fire
that aches inside
a wall of ashes

and what would become of your eyes.
But your pen cut Mayan stone.
Your tongue released the red fire bound
since Tecun Uman in a husk of corn.

Guatemala

Lesley Kruger

The lake was shaped like an anchor thrown between the volcanoes. Lake Atitlán; blue-black, flat and shimmering. On the shaft of the anchor, where water lapped against the east side of the San Pedro volcano, it grew golden from reflecting back the winter cornfields on the mountainside; cornfields planted so far up that the slope seemed nearly vertical, and the desiccated, honey-coloured stalks seemed to have been left there to hold down the soil. Monroe saw he had a picture. Villagers were fishing in the golden reflection from rough canoes hollowed out of logs. Behind them were some green reeds. The gold dimmed out to blue-black at the water's shifting margins. He got out a long lens, then remembered what the art director at the magazine had said and wondered if he should screw on the sparkle filter too. He could make it pretty-pretty. Pretty-pretty fishermen holding big nets, wearing straw hats, their canoes lost in glitter like the floor of a disco. But they were probably from Santiago Atitlán, where Monroe's boat was headed, and near which a twenty-year-old schoolteacher had recently been disappeared, presumably by the army, then found dead with signs of torture on her body. Monroe took the picture straight. Then he swore and screwed on the filter for a few more shots. If it turned out he wasn't good enough to give them the pictures he hoped for, he was going to have to give them the ones that they wanted.

Monroe's assignment was to photograph the beauties of Guatemala. "I agree it's superficial," the art director had said. "Or at least, I did at first. But then I thought, the killing's pretty well over; the death squads have been disbanded, the people probably want to just put it behind them. And one thing that's gonna help is the tourism dollar."

She was new at the job, but Monroe gathered that her predecessor had left some crib notes about the freelance photographers. "Bypass Monroe's lug head," he apparently said, "and go straight for the bleeding heart."

"Leave us not be sentimental," the art director told him. "When my Dad died the insurance money made all the difference in the world to my Mom."

Her crewcut, new wave off-handedness irritated Monroe, but he decided to ignore her and look hard at the assignment to see if there was any way to do a good job. The problem was, he seldom knew what was in an assignment until he saw it through his viewfinder, and sometimes after that, after he lifted the best slides off his light table and projected them on the wall above his bed. That was how he found he had a locust shot. About a week before then he had been driving around the back roads of the Yucatan when he began to see one or two locusts in a henequen field, then more and more until the sky was pink and he stopped the car. He stuffed his jeans inside his boots, tied a spare strap around his collar and rolled up his sleeves until they were like tourniquets on his biceps. The he leapt out to the car and slammed the door. Normally Monroe prided himself on the amount he could take. But locusts knocked against his bare arms. They crawled behind his sunglasses, touching his eyes. He began to shoot wildly, holding his camera straight out in front of him and bending his knees, half squatting to keep his legs from shaking. Then he bolted back to the car. He only knew what he had shot when he saw the slide of the oppressive pink-brown sky with the field of cactus blurred as grey as his hair by the insects flying in front of him. Only one plant was in focus. But it was perfectly in focus, and had insects sitting on the tip of each grey-green leaf looking as bleak and wrong as dead lights on a Christmas tree.

There was another time like that. Monroe had seen his girlfriend sitting in a garden chair in an attitude which had struck him, although he grabbed a shot almost absently as he walked by, and only knew when he saw the slide that he had taken a picture of the anniversary of her husband's death. Which was a hell of a thing to project life-sized on the wall above your bed.

"What I would want to do in Guatemala would be to shoot not what was there so much as what isn't anymore," he said, then stopped.

"My God, we're talking Art with a capital A," the new director told him.

"Aw hell," Monroe replied. One thing. Having taken the assignment, he found that whatever contempt he had for it or her or for the magazine had to extend to himself.

The crossing to Santiago Atitlán took an hour and a half. Monroe was glad of the rest. He had landed in Guatemala City the previous afternoon planning to spend a few days reconnoitring, but he had quickly decided to get out. It was a creepy place. Two places, really; a rich zone of fortified mansions butted up against something like a rundown Mexican provincial town. Before he had left, some people at home had schooled him about what they called the disastrous gulf between the rich and poor of Guatemala, but he hadn't sensed a gulf so much as claustrophobia coming from the abutment, the rasping and impingement which made even the dust on his boots seem like something the rich bricks made grinding against the poor ones. Of course thirty-eight thousand people had just been killed in a very dirty war and it was hard not to see things through that prism. Or to assign another, more Biblical provenance to the dust.

Most of the other people on the Atitlán boat were German tourist couples. Like him, they were staying in the resort town of Panajachel across the lake. Like them, he carried a camera casually by its strap as he clambered onto the Santiago dock, being careful to look as if he didn't care about it, and keeping most of his equipment hidden for now in a bag underneath his jacket. He felt a bit funny coming to gawk at a town where people were having a hard time. Dionisia Matzar: the murdered teacher's name came back to him, although the image he had formed of her dried up when he stepped onto the path leading from the lake and looked up at the little town. He had pictured a Ladina girl with high-heeled shoes, a tough red mouth, wicked fingernails and bruised brown eyes; a very sexual picture which he was ashamed to realize came from her probably having been raped. No one could wear high heels there. The streets were either dirt or cobbled. It was an Indian town, with thatched-roof houses. Naked children. Chickens. Dogs which suddenly reminded him of Mayan figures dug out of pyramids not too far away.

Monroe walked towards town, passing some rocks on the lakeshore where women were doing their laundry. They were dressed in the local native blouse of bright, loose intricate striped cotton; red and white, or black and white, or blue and black and yellow and white, each with its band around the neck of hand-embroidered flowers. They had shawls, thrown now on some bushes, and long striped skirts of astonishing weave that were drawn up high between their legs so they could wade knee-deep in water. Monroe forgot his hesitation and quickly got to work. He took pictures there, pictures down the street where a woman knelt in her swept brown yard and wove some startling fabric on a back loom hitched to a tree. It was exhilarating. Drying beans lay piled on a porch. Corn was stacked beside some rocks. Here a tray of bright red chillies lay on a yellow windowsill. There some fraying pink and green striped fabric was thrown on a grey stone wall.

"Hey, look," one kid yelled to another. "Now he's taking a picture of Hugo's shorts." An old woman watched him from a blue casement window high in the opposite wall. Monroe held out his camera in both hands to ask if he could take her picture, but the woman shook her head and closed the window. Monroe shrugged. He was on a roll. As he walked up the narrow street, he told himself that if he could find a way to put it all in context for the people who saw the magazine, he had a chance, her only chance, of bringing Dionisia home.

It was a hot day. Monroe was sweating by the time he reached the central market. The amazing market. All around the town square, people gathered in costumes that made the streets look like they were filled with the waving of a hundred closely-packed flags. Monroe blinked and wiped his forehead, sensing a pride in local traditions he could play on. But when he lifted his camera they all turned away, and the women drew their shawls over their babies' heads. The scene looked strange then, a dozen Lots turning from Gomorrah, and Monroe dropped into a store to get a drink while he figured what to do. Hanging back in the doorway, he saw so many tempting faces. Then he realized that they didn't notice him there, and took a final pull on his drink before getting back to work. A girl passed him carrying a load of oranges on her head. Some men walked by holding rope. Then soldiers. Suddenly he had soldiers marching through his frame. Before he knew it, Monroe had a picture of a girl's eyes looking at the soldiers through the crowd. Then he dropped his camera into his bag so he wouldn't get caught taking unauthorized pictures of the army. He didn't want his film to be confiscated, particularly the last shot, although he realized the art director would never use a military picture. That would be his; his idea to play with, to refine. Next time he would cancel the soldiers, but get the eyes.

Monroe ordered another drink, and this time got the girl to pour it into a plastic bag so he could go check out the army. It wasn't hard; he only had to turn a corner to see the place was crawling with soldiers. They stood at the ready guarding the construction of a martial-looking building that would never rank among the beauties of Guatemala. They hung around what he presumed was a command post. Monroe wiped his forehead again and sat down on the church steps. A few kids were shooting basketball on a court nearby, ignoring the army, but Monroe wasn't sure he could be so blasé. It might not be smart to start taking more pictures than a tourist would take when he had no idea what was going on. Why had they killed the teacher? The human rights report he had read was short on reasons, although it quoted a senior army officer as telling the local people to expect reprisals when there was any guerrilla activity in the area. The officer had told them that after the killing, but the way things seemed to go on around there it might be an explanation as well as a warning.

Monroe was still wondering what to do when a girl with a German accent came up behind him.

"If you would be so kind?'

He turned and saw two university kids who wanted their pictures taken in front of the church.

"Why not?" he replied. A delay might help him make up his mind. "With both cameras?" But instead of answering, the girls seemed to look right through him. Monroe turned and saw that a platoon of soldiers was marching into the churchyard.

"Porci," the bigger girl called. Pigs. But in Italian; she had mixed up her languages, and spoke in such a wavering voice anyway that Monroe could pretend she was speaking to him.

"With both cameras, then," he answered her in Spanish. Then he frowned at the girls, so they took each other's hands. Monroe doubted anything serious would happen, but unpleasant things might, and he kept his eyes on the girls as he backed up to take their pictures.

"Smile," he warned.

The girls smiled wanly.

"Come on, smile," one of the soldiers told them.

Monroe glanced back quickly. The platoon was standing in a semi-circle behind him.

"Smile," another soldier called. "Smile at the birdie." Then they all began to whistle and make cheepy bird noises, kissing their lips and knocking Monroe right off kilter. He wondered what would happen. Then he glanced back again and realized this was just a group of sixteen-year-old boys. They didn't mean any harm. They were only curious. Monroe grinned back at them and took the pictures quickly. One. Two. Three was his camera. He turned around hoping to get a couple of shots of the soldiers, but their sergeant caught his eye. He nodded at Monroe, then lifted his chin at the bigger of the two girls.

"That's a lot of ham for two poor eggs."

Monroe grinned broadly at the line, then took another look at the sergeant and felt so cold he had trouble giving the expected wink. The sergeant had never cracked a smile. He was too proud of himself. Seedy. Older. How old? Evidently old enough. The whistles had a tendency to echo in the churchyard. Monroe turned and saw the frightened girls. They looked about twenty years old. One. Two. Not three of them.

Monroe had a pretty good idea that his girlfriend, Joanna, didn't waste too much time thinking about him while he was away. He liked to tell himself he was just as glad if that meant she didn't get into one of her monologues. Pacing, smoking, her curly hair wild, she sounded hilarious to anyone who didn't notice her dilated pupils, or her trick of gnawing a thumbnail while holding the cigarette up against her mouth. She went in for lists of things that could happen to him. He might be bus plunged, struck by a falling suicide, mistaken for the middle class and taxed half to death.

Joanna said that the way her husband had been electrocuted while drilling new holes in a wall unit had alerted her to all the possibilities inherent in everyday life.

Yet really, Monroe didn't like to picture the way she rushed obliviously from her occasional jobs as a set designer back to her studio, to the sculptures and constructions which showed how far her line of thought carried her away from him. As he sloped through Panajachel on the way back to his hotel, Monroe thought about the time he got home and found something called Recovery, A self-portrait. Joanna had shopped the junk stores until she found a sofa of about the same vintage as herself, then slashed off the conventional tweedy brown fabric about a quarter of the way along and began to build it up again with raw patchwork pieces of fabric, first from her parents' basement, from the trunks of old clothes she had initially rifled when she went back to stay with them after her husband had been killed—pieces from old bowling shirts, felt skating skirts, a swatch from the hem of her prom dress—then increasingly nutsy fabric from her wildcat days, leather and spangles and a forest of pocket-like zippered flies which Monroe tried not to count—"Go on," she said, "open them"—all this giving way to pieces of fabric handwoven by her feminist craftswomen friends; pieces which got bigger and bigger until that whole end of the couch was covered with handwoven tweedy brown material that stood in contrast to the original, more conventional upholstery, being thicker and richer, but also more flawed.

"I could tell Monroe was impressed," Joanna said later. "His jaw must have dropped a quarter of an inch and he pumped his biceps once or twice."

Alone with him she was more conciliatory. "You can sit on it too."

But the flaws had bothered him. Not because they referred to him, but because they obviously did not. Nothing referred to him; he was entirely absent from the piece. Not absent like the husband, not merely invisible, but completely non-existent. Nada. And he couldn't help thinking that the flaws were a reference to her husband, or rather to his absence, since what were flaws but the absence of perfection? And what conclusions could he draw from that?

Panajachel was a hippie town, a strange place to find so close to a village like Santiago Atitlán. But Westerners—mainly Germans and Americans—had been settling near the extraordinary lake for about twenty years. By that time the town was full of crafts boutiques which Monroe began sloping into, shopping for Joanna, feeling all too conscious that she was probably oblivious of him, and cherishing a little feeling of wounded righteousness which tended to make him extravagant. In one shop he bought Joanna a dressing gown which seemed to have been designed by the exotic young German girl who sold it, or maybe for her by the artist whose sexy paintings of the girl covered the walls, a dressing gown made out of local fabric shot through with silver, lined with imported silk and cut to the latest vogue.

"My God, just look at the price," Joanna would have said. "Feeling connubial, are we, my dear transparency? In payment for what evil thoughts? Those concerning the fraulein, perhaps?"

Monroe had never caught Joanna feeling jealous, however much he might have liked to. But when he looked, she saw. She saw right through him, and he sometimes heard her commenting on it all.

"But which fraulein, might I ask? The one in the boutique, or the one in churchyard? I mean, of course, the one you laughed at when that horrible sergeant cracked his joke."

Even at the time, Monroe had seemed to hear her speaking for the two girls he had helped frighten into silence, and for poor Dionisia Matzar. The echoes hadn't gone away.

"What were you *doing*, Monroe, laughing at a joke like that? Then winking at the bugger. You didn't need to wink. Don't let's be melodramatic; what would he have done if you refused? My God, Monroe, you owe for that one. How do you propose to make it up?"

How about a dressing gown?

"How about doing a good job?"

In his hotel room that night, Monroe lay on his bed trying to bring into mental focus the kind of pictures he needed. Joanna's present lay across from him on the dresser, serving as a bit of a goad. Underneath it all, of course, was the fact that she had already demonstrated her mastery over the implicit in her art while he still lay there struggling. They weren't in competition. He had never thought of himself as competing with her. But that only made it seem unfriendly on her part to have already beaten him.

The next morning Monroe got up before sunrise and drove on as soon as it was faintly light. He headed westward, driving up into the mountains on a solid climb that soon took him into the cold. He kept looking out for pictures, of what he didn't know. But then he came across a farm very high in the mountains on undulating ground. A little wooden house stood in the middle of a cornfield, the stalks dried and yellow-beige in this light, the soil a powdered terra cotta, the sky almost ochre; matte, flat colours. And from the chimney of the little house smoke spread levelly and strangely through the field at the height of a man, held down by the cold so the tops of corn stalks were above it. Monroe stopped the car and got his tripod out of the trunk.

Is this it? he asked. Is this? Is this?

Ten days later Monroe drove back into Panajachel, feeling tired, dusty and dissatisfied. He had driven westward to Quetzaltenango, Chichicastenango— all the Mayan highland towns then out to the coast, where they grew coffee and sugarcane. Along the way he had taken a mountain of pictures. Beautiful things. Mist in empty villages, religious processions, named and decorated trucks—one called The Owner of Nothing. Then he began to get volcanic hotsprings, the bathers all with little heads; mud pools he shot early when the shadows were hard and they looked grotesque. Strange things, striking; but they were about his mood more than the country. He was getting impatient that he couldn't find a central image to tie it all together. At first he told himself he would find that when he got back to the capital, but all he got there were orchid vendors, shop signs crowding the tight little streets; more pictures in the succession but no fulcrum, no pivot; shapes more than information. He knew he was being hard on himself. Most people would have been proud to turn in his shots, and they were certainly what the magazine had wanted. But he had promised more, and he could almost hear the art director laughing at his presumption, joining the chorus of female voices in his head. Derisive. Demanding. To make decent money on the assignment he should probably have hopped a plane home from Guatemala City. But he had an idea that if he went back to Santiago Atitlán he could do it, he could force something, he would show them all.

When Monroe got off the Santiago boat for the second time he had three cameras with different lenses hanging around his neck. He knew it was all or nothing, and walked quickly up the slope. Then he stopped in the plaza, seeing he had nothing. He'd forgotten it wasn't market day, and on other days these towns were dead. Wandering through the dusty streets, all he saw were tourists. And corn, of course, against the rocks. Chillies drying on a windowsill. But he had done all that. He had already stripped the surface off Santiago Atitlán, used it up—or maybe just used up his enthusiasm. In any case, he had used something. When people asked if he didn't exploit the subjects of his photographs, he said no, not if he did a good job. But as he circled through the town, brooding and increasingly angry, he couldn't fool himself into thinking he had done a good job anymore than he could see how to improve on it. He decided he might as well go back to the dock.

"Diddums," he could hear Joanna say.

Then something caught Monroe's eye. Three local teenage girls were rounding the corner, each with a bundle of fabric on her head. The composition was lovely. The complex vertical line of clothing, cloth and embroidery was broken by three distinct swaths of bronze—which is how he first saw their faces. Monroe had already put a yellow filter on one camera which would deepen the reds and blues and browns until you could hardly stand it. He stepped in front of the girls and started to take their pictures.

"You've got to pay us for that," the middle girl yelled immediately. Monroe usually resisted paying his subjects, but this time he pulled a fistful of the local currency out of his pocket. He had seen something through his viewfinder, although he wasn't quite sure what.

"Five quetzals apiece," he answered. Nothing to him, a feast to them. They stopped where they were and began to smile.

First he tried group shots. But whatever he wanted wasn't there and he quickly moved on to close-ups. Two of the girls were obviously sisters, although they wouldn't tell him their names. The older one was slim and shy, the younger the one who had asked for money. But the picture wasn't there either. Monroe turned impatiently to the third girl. She was taller and plumper than the sisters, with a pleasant longish face. But Monroe quickly found she wouldn't show it to him. She kept giving him her profile, until he finally realized she was the one who had torpedoed the group shots by staring off into space. He wondered what he had to do to get women to pay attention to him.

"Look at me," he ordered. But she would only look when he let his camera drop in exasperation. Then he realized she was trying to keep him from photographing her right eye. It was cloudy, and the pupil stared off to one side. Wall eye, he thought it was called. Monroe wondered if there was any point in going on, when all that had probably struck him in the first place was this one odd eye. But he felt a bit bloody-minded. He had started this and he wasn't going to stop until he had her picture.

"Look at me," he repeated, raising his camera. But the girl looked off again, so he began to dance around her, shooting one exposure after another and making sure if she wouldn't cooperate, at least she had to dance with him.

"That's too many," the younger sister said. "If you want any more, you have to give her more money."

Maybe she thought that would stop him. But Monroe just fumbled in his pocket and came up with a fifty quetzal note—a fortune in Guatemala. He stopped dancing long enough to fold the note in half lengthwise and weave it between his fingers like a teller. Then he raised his camera again and saw he had his picture.

He would use the word "haunting." Distress haunted the girl's face as it did the country. You wouldn't be able to look at the rest of the pictures without seeing it. Without knowing how much was still going on underneath the surface. What he had was rich fabric and expression, killing blues, living bronze. And that eye, like the eyes he had seen looking at the soldier. That eye, he would say, looking at the dead.

All fake, of course. It was only vanity which distressed her, and all she had her eye on was a fifty quetzal note. Not that Monroe would tell anyone. He circled her more slowly now, stalking the perfect angle. Crouching, level, wheeling, he made her his pivot too.

134

Some fisherman whistled derisively behind them. Monroe looked up for an instant, then dismissed them. They were like the soldiers. Then it occurred to him that he was more like the soldiers than they were. Or maybe like the sergeant. Bullying the girl. It was for her own good, of course. If more tourists came, she would sell more cloth. So they said, although Monroe wondered briefly if all solutions were so closely related to the original problems that they echoed the problems in a minor key. He was beginning to dislike what he was doing. Imposing meaning, interpretation; that was where you got into exploitation. He felt diminished, and could not help thinking that the cliché was all wrong. When you took peoples' photographs you didn't capture their souls. You gave them a piece of yours instead.

Monroe had already used up half a roll of film on the girl. He wondered if he should stop, cut his losses. On top of everything else, he was sweating and exhausted. He thought how good a can of beer would taste. He wanted to sit down.

Then something happened. Very quickly but firmly, the girl turned fully towards him. Monroe couldn't believe it; she had decided to give him her face. Bravely, so the bravery showed around her mouth. Proudly, so the pride showed through her distress. Shyly too; she was still very young. It added up to something extraordinary, and average. An everyday face rising to a challenge. A kid deciding she could take it. Even with that one eye looking at the dead.

Thank you, Monroe thought. Thank you. He took several pictures. Then his job was finished and he dropped the cameras back into his bag.

The body of Dionisia Matzar was found on March 29, 1986, near kilometre five on the road from Almolongo to Quetzaltenango, Guatemala.

Moveable Territory

Alfredo Lavergne

The pain of the Quiché language
Prayer in the pre-Columbian fields
A name spread in taxes
        briefly Alvarado (1524)

135 horsemen
        slash through a civilization
Mnemonic pictographs in neon
Rapids in sumptuous structures
The volcanic origin of hunger

And the dispersed villages of light.

The Market at Atitlán

Whether she sells or not
        The Indian woman sits
Along the path
        To the hut
        Embroidering
A wound.

The Lake

They wash clothes on the shore
    Dry them on the rocks.

While their daughters
    Distract
        The lake.

The Ceiba*

One by one I count
        Cornfields
    Burial mounds and soldiers.

Their mountains
      land of fruit trees.

*National Tree of Guatemala

Reversible

The shadow
    slips by
        the soldier
fires on hunger.

At night or
    at the end of the day
The earth covers the peasants.

Parallel

The Cakchiquel couple
      walks to the lake
          their footsteps
Suffer through the seasons—trucks
      in Spanish
          burst across
              the dust

The soldiers are hurrying
          to the south of Atitlán
To fight against
      The Tzutujils.

Where The Sky Is A Pitiful Tent

Claire Harris

Once I heard a Ladino say " I am poor but listen I am not an Indian"; but then again I know Ladinos who fight with us and who understand we're human beings just like them.

Rigoberta Menchu (Guatemala)*

All night the hibiscus tapped at our jalousies
dark bluster of its flower trying to ride in
on wind laciniated with the smell of yard fowl
Such sly knocking sprayed the quiet
your name in whispers
dry shuffle of thieving feet on verandah floors
My mouth filled with midnight and fog
like someone in hiding
to someone in hiding
I said *do not go*
you didn't answer
though you became beautiful and ferocious
There leached from you three hundred years of compliance
Now I sleep with my eyes propped open
lids nailed to the brow

After their marriage my parents went into the mountains to establish a small settlement . . . They waited years for the first harvest. Then a patrón *arrived and claimed the land. My father devoted himself to travelling and looking for help in getting the rich landowners to leave us alone. But his complaints were not heard . . . they accused him of provoking disorder, of going against the sovereign order of Guatemala. . . they arrested him.*

Ladino: descendant of Spanish Jews who came to Guatemala during the Inquisition

* From the testimony of Rigoberta Menchu, translated by Patricia Goedicke, A.P.R., January/ February 1983.

In the dream I labour toward something
glimpsed through fog   something of us exposed
on rock and mewling   as against the tug of water
I struggle under sharp slant eyes
death snap and rattle of hungry wings
                              Awake I whisper
You have no right to act
you cannot return land from the grave
Braiding my hair the mirror propped on my knees
I gaze at your sleeping vulnerable head
Before the village we nod smile or don't smile
we must be as always
while the whole space of day aches with our nightmares
I trail in your footsteps through cracks you chisel
in this thin uncertain world
where as if it were meant for this mist hides
sad mountain villages   reluctant fields
still your son skips on the path laughing
he is a bird   he is a hare
under the skeletal trees

My mother had to leave us alone while she went to look for a lawyer who
would take my father's case. And because of that she had to work as a
servant. All her salary went to the lawyer. My father was tortured and
condemned to eighteen years in prison. (Later he was released.)
But they threatened to imprison him for life if he made any more trouble.

I watch in the market square
those who stop and those who do not
while my hands draw the wool over up down
knitting the bright caps on their own
my eyes look only at sandals
at feet chipped like stones at the quarry
There are noons when the square shimmers
we hold our breath while those others
tramp in the market place
Today the square ripples like a pond
three thrown   what is left of them
corded like wood   alive and brought to flame
How long the death smoke signals
on this clear day
We are less than the pebbles under their heels
the boy hides in my shawl

The army circulated an announcement ordering everyone to present themselves in one of the villages to witness the punishment the guerrillas would receive . . . There we could observe the terrible things our comrades had suffered and see for ourselves that those they called guerrillas were people from the neighbouring villages . . . among them the Catequistas and my little brother . . . who was secretary to one of the village co-operatives. That was his only crime. He was fourteen years old . . . They burnt them.

As if I have suffered resurrection I see
the way the grass is starred with thick fleshed
flowers at whose core a swirl of fine yellow
lines disappear into hollow stems
so we now into our vanished lives
Dust thickening trees we turn
to the knotted fist of mountains
clenched against mauve distance
Because I must   I look back
heartheld to where the mudbrick huts
their weathered windows daubed with useless crosses
their shattered doors   begin the slow descent
to earth   my earlier self turns in
darkening air   softly goes down with them
The boy only worms alive in his eyes
his face turned to the caves

When we returned to the house we were a little crazy, as if it had been a nightmare. My father marched ahead swiftly saying that he had much to do for his people; that he must go from village to village to tell them what had happened . . . A little later so did my mother in her turn . . . My brother left too . . . and my little sisters .

If in this poem you scream who will hear you
though you say *no one should cry out in vain*
your face dark and thin with rage
Now in this strange mountain place
stripped by knowledge
I wait for you
Someone drunk stumbles the night path
snatching at a song or someone not drunk
I am so porous with fear
even the rustle of ants in the grass flows through me
but you are set apart
The catechists say *in heaven there is no male
no female*   that is a far foolishness
why else seeing you smelling of danger
and death do I want you so
your mouth   your clear opening in me

---

*We began to build camps in the mountains where we would spend the night
to prevent the troops from killing us while we slept. In the daytime we had
taught the children to keep watch over the road . . . We knew that the
guerrillas were up there in the distant mountains. At times they would
come down in order to look for food, in the beginning we didn't trust them,
but then we understood that they, at least, had weapons to fight the army
with.*

You will not stop what you have begun
though I asked in the way a woman can
Since you have broken thus into life
soon someone will make a pattern
of your bones   of your skull
as they have with others
and what will fly out
what will escape from you torn apart
the boy and I must carry
In your sleep I went to the cenote*
in the moonlight I filled my shawl with flowers
threw them to the dark water
the ancient words fluting in my head
your son pinched awake to know what must come

---

*My mother was captured (some) months later . . . when all she could wish
for was to die . . . they revived her, and when she had recovered her
strength they began torturing her again . . . they placed her in an open field
. . . filled her body with worms . . . she struggled a long time then she died
under the sun . . . The soldiers stayed until the buzzards and dogs had eaten
her. Thus they hoped to terrorize us. She doesn't have a grave. We, her
children, had to find another way of fighting.*

*cenote: a well occasionally used in ritual sacrifice (pre-Columbian)

Oh love this is silence   this is the full
silence of completion   we have swum through
terror that seared us to the bone
rage lifted a cold hand to save us
so we became this surreal country
We have been bullet-laden air   fields that sprout
skulls   night that screeches and hammers
we have been hunger   whip   wind that sobs
feast days and drunken laughter
a rare kindness and pleasure
We have come through to the other side
here everything is silence   our quiet breathing
in this empty hut   our clay jugs full of light
and water   we are our corn our salt
this quiet is the strength we didn't know we had
our humanity no longer alarms us
we have found who we are
my husband our silence is the silence of blue steel thrumming
and of love
Our deaths shall be clear

Our only way of commemorating the spilled blood of our parents was to go on fighting and following the path they had followed. I joined the organization of the Revolutionary Christians. I know perfectly well that in this fight one runs the greatest risk . . . We have been suffering such a long time and waiting.

Your death is drenched in such light
that small things   the sky   branches
brushing against the cave mouth   the boy
stirring   make my skin crackle against damp blankets
As one gathers bullets carelessly spilled I gather your screams
all night I remember you   utterly lovely
the way you danced the wedding dance
rising dust clouding your sandals
your slow dark smile
You return to the predawn   leaving us
what remains when the flames die out of words
(small hard assertions
our beginnings
shards of the world you shattered
and ourselves)

---

*Their death gave us hope, because it is not just that the blood of all those
people be erased forever. It is our duty on this earth to revive it . . . I fight
so they will recognize me . . . If I have taken advantage of this chance to tell
the story of my life it is because I know that many people cannot tell their
own stories. But they are no different from mine.*

In a Black Wind

Jan Conn

We crouch in the courtyard
where a wind picks up
a few last rain drops and dusty
papaya leaves, driving them
against a white plaster wall.

This is the day of the Festival of Soldiers
and military planes fly low overhead
celebrating more than a year in power
without a successful coup. You ask me
what I'm thinking.

Last week in Panajachel I heard
the firing squad, wanting to believe
in firecrackers.

I was in the garden. A group of children
arrived at the gate.
They told me a man was dead in the street.
On his feet are expensive shoes.

Hibiscus fell during the night
onto his dark shirt and hair.
Someone dragged him
down a dirt road by his heels.

I went down to clean my hands
in the lake still black as the road
to the north in the *Popul Vuh*

or all the bars on windows
behind which faces are peering out,
faces that slowly flicker out,
candles in a black wind.

Sonsonate

Larry Towell

We've come far enough to know
that while the birds sing
in their freedom, we've abandoned no one
It's not a matter of abandoning
We are prepared—
If you see me on the street
with my violin, I play
to abandonment, retaliation
papayas & mangos, hoping no one
will remember the small dark face
of a man who once climbed
the stiff uplands—
The trees remembered your face;
clouds promised names
Even the stones had eyes
I have transcended the mountains
with their permission
'Let him pass' Nothing
Nothing ever answers me now
There was Antonio Paz
starved in the mountains
wind entering his guts
his diary turning of itself
'Patria Libre o Morir' &
'... the stars ... city of the dead ...'
his pitiful empty gun
pointing as all guns must
The mountains have their debts
They hide some & kill the rest
who cannot be changed into mountains—

Olivia, how many times
did they fuck you
their penises like rifles
& then used a rifle?
You did not die
I have kept everything
you insisted of me
sliding your hand into mine
one last time, these hands
assigned to protect us

especially in the coffee—
the scent of tortillas & wood smoke
& frying fish
with black coffee in the dawn
This is not a revolution
It is a mass grave
one hand protruding
the sound of bones
touching each other in the trees
the transfiguration of darkness
into phosphorescent bombs
children running naked in the flash
People, you are powerless—
In Jujutla, Victor, brother, poet
forced to dig his own grave
'Why am I digging?
There is no one dead'
The earth knew nothing
He descended into the earth
to hunt mice in its nightmare
He searches until he finds them
& then kills them—

The screams of those tied
naked to tables, grease
smeared on their testicles
so the dogs would eat them
have not reached me here
I am too far north
I listen in the silence
until I become so small
I will not exist
How much further
into a little hole
can a man go?
The names of those who vanished
their bodies never turning up
that nest only south of Metapán
I do not remember their names
so I keep my silence
This is why we sell iguana
in the markets of Izalco
their legs broken
so they cannot escape
This is why fifteen year old girls
suckle babies

Living Picture / March 18, 1982: El Salvador

Paul Wilson

the cameraman is hit
      picture
thrown to sun

scraping blue
        the spine
of a red clay roof
          empty window
focusing black   panning
to the soldier   who fires
who kills the picture

       a second
time slow
motion
soldier   aims straight/fires
         at the camera/drops
         picture/camera/
          man

One of My Dead

Salvador Torres

You are one more of the unruly dead
who fight among the living;
you are the rubbing and lubricant
in the act of love that creates
an imitation of the new man
bastard Son of God
——or whoever——
and the dialectic whore.
Café companion in splendid binges
of galactic proportions
today your words rise up
jubilant from your bones
and spread irrepressibly
through homes filled with flowers
where the fearful magic of passion
transforms the night into a beacon.

Poet with the soul of a mountebank,
charlatan swindler of muses
and sarcastic blasphemer
of timeless hours,
your incandescent words
flash in the rebirth
of the liberated homeland.

Roque
creator of poems with gunsights, triggers, and trenches
Dalton
outlaw of the dawn.

Because you are needed here,
I believe,
poor little poet,
that your one-way trip places you
among those never reached
by oblivion.

> Is it because life
> without a carcass is wings?

Poem with Corrosive Intentions

Guanacoligarch of the grim look given away by your macabre vices,
I take the liberty of showing you that everything indicates
that your orgy of blood is leading you straight to the bitter end.

Fetidoligarch standing proudly over piles of cadavers like unthreshed corn,
your stench has so rarefied the air that imperial
buzzards and falcons flinch, stunned.

Because you've always asserted yourself with blood and fire,
now you're fucked forever: there are no more tricks that will work
for you, nor any packs of hounds to help you,
nor any apocryphal saints to protect you.

Since you're really nothing more than a one-legged jackal
grown fat in the shade of infamy,
I foresee a mortal trap waiting for you
at the edge of history, which is sometimes late, but never forgets.

Oligabeast, the air you breathe
is saturated with the best-loved dreams of all those
torn apart by your insatiable claws.

For you, such air is poison without antidote,
like the bite of the black widow spider in a shitless universe.

Arrogant malificoligarch, the future will not stop
corroding you even when all that's left is a pile of dust
holding up this epitaph:
        Here lies an oligalizard
        who marches onward toward nothingness
        having succumbed to the turmoil that he began.

¿Qué Hi?

Alfonso Quijada Urías

. . . and there I was, my friends, walking in a night full of diamonds with my buddy Suncín, both of us drunk as farts, staggering one Sunday through the Escalón dropping our money in night clubs and our hands into drunks' pockets, a great fantastic life eating like kings and screwing rich old ladies, rapping and flying around in the latest wheels, living it up. Man, I felt almost like Marlón Brando himself in one of his best takes, and so between one bash and another it was finally midnight and the old ladies took off back to their old men and we ended up near the Safari and looked in to see what was happening and inside there were some rich bastards talking business and at another table some really old guys with their decked-out elegant old ladies and we started to set something up because, you know, right there in the dark in the middle of the show starring Zaza Gabor and the Salvadoran Briyit with spicy salsa music, the Animal was keeping watch, and you can never tell who they're going to come down on next and so we kept on checking things out till we saw some other suspicious-looking characters drinking endless beers and Suncín gave me the sign that they were cops and we split back out onto the street to get some fresh air just when the Areta Franklin of Panamá was winding up her show by smoking a Havana cigar with her cunt.

Outside everything was cool as usual with a nice little breeze coming down from the volcano and we began to walk and walk tripping out on the unbelievable wheels that seemed newer and shinier than anything I'd ever seen before and we cased out an MG and opened the door with a wire without being spotted by the Animal or any night watchman, and bam! we got into the car and inside that new-car smell hit us superfine and even better when we slipped the pass-key to her and she started up clean and I pushed down on that little virgin accelerator and we blasted out of there, man. And then as we were going down Beethoven Street I put on the radio just when Mama Katch's beautiful voice came belting out with a tremendous wail and after that it was Hendrix with riffs like bursts of machine-gun fire spraying our ears, unbelievable and totally out-of-sight. That's what we were into when we heard the Animal's siren behind us but when were they ever going to catch us with a wonder car like that? So we danced them a mambo through the city and traffic, flat out down the boulevard all the way downtown where we messed up their heads and lost them and then took off north down Trunk Road in that car that hauled ass like a mother and leaped over potholes like cotton clouds. We were just starting to imagine how sweet it was going to be showing off to all the chicks and brothers in the neighbourhood when the cops suddenly appeared bouncing out of the darkness onto the Trunk. I punched it to the floor and jammed it left and we took off down Atlacatl Road where we finally ended up smashing that beautiful machine into a wall.

When we opened the door we were met by a storm of punches, kicks, and blows with billy-clubs; one cop put a gun barrel in my goddamn ass and got so worked-up that he was frothing at the mouth. They knocked Suncín to the ground with a pistol-butt and kept screaming "fuckinhippietroublemakers terroristcarthieves kidnapperobbersonsofbitches" and they lifted him up off the ground by the hair and tied us up so tight that the rope broke and the second time we lost all sensation in our hands because they turned purple and went numb.

They took us to a basement where the Head Animal took charge of the third degree: so where was the minister, what faction did we belong to, who did we rob cars for? The whole thing turned out to be a huge fucking hassle because as the cop ranted on we found out that the same night somebody had dragged the minister or whoever the fat cat was out of his house and that every cop in the city was hunting for the guys who'd done it, and since we didn't squeal the guy put wires on our balls and gave us a Russian salad hooking us up to electrodes that sent a current up from our feet to our ears by way of our noses and the first jolts made us bleed like crushed strawberries and at the same time another fucking cop kept hammering us with his truncheon.

And that, brothers, is how we woke up and after beating on us some more they left us in a pile, gasping like fish in pools of our own blood. Then I went into a long black dream, and after that a heavenly song came out of the night and suddenly it was as if the sky were opening and Number One Himself and His archangels and the whole orchestra of bugles and electric guitars was announcing the end of the world and then it was like in a movie or a mirror I saw myself the night I stabbed the old lady who caught us robbing her grimy little store and we tied her to a chair and emptied all the beer in her refrigerator just for fun until the neighbours came to see what was going on and the old lady's sons showed up with guns and we split like lightning into the night jumping over backyard fences and then fell into the street on top of some guy who happened to be walking by—and they never picked up our scent because we took off a second later in the yellow Beetle. About a century or maybe a minute later I woke up to the screams of Suncín who was rolling around on the floor covered in blood and then I saw everything in blue and on the horizon there was a superfine park full of green and my old lady was sitting on the grass in a blouse with a picture of Che Guevara on it that kept goddamn moving and then the whole landscape suddenly began turning into a ball of thread that was being dragged along by the foot of a red bird that came zooming down into my navel and then I saw myself inside a car getting it on with that girlfriend I used to have in Number 16 and I heard her delectable moaning and the radio playing "Lucyenescaay/güitdaimons" and you could see the waves of music coming through the air. But then everything became dark and goddamn depressing again and the sun appeared out of the darkness like a black disk and you could hear it fall into the waters of the sea that came roaring up in gigantic waves that splashed over the mountains and were so enormous that they demolished eighty-storey buildings and followed us with huge toothless mouths.

At that moment the cop had tossed a bucket of cold water in my face and I began to remember that I was locked up and I saw Suncín shaking the water from his head and they'd worked him over so bad that his face looked like somebody else. Then the cop punched us in the head to show us that we had to stand up and after about a thousand years we finally managed to get up on our legs that were shaking like crazy and once we were standing everything began whirling around again and I puked for hours and hours and when I'd finished they dragged us back for interrogation.

And it began all over again the whole spiel with him showing us the photo of the minister and offering to set us free and send us outside of the country if only we gave him important information about our cell and the other terrorists and when we couldn't answer he sent us back down to the basement and they put us through the Russian salad I-don't-know-how-ma-ny-times again with shocks to our balls every fifteen minutes and with the radio on full blast until that night they put us in some special kind of cop laboratory where a shrink shot us up with a drug that makes you tell the truth and a few minutes later I saw the heavens opening up again but this time full of blood because the whole earth was spattering them and then came German tanks and millions of soldiers with faces like Hitler and a huge rotten green fish as big as a country while I heard a voice yelling questions at me again about the terrorist cell and the minister, the terrorist cell and the minister, the terrorist cell and the minister. In the middle of all of this I saw a great thick cloud that my old man fell out of, he fell out and ran off down a blind alley of some city in the States like New York where my old man actually lives and then for some reason he came running back out. Everything was like a huge noisy movie because you could hear "Black Dog" in the background. And so after about half a century I heard the cops screaming at us and I woke up in a cell where other guys were laughing at us like crazy and I couldn't handle it so I got up as well as I could and kicked the worst one of them in the face and then everything broke loose in a huge brawl and all the prisoners began to yell until a couple of cops came and opened the cell and dragged us out of there hitting and hitting us and threw us in another cell and from there on I never saw Suncín again, my friends, because then they put me in the nuthouse and broke me down with electroshock every time that I told them that I am El Salvador and here I am brothers they've got my number and know that I'm not lying or bullshitting when I tell them that I am El Salvador, the goddamn Saviour of the World.

from The Ides of March

Henry Beissel

Here the scream was a skyblue flutter
in bleak branches, a puff of snow—
a pair of jays warning the stillness
against predators. Birds
are forever startled
into flight sudden as
death because they know
freedom is in the air.
Or have they been frightened
by the coming of creatures
who hunt the hunted
for a fee for a trophy for a
laugh kill partridges polar-bears
people?—I have a message
for you: the killers
are here. What happens
in El Salvador happens here in our hearts.

> Gunships erupt over Guazapa.
> The ancient volcano is still
> but not the violence in the eyes
> of men screaming bloody
> murder blossoming into bullets
> rockets bombs bursting into
> fire Fire FUEGO!
> consuming those who seek
> freedom on this scorched earth.

Vietnam. Afghanistan. Poland. El Salvador. The redhot lava
of violence has seared every side of the mountain of history
and still flows into the streets of villages, towns and
cities, threatening to suffocate and burn us all. The ashes
of unbridled power that bury us preserve our minds forever
twisted like those contorted bodies of Pompeii still clutching
their gold with their last charred cry. Cry, my beloved,

> cry to the stars!
> The morning is turning
> its back on Andromeda
> our next-door galaxy
> a couple of million light years
> down the road to eternity
> where winter is not a season
> but a destiny for every sun.

But here dawn and dew begin
their rousing glassbead game.
A flock of redpolls is pecking
a patch of hard ground
as if impatient to wake up
the earth where deep in darkness
the roots of maples sense
the sweetness of another season.

                    The snow is melting.
                    The sap is running.
                    The light will soon
                    match the darkness
                    and we must take sides.

Slowly the sun is hurtling
through the constellation of the fishes
that will not feed the multitude.
Soon it will reach its vernal equinox
to plant a garden in the north
that is the toil of many
but the delight of few.
The poor are poor
because the rich are rich
in a world divided
into hemispheres of power.

                    This is the month Champlain
                    sailed for a new and better
                    world and found Cain's land.
                    Others sailed before and after
                    on the tides of gold and glory,
                    somnambulists of freedom
                    bent on divine rule, driven by
                    the prevailing winds of politics
                    their hopes inflamed by a fever
                    of conquest and curiosity among
                    drifting continental plates
                    to spread a deadly virus
                    that hollows the heart and
                    strikes the mind with blindness.
                    Columbus was a carrier. So was
                    the Mayflower with its cargo
                    of heavenly pride. Half a millennium
                    of blood and bondage as the blind
                    led the blind up and down the Americas
                    into darkness. Civilization put to
                    the sword as far south as *Tierra del Fuego*

And still men and women
drag the chains of their poverty
up and down the continent.
And still El Salvador is un-
redeemed—even in the sleep
of children who starve to death
in a nightmare of paradise
which Fourteen Families have turned
into hell. Land of plenty plundered
by the few. There is always a lord
to make a slave of his brother
by the blood ties of fear. Fifty
years of military dictatorships—
and still their dreams live on.

Fifty civilians now murdered
every day and night between
hibiscus and banana flowers
by the national security forces up
and down torturing volcanic
slopes cane and coffee in
pursuit of steaming sweat river
valleys balsam hiding in cacao
millet hunting grapefruit beans
helicopter sesame—and everywhere
Rosita's rigid eyes watching
the seeds of freedom grow.

Mornings scream into consciousness
on the blue wings of jays.
Patches of snow are still holding out
deep in the north shadow
of spruce and cedar where
the sun cannot reach yet.

Heat and light are points
of violence in the brutal
wasteland of interstellar
space, a caprice of the cosmos
beyond our ken, a quick gesture
into the void. The sun is a nuclear
explosion among a hundred billion
others burning into extinction
at the speed of light.
Remember the moon.

The dying of a star quickens our hearts.
This galaxy has granted us a niche
on the edge of one of its spiral arms,
a space of time measured in generations
only, an equilibrium of day and night,
a balance of elements compounded
to flower into love and comprehension. It's that
or ashes. Mind or mineral—that is the question
in Rosita's eyes, and you and I must answer
to the difference between spring and winter.

                        Beware when eagles spread
                        their wings. This is the two-faced
                        month of Mars, god of warriors
                        and ploughmen. Blood is his
                        colour. A virgin was his
                        bride. And they danced
                        beating time
                        on the ground
                        with sword and share
                        as the sun entered its season.
                        We cannot escape spring.

Already the crocus bulbs
can feel the distant
light and shoots begin
to push the darkness
the whole length
of an owl's cry.
Sap runs to the ends
of poplar branches and
pussywillows punctuate
the budding bush
that gives refuge
to all the hunted
creatures of the world.
Here where honking geese put down for the night
on their annual pilgrimage to the pole, the partridge
struts with dogged stealth the ancient mating paths
and deer shelter their vulnerable births against death.
Beware the Ides of March.
In the twilight eyes are
trained in the sights of blood.

Notes Towards a Poem That Can Never Be Written

Margaret Atwood

for Carolyn Forché

i

This is the place
you would rather not know about,
this is the place that will inhabit you,
this is the place you cannot imagine,
this is the place that will finally defeat you

where the word *why* shrivels and empties
itself. This is famine.

ii

There is no poem you can write
about it, the sandpits
where so many were buried
& unearthed, the unendurable
pain still traced on their skins.

This did not happen last year
or forty years ago but last week.
This has been happening,
this happens.

We make wreaths of adjectives for them,
we count them like beads,
we turn them into statistics & litanies
and into poems like this one.

Nothing works.
They remain what they are.

iii

The woman lies on the wet cement floor
under the unending light,

needle marks on her arms put there
to kill the brain
and wonders why she is dying.

She is dying because she said.
She is dying for the sake of the word.
It is her body, silent
and fingerless, writing this poem.

iv

It resembles an operation
but it is not one

nor despite the spread legs, grunts
& blood, is it a birth.

Partly it's a job
partly it's a display of skill
like a concerto.

It can be done badly
or well, they tell themselves.

Partly it's an art.

v

The facts of this world seen clearly
are seen through tears;
why tell me then
there is something wrong with my eyes?

To see clearly and without flinching,
without turning away,
this is agony, the eyes taped open
two inches from the sun.

What is it you see then?

Is it a bad dream, a hallucination?
Is it a vision?
What is it you hear?

The razor across the eyeball
is a detail from an old film.
It is also a truth.
Witness is what you must bear.

vi

In this country you can say what you like
because no one will listen to you anyway,
it's safe enough, in this country you can try to write
the poem that can never be written,
the poem that invents
nothing and excuses nothing,
because you invent and excuse yourself each day.

Elsewhere, this poem is not invention.
Elsewhere, this poem takes courage.
Elsewhere, this poem must be written
because the poets are already dead.

Elsewhere, this poem must be written
as if you are already dead,
as if nothing more can be done
or said to save you.

Elsewhere you must write this poem
because there is nothing more to do.

¿Te Duele Todavia?

Joan MacNeil

They file into the office quietly
A dozen men and one woman
It is a meeting of progressive politicians
And their assistants—some dressing for success
to hear two Salvadorans speak
About Salvadoran political prisoners.

The son of the junta member speaks first.
He was lucky, he says
He was only tortured for two weeks
Then his father found out
So, he wasn't tortured anymore.
He got out two years later.
His father and he "do not agree politically"
The woman listening thinks of her own son
And wonders what the father told himself
In the middle of the night
For two years.

The MPs grow more silent
Their assistants fumble with their notes
The woman fixes her eyes
On a particular molecule of air
Suspended in the centre of the room
And listens.

Then it is the turn of the second,
The poet's son.
Misunderstanding the silence
Thinking they do not believe
He goes into more detail
Carefully trying to chip away
At what he thinks is indifference.

I was given *el avioncito*, he says
The little plane.
That's when they tie your hands behind your back
And hang you from the ceiling

Suspended by your thumbs and ankles
And swing you back and forth
Head crashing into the cell wall in front
Caked with the blood and hair
Of those who went before you.

Then they gave me *el avioncito con pilote,*
The little plane with a pilot.
That's when one guard sits on your back
While the others swing you,
Back and forth.

The woman's eyes fall
On the face of one MP
A railway worker, from the West
His face is pale now, staring.

The woman's hands lie in fists
On the carved oak arms of her chair.
The carpet under her feet is too soft
The silk scarf knotted around her neck seems suddenly obscene.

Then the poet's son
In a final effort to dispel any doubts
Lifts up his shirt
To show a scar.

His body is thin and brown
Like a young boy's in August
There is a gouge out of his chest
Fist-sized
Close to the heart.
Bone, muscle and skin
Beaten away.
A Hiroshima for your body, Juan José Dalton

The woman feels her fist unclench
Her hand almost reaching across
To lay three fingers in the scar
Softly
To say
        ¿Te duele todavia?
                Does it still hurt?

Tito

Alison Acker

Unripe bananas give you stomach-ache. Tito should know, because he eats them a lot when there is nothing else to eat, and that happens often. On good days, there are beans and corn tortillas. Some days there are just tortillas. And sometimes there is nothing at all. So kids like Tito grub around for whatever roots or fruit they can find.

Yet Tito lives on what we might call a farm. His family has a *milpa*, all two acres of it, with a patch of corn and a goat and a few chickens.

"The goat is no good. She has no milk. She's sick," Tito tells me. And eggs? "Mama sells them in the market."

He is a skinny kid, just eight years old. His T-shirt is torn and he has dirty shorts, knobbly knees, and no shoes. It is difficult to see him at all because he's hidden under an enormous load of firewood carried on his shoulder. I met him trudging along the highway twenty kilometres from Progreso, in the heart of the banana lands. Tito has a machete, too, wrapped in a rag, under the firewood. He uses it to cut the wood himself. He has to walk "a long way" to get it, and a long way to get home. His thatched-roof home is indeed a long way—four kilometres—from the stand of trees. The trees are private property.

In a country where pine forests abound and mahogany, rosewood, Spanish cedar, and balsa are national riches, there is no wood to gather for a fire. As well, there is no land for Tito's family, in a country with 112,088 kilometres of land, and only thirty-two people on each square kilometre. The land belongs to either the sugar plantation owners and the banana company or the cattle ranchers. Families like Tito's get the leavings. Their two acres are rented. As rent they hand over most of the corn they grow. During bad years, they often go in debt because there's not enough corn to pay the rent.

Tito lives in a little village outside Progreso, inland from the north coast of Honduras. This area has long been a centre of rebellion by peasant groups enraged by the landowners. Up the road, at El Bálsamo, I saw the four graves of local men who were shot down by one of the many private police forces when they tried to take possession of land involved in a legal dispute. That was in the summer of 1983.

What would Tito do if a man with a gun saw him cutting firewood on someone else's land?

"Run away as fast as I can," he answers. "But I always watch out before I start cutting. I'm afraid of the *hacenderos* [the landowners]."

My romantic notions of rural simplicity are making it difficult for me to comprehend the harshness of life in Tito's village. I keep thinking the place is picturesque. But no, I would not like to live in a leaky thatched-roof hut, without windows, and with rats. Yet the illusion of tropical simplicity remains.

The main "street" of Acaya is fringed with flowering trees. Bright salmon-pink clashes with turquoise blue, so much that my eyes miss at first the garbage and ruts in the road, the stagnant water, and the rusting remains of a truck. The village boasts a church with a bell tower and a store; there is no electric light, no water, no bus service, no school, no telephone. Whenever the kids go to school, which is not often, they have to walk four kilometres to the next village. The women cook on open wood-fires.

Tito doesn't know anybody who has a truck or car, except the police, the *hacendero*, and the priest who comes every second Sunday. A literacy teacher comes on foot once a week. He brings his own lantern and chalkboard. Tito's mother goes to the classes "sometimes" when she is not busy with the kids. She has nine other children besides Tito. His father is usually away either working for a banana company or cutting cane, depending on what work is available.

The banana lands to the north extend further than I can see. Each plant stands eight feet tall, a fierce green row upon row, behind barbed wire. A single line of railroad snakes toward the banana ports, and the train whistle breaks the silence twice a day. Tito's grandfather used to work as a *venenero,* he tells me—the man with the "poison" who sprayed the banana plants. He worked in a gang that lugged the hoses carrying the blue pesticide that dyed their clothes and made them cough up their lungs and become old men at forty.

"My dad says the banana bosses are millionaires. But they don't want any workers now," says Tito. It is true that the "yellow gold" is grown less now in Honduras, as banana companies find other more profitable land in South America. The Honduran land is worn out. Sugar plantations offer back-breaking work for a couple of months a year. Cattle ranches need very few workers. So most of the peasants in Acaya have very little work and very little income. They make less than $10 a week, on a year-round average.

Tito tells me his mother keeps "a few *lempiras*" [worth roughly fifty cents] for some medicine or if somebody has to go to the nearest town, Progreso, in an emergency.

One of his sisters is blind. She was bitten by a *bicho,* an insect. When people are sick, they usually call in the *curandera,* the local healer. She doesn't cost much and she is someone they know and trust. Tito has never been vaccinated against childhood diseases and has never visited a doctor. He's never been to school either.

He refuses to take me inside his little house. I call out, but the voices from inside hush quickly and nobody comes to the open doorway, so I do not intrude.

Later I talk about Tito to a nun who works for a church rural training and development program, not far away. She has lived there for five years and now identifies completely with her peasant community.

"They live like they did two hundred years ago, and they seem so apathetic, right?" she challenges me. "So would you if you suffered from parasites and malnutrition. In the countryside, three out of four people live in extreme poverty. There isn't enough money for food, let alone school books or shoes. This is why the children don't go to school; it is a vicious circle. Without education, they can't climb out of poverty, and without money, they can't get an education.

"When the men try to organize to defend themselves, they are called Communists and cut down by the landowners or the police. I have seen twenty different political murders in this area in the last twelve months. The graves you saw at El Bálsamo are those of four ordinary peasants, who went to help fellow workers on strike at a banana plantation. They had a truck and were driving home when two members of the territorial forces stopped them for a ride. The soldiers shot four of them; the other three ran away. They piled the four bodies into the truck and drove off. Other peasants saw the bodies when the truck passed through a village. They stopped it, and the soldiers ran off. They were never prosecuted, though everybody knows who they are."

She did not want me to use her name. "This quietness you see everywhere isn't peace," she says. "It is fear and despair. The children may talk to you because they are not yet aware of the reality."

But even the children in Tito's village are quiet. A very small boy battles a large pig on the end of a string; the pig oinks and scrabbles on the gritty road. The other kids just watch. Most of the day they fetch and carry and look after the little ones, and plant seeds in the bare ground with a digging stick. When the chores are done, they sit listlessly in the dirt.

What sort of games do you play? I ask Tito, But I don't get any answer. Maybe the words are wrong. What do you do when you are not busy doing chores? "I go to sleep," he replies.

The International Labour Organization in Geneva estimates that more than a third of the world's children work, most of them as unpaid family workers. Tito's chores would not even class him as a worker. He is lucky not to be making bricks in forty-degree heat, or working in a carpet factory, or pulling a cart. He has a home, a mother and a father, brothers and sisters. He is not sick or in jail or a victim of war.

Tito is just a typical child of Third World poverty. Nothing special. No emergency. A common case.

Insomnia & Lovers, Solentiname

Larry Towell

Sometimes when I listen to the distance rattle
its ten pound heart-of-stone vibrates in my
throat
You would have to sit at this bedroom window
or wander to the pier with your mother's Bible
a distant motorboat violently blowing bubbles
to keep out the screams—sniperfire of stars
here & there a spatter of blood
A *compa** with his lover walks in the garden
He kisses her hands
They put their lips together and breathe each
other
lungs crushed together like a bloodclot
He holds her limp hands
two dark figures with white gloves on

* *compa:* comrade

The Visit

Larry Towell

When I got up this morning Sister Joellen was washing dishes. A small bird sang, 'Will you marry me?' The slow wind picked up its song & brought it away. She cut the papaya into four breakfasts. A car passed, windows down, watching us as we watched them. One grey hen pecked broken glass that blinked in the gravel like moth eyes. The horizon rose hard & clear. Rita came from the bath blooming in a red housecoat. 'Damn it! No water again!' We went to the gas station for water to do laundry. Clouds began to move & thick air soon smelled like fresh towels.

After breakfast we drove to the camp: two nuns, myself, & Myra. Three girls hugged on the road, the likeness of lovers. We swerved around, sucking dust & skirts into the undertow. A heavy orange leaf caught on the wiper. An animal's vertebrae lay on the roadside swooning with brilliant yellow butterflies. Rita coughed into a white hankie & stuffed a comb into her sweater pocket. 'Hey! What is that red stuff . . . blood on the windshield?' We pulled into the yard of Salvadorans, a cloud of dust & grasshoppers.

Chepé rocked my wrist like a fruit tree shaken by a good wind. Loose skin hung on his arms like a baggy shirt. His daughter peered down from her tree. Elvis swung in a hammock cracking sunflower seeds between his front teeth, spitting the shells into an empty can used to measure rice. Chepé answered my questions with the music, wheezing like a harmonica. On his left leg, tincture of iodine bled through gauze. 'I'm getting too old for the fields, & see, I've cut myself.' He occasionally stopped to suck at the air, breathing out the black notes. He coughed, then waved at the girl in the tree. His wife stopped scrubbing the burnt rice from the bottom of the only large pot in the camp & looked at us, then back at the black bottom of the pot. She threw it into a cistern of water. A dog barked itself into a frenzy.

In the distance, I noticed a man in a plowed field. He was running. Was he being chased? By whom? Who was this man? Vultures pranced around a dead horse, mothwings fluttering in twilight. Ribs of earth lay open like raw meat around us. I could hear a motor starting, stalling, the grating of steel on steel wheels, a tractor in the sundown of its own life. I could hear it coughing, praying in the Third Light, the earth confessing to the dead horse. 'It is Salvador running across the field,' someone said. Someone else, 'The dogs are the people.' & someone else, 'The vultures are the people.'

I went back to the shade. I was afraid & wanted to go home. I needed some good Irish whiskey. I heard the child gently sucking her fingers. Chepé clicked his tongue & caught his little girl as she dropped. Then I noticed what seemed to be the tracks of a chainsaw around his neck.

We toyed with this mystery on the drive back, the world succeeding to resemble this pain. When we reached the main road someone yelled, 'Hey! It's those three girls! For God's sake!'

The Correspondence of Leonel Rugama of Nicaragua and Roque Dalton of El Salvador

Jim Smith

Letter One

We are both still alive. Yet it is taken for granted that our mail is opened by others, read by others and disposed of. *Does it make you want to scream, as I do?* After all, this is the throat of Americas, even if they treat it like the toilet's bowl. Surveillance—always to be under surveillance. How do we come to cope with it? Every day someone we know is picked up, and taken to the edge of the city, where the garbage builds up in heaps, and they are hacked into pieces, or kicked into the other world (wherever that might be), and usually their hands are cut off—do you ever sit there in the heat and imagine what it actually feels like to have a machete descend through the flesh and the muscle and the tendon and finally the bone and through flesh again—and there they lie until some kid comes along and watches the flies. My vision of those flies is a horde of little green *guardia,* buzzing and attacking and consuming and laying their evil eggs. In someone we know. Over and over and over again, every day that we live. This is what we must live with, the certainty that there will be a day when it will be us on the floor of that car or that jeep and they will be taking us to that place that smells. My *compañera* asks me why I carry a gun if I am a poet and if I am searched it will mean the end. You know why, don't you? We both know, and it was Rigoberto López Pérez helped teach us the value of arms here in the throat of the Americas. When I write, it is the words themselves, every one of the words, so unlike the *guardia* flies, which ask me whether . . . well, I am not at all sure what it is that they ask. That is part of the struggle, and part of the presence I feel outside the door of this hut in the *barrio.* I am enclosing a pamphlet.

Leonel

Letter Two

Why do we bother writing to each other? So that a letter finally gets there and sits because the other has been murdered? Because in the composition we explain our ideas to ourselves? Because you will die, I will die, they will die and it will or will not make a jot of difference in the world around us, and we want some record to be available someday that we were indeed on one side or the other? I have learned so very much from reading your booklet, that there is no difference between our struggles, in one sense, and that there is a world of difference in another, or many others. You have Sandino, we have Farabundo Marti. Virtually the same year, they died, were murdered. Our *matanza* claimed how many lives, 35,000? You have lost the same number in the course of more years. Do we write then because we are the same person, grown up only several hundred miles apart, carrying out a doppelganger life in which the same character gets to do different things but within a limited frame? As I decide it is time, and close the doors and pull the shutters on my mother's house, lift the material from its place in the corner and begin to tune the shortwave, do you speak nervously around the corners of your mother's house,

 and approach the corner where you will await a poem?

Will my next letter tell you of a broadcast I heard, or will one never arrive? Will your next enclose a poem or two, or blank sheets?

Why when I thought of you last night did I see myself?

Is the knock on the door innocent?

There are so many questions, why do we await the subset which depends on pain?
     The fact that others die, not just us, but dependent on our actions, or absolutely independent of our actions, and worse than that, in spite of our actions.

What is the sound of the knock on the door of the innocent? The living need us. As long as we do not forget the dead.

Please excuse the morbid tone.   *Con un abrazo fuerte*

                              Roque

Toxicity

Erin Mouré

Can acupuncture cure the sadness of organs
Can the liver forget sadness when the needles enter,
its field of memory,
words of politic, the mining this week of the ports
of Nicaragua, Corinto & Puerto Sandino
Nicaragua of the liver & the pancreas,
Nicaragua of the heart,
the small cells of the kidneys teeming
The cords of energy severed in the body,
the body poisoned by underwater mines
In a country never seen, fish boats
pulling drag-nets under water,
risking explosion,
can acupuncture cure the sadness of the liver, now?

What is fucked-up in the body, what is blocked
& carried rolled in the intestine,
what suffocates so badly in the lungs,
adhering, we talk about it, *toxicity*, your body standing
at the sink & turned to me,
near but not near enough, not near enough, Gail
What if the blocked space in the liver is just sadness,
can it be cured then?
Can the brain stop being the brain?
Can the brain be, for a few minutes, some other organ,
any organ, or a gland, a simple gland with its fluids,
its dark edges light never enters, can it let us alone?
When I think of the brain I think
how can something this dark help us
together
to stay here, as close as possible, avoiding underwater minefields,
the ships of trade churning perilously toward us,
the throb of their motors calling the mines up,
as close as our two skins

IV Colombia, Peru

Cartagena de Indias

Earle Birney

Ciudad triste, ayer reina de la mar.
—Heredia

Each face its own phantom
its own formula of breed and shade
but all the eyes accuse me back and say

There are only two races here:
we human citizens
who are poor but have things to sell
and you   from outer space
unseasonable   our one tourist
but plainly able to buy

This arthritic street
where Drake's men and Cole's ran
swung cutlasses   where wine and sweet blood
snaked in the cobble's joints
leaps now in a sennet of taxi horns
to betray my invasion
All watch my first retreat
to barbizans patched from Morgan's grapeshop
and they rush me
three desperate tarantula youths
.waving Old Golds unexcised

By an altar blackened
where the Indian silver was scratched away
in sanctuary leaning   on lush cool marble
I am hemmed by a conga drum-man in jeans
He bares a brace of Swiss watches
whispers in husky Texan

Where gems and indigo were sorted
in shouting arcades
I am deftly shortchanged
and slink to the trees that lean
and flower tall in the Plaza
nine shoeboys wham their boxes
slap at my newshined feet

Only in the Indio market
mazed on the sodden quais
I am granted uneasy truce
Around the ritual braidings of hair
the magical arrangements of fish
the piled rainbows of rotting fruit
I cast a shadow of silence
   blue-dreaded eyes
   corpse face
   hidalgo clothes
   tall one   tall as a demon
   pass O pass us quickly

Behind me the bright blaze of patois
   leaps again

I step to the beautiful slave-built bridge
and a mestiza girl
   levels Christ's hands at me
   under a dangling goiter

Past the glazed-eyed screamers of *dulces*
swing to a pink lane
where a poxed and slit-eyed savage
   pouts an obscenity
   offering a sister
   as he would spit me
   a dart from a blowpipe

Somewhere there must be another bridge
from my stupid wish
to their human acceptance
but what can I offer—
my tongue half-locked in the cell
of its language—other than pesos
   to these old crones of thirty
   whose young sink in pellagra
   as I clump unmaimed
   in the bright shoes
   that keep me from hookworm
   lockjaw and snakebite

It's written in the cut of my glasses
I've a hotelroom all to myself
with a fan   and a box of Vitamin C

176

It can be measured
in my unnatural stride
that my life expectation
is more than forty
especially now that I'm close to sixty

older than ever bankrupt Bolívar was
who sits now in a frozen prance
high over the coconut trays
quivering on the heads
   of three gaunt mulatto ladies
   circling in a pavane of commerce
   down upon spotlit me

Out of the heaving womb of independence
Bolívar rode   and over the bloody afterbirth
into coffee and standard oil
   from inquisitional baroque
   to armed forces corbusier
He alone has nothing more   to sell me

I come routed now   scuffling
through dust in a nameless square
treeless   burning   deserted
come lost and guiltily wakeful
in the hour of siesta
   at last to a message

   to a pair of shoes
   in a circle of baked mud
   worn out of shape   one on its side
For a second I am shaken by panic
heat? humidity? something has got me
   the shoes are concrete
   and ten feet long

   the sight of a plaque calms
   without telling me much
     En homenaje de la memoria de
       LUIS LOPEZ
     se erigió este monumento
     a los zapatos viejos
     el día 10 de febrero de 1957

Luis Lopez? Monument to his old shoes?
What??? There was nothing else

Back through the huckster streets
the sad taxi men still awake and horn-happy

  Si señor   Luis Lopez el poeta
  Here is his book
  Unamuno praised it   *sí sí*
  You have seen *los zapatos?*   Ah?
  But they are us, *señor*
  It was about us he wrote
  about Cartagena where he was born
  and died   See here this sonnet
  always he made hard words
  Said we were lazy except to make noise
  we only shout to get money
  ugly too, backward . . . why not?
  it is for a poet to say these things
  Also *plena*—how say it?—
  plena de rancio desaliño
Full of rancid disarray!
  Sí, Sí, but look at the end, when old
  he come to say one nice thing
  only one ever about us
  He say we inspire that love a man has
  for his old shoes—*Entonces*
  we give him a monument to the shoes

I bought the book   walked back
sat on the curb happier than Wordsworth
gazing away at his daffodils
Discarded queen   I thought   I love you too
Full of rancid disarray
city like any city
full of the stench of human indignity
and disarray of the human proportion
full of the noisy always poor
and the precocious dying
stinking with fear   the stale of ignorance
I love you first for giving birth
to Luis Lopez   suffering him
honouring him at last
in the grand laconic manner
he taught you

—and him I envy
I who am seldom read by my townsmen

Descendants of pirates   grandees
galleyslaves and cannibals
I love the whole starved cheating
poetry-reading lot of you   most of all
for throwing me the shoes of deadman Luis
to walk me back into your brotherhood

This Labyrinth of Entrapment

Yvonne América Truque

          I walk
alone, my steps lost
in the interlacing streets
of the sleeping city.

          I breathe
air of cars honking
nauseous gas
fetid rotting garbage.

Tango music comes
from an ancient bar on the corner.

          Arcades
cradle curled-up children, the homeless, drunks,
one man hidden like a hungry wolf
lying waiting for its prey.
Someone's just been knifed!

          Whores
and customers in the shadows
all blur into the night.

               Stoplights, streets
               streets, noise
               noise, bars
               bars, soldiers
                    Bullets!

          I walk
silently
on the humid asphalt.
The clocks have stopped.

          Tomorrow
I'll read the newspapers, and on the front page
the headline will be
"NEW QUEEN CHOSEN FOR COFFEE FESTIVAL"

The Miners of Caruquia

Luis Pérez Botero

It was impossible not to know the miners of Caruquia by their glittering black eyes, parched skin, broad hands, bony feet, heads held high, sunken stomachs, hoarse voices and quick words. One could calculate exactly how many years a man had been in the mine, for the earth gave each one his due and etched the years on his face with unmistakable signs. To be from Caruquia was to carry an indelible mark.

Don Rubén Restrepo Rojas, the schoolmaster most admired by those who couldn't read, was the first to recognize for what they really were. It was this teacher who taught his students that the men of Caruquia were of a different race, unlike that of their own forefathers, unknown to their contemporaries and distinguished by the unique fact that they were capable of shaping their own destiny on this earth.

José Domingo was the boy most excited by the secret story of the miners of Caruquia. Don Rubén told him that down there the earth is not kneaded with blood, but with sweat and tears. He also taught him to write well, copying in a good, round hand the example so carefully executed on the blackboard: I am a miner of Caruquia.

For that reason, José Domingo lived only for the day when his father would pronounce him free to leave home and enter the mine in Caruquia, where he would devote the rest of his life to extracting gold. And the day came when he was to see Caruquia. All that José Domingo found there was soaring mountains, deep, silent rivers which were unnavigable, and infinite roads that disappeared into the distance. When a man leaves Caruquia he is never seen again, unless he returns one day, full of nostalgia and sins, hauling a truck or train through the mountains. None of this frightened José Domingo; on the contrary, when he spied the gold-mine on the far horizon, he shouted joyfully with all the potency of his youthful years: "Caruquia!" And the echo rebounded from the mine: "...quia!"

When he heard that echo, José Domingo felt that the earth recognized him as one of its own. It was there that he observed how the rocks were covered with immense thickets of blue and red leaves. Years spent in the sun had made them so invulnerable to the heat that they never dried up. The river had a black water of interminable pain that was heard to moan on silent nights with the voice of a soul in Purgatory. The air was hot, like the breath of a runaway horse. It was then that José Domingo felt that he would have to be strong to survive in this stretch of land set among water and blue and red rocks.

It made no impression upon him to learn at the roadside inn that those who came to this place were beggars who, with outstretched hands, asked for alms for the love of God, spoke like souls loosed from Purgatory, hobbled on twisted feet, bent broken backs, walked with faces that looked back, with veins that shone with an inner light. But when they were taken with gold-fever, then they covered their heads with great, gold-brimmed hats, tied round their necks red kerchiefs woven with threads of gold, and bounded into the air astride horses made of moonbeams that leapt from summit to summit as if their hooves clattered on the stars. Then everywhere a great cry could be heard: "Caruquia!"

José Domingo did not regret having come to Caruquia, for there one was never still for a single instant. From the moment of his arrival he began to learn the secret art of extracting gold from rocks, grinding them in the immense stamp-mills that old Pepe Botero set up at the back of the crevice. That was where Francisco Vinagre was stationed, the negro with the face of Jesus Christ, who sweated so prodigiously when he brought up a car-load of rock under the sun's full glare. It was he who knew where to open the rock and lay bare the veins of gold. When he arrived at the stamp-mills with his cart of oaken planks, he raised his voice and announced: "Load!"

At that moment, José Domingo released all the water in the mill-race, the immense wheel began to turn slowly, the rammers went up and down and the rocks containing gold were split and converted to a dust that was swept along as the water shot down the board chutes. At the end of this process only gold remained in the drainage troughs.

From above, José Domingo shouted: "Another load!" Once again the rock-laden cart emerged from the cave and emptied its mineral load into the stamp-mills; once again the rammers ground the rock and the water washed away the sand and left the gold in the troughs, all without a moment's pause, as if the entire operation were carried out by an internal force that made the earth tremble with the thud of rammers, shatter with the splitting of rocks and catch fire with the sun reflected by the flecks of gold.

The evenings were silent. When the shadows obscured the rocks and everything became confused in a dark mass, the men went to the foreman's house, ate venison with Caramanta beans, drank *guarapo* and began to sing and dance. It was the time when the witches came flying through the air to alight beside young miners. With their long, pointed noses, they hung from tree branches and made the air whistle with their tumbling until they fell into the water, emerging almost naked to dry themselves by the fire. They could always be seen there, with their protruding eyes, long, bony hands, backs curved like enormous tobacco leaves and lips pressed tight as they sang an old song between their teeth.

It was the time when the miners fought to sit beside the prettiest girls in Caruquia, to look at them from up close and say that they loved only them, even more than their own dear mothers. Since many young women refused to sit with anyone, the men fought for those few who weren't particular about having by their side a miner who reeked of earth. Many miners would slash their faces with machetes if a girl paid them no attention. It was all blood on those nights of carousing and revelry, but afterwards calm was restored and all that remained were sweet memories of lost loves.

182

It was then that Marceliano went out onto the patio and saw the Devil cooking condemned souls in the mine's own pots. It made him so angry to see Satan's boldness that he snatched a broom from behind the door and confronted Lucifer with only this poor weapon in his hands. Marceliano was so fortunate and so valiant that after an entire night of battle with Old Nick, wielding his broom throughout, he at last left the Evil One cross-eyed and stub-tailed for all eternity. From that time on, according to popular belief in Caruquia, he never again tormented the hearts of women who didn't care for men.

One day those in charge saw men with eyes like cold, blue water arrive at the mine. They came saying that they, too, were very fond of the earth and, for that reason, had come from their distant land to see these enchanted mountains, this marvellous water that cleanses sins, this immaculate sky where the souls of children and pretty women go, and these strong men who have been capable of breaking and dominating the mountain with only the strength of their arms.

Nobody believed the endless story told by the sad-eyed visitors. Malice welled up within the Caruquians at the thought that these cold-eyed men had come from where people eat well, dress in silk and wool, wear goatskin shoes, perfume their hair, utter nothing but niceties, and bow before each other as if life were no more than a round of ceremonies.

Uninvited, the sad-eyed men pried into everything, asked no end of questions, sniffed round everyone, confirmed that there was indeed gold and, when there was nothing else to investigate, announced that they were returning home. But, far from going anywhere, they only ventured further into the caverns of the mine, measuring the rocks with diabolical tenacity. In this way they arrived at the mine's largest vein and measured it with meticulous care. The foreman found them there, their noses in the vein, licking the pure gold. He asked them what they were doing and they responded that they were just taking measurements. The foreman told them that he didn't at all like them taking so many measurements, that nobody in Caruquia liked the measurements and that it would be better if they left the same way they had come, without taking anything that wasn't theirs or harming anyone.

This time the sad-eyed men did leave Caruquia, but the next day the army arrived, with ten majors, two hundred lieutenants and thousands of soldiers. They were looking for the terrible thieves of Caruquia, those that devour the flesh of newborn infants, those that hold up innocent travellers in the mountains, those that suck the blood of pretty women, those that perform mysterious ceremonies on moonless nights and leave the woodlands burnt and the crops barren; in short, those that neither go to mass on Sunday nor hear the word of God and, what is even worse, those that have never read the *Torah*. In Caruquia, they found Francisco Vinagre, Feliciano, Gregorio, Felipe, Marceliano, Macario, and Santos. They were all loaded with chains and taken away.

In Caruquia, only women remained. It was then that two thousand technicians arrived to set up a plastic hospital where all the sick were to be cured, even the children who only had mange. It was when they were starting work on the hospital that an army major realized that the only one who had escaped the chains was the half-breed, José Domingo, the one who did the unloading. His men were ordered to search for him through all the galleries of the mine, but after a day and a half they had found only his shoes, intact, wedged between the boards down which the water rushed to the stamp-mills. The silly fool had fallen to the bottom of the hollow beneath the rammers, the stamp-mills had ground him up, and that was all that was left of José Domingo...a pair of hemp sandals. So they gave him up for dead and went on to present their report to the effect that the savages of Caruquia had been reduced to a civilized state.

The hospital project turned out to be nothing more than smoke with no fire. What they did set up for all eternity was a great, mechanical mill that hoisted rocks and ground them, gleaned the last grain of gold, then let fall what remained—a foul-smelling gravel, like devils' droppings. Little by little the earth grew poorer. Now there were no great, dream-like thickets of blue and red leaves; instead, there was only a filthy quarry, bristling with thorns like old misers' claws.

Never again was the blessed name of Caruquia heard. Had it not been for the monotonous noise of the dredge eating away at the mountain, one would have said that in all that expanse of land nothing remained of Caruquia. The women shut themselves up in their houses. One could hear them continually praying the litanies of all the saints, for they said that this was the best remedy for the loneliness that never ends. The truth, it was later discovered, was that they wished to ascend to God, that He might help them, bring back their husbands, once again give them sons, and banish the horrible nightmare of the dredge that was eating up the mountains.

One day, quite unexpectedly, the immense dredge ground to an abrupt halt. No one had stopped it; of its own accord, controlled from eternity, it ceased to eat rock and spew gravel. It was then that Caruquia became total silence. One could hear not only the sweep of the wind, but the emergence of the moon, like the leap of a small, white frog; the coming dawn had the sound of crystal shattering, while nightfall was akin to the whistling flight of a black vulture. One could hear the beating of one's heart, the crackling of grass growing, even the rustle of clouds, like young girls dressed in white chintz. In that silence, the earth yielded no corn, no beans of any kind, nothing. Only the rocks seemed to flourish and breathe, as if to stone each other to death.

One evening, they saw the men from the mine returning along the long-deserted road. At their head came Francisco Vinagre, the foreman. They came with hands that were empty, broader, harder and stronger than ever. They wore the same clothes as when they had left. They all came sadly contemplating the dead mountain, transformed into dirty slag by a machine of which they knew nothing, because they had been loaded with chains, accused before a blind judge, convinced that they were thieves, isolated, condemned, and put to work like beasts. Now they were returning from death like invincible shadows.

Once again the men entered their houses and found their wives just as they had left them when they had been collared and dragged away, lashed together. The women remained in the same sorrowful attitude that had possessed them on that unfortunate occasion. Seeing the men return, they began to make vague, fluttering movements with their hands, awoke from their dreamy stupor, wanted to renew the tasks they had put aside; but the mountain no longer existed, the river had fled, the road had been erased and only wandering spirits remained. The entire expanse of land was full of dirty slag.

Macario was the first to express a desire to abandon that godforsaken place where those from outside carried away the earth's riches, accused those who had the land of being thieves, made prisoners and beasts of them; a place which, when nothing remained to be looted, the intruders calmly abandoned, counting their money as they went. No one wanted to remain in that desert left in the wake of greed. Before nightfall, without taking anything from their homes, the miners of Caruquia slowly set off and followed the old mule-trail. Perhaps there would be another, free mountain beyond the heaps of slag; perhaps somewhere else dream-like thickets would cover the rocks, and in that place their women would once again give birth to sons.

A little way into the desert, they saw a mining truck coming along a recently opened road. It was one of those hated monsters that carried off people, health, women, music, joy and wealth. When they saw it approach they stopped, powerless. They could do nothing against this apparition of iron and lights. They could only throw a dirty stone at it, in sign of protest. But they would be accused of insulting the authorities, of rebellion, insurrection, armed robbery and the destruction of government property. However, they stopped for none of those reasons; they simply wanted to know where it would all end, wherever that might be.

The truck did not go by, but brought its enormous, black tires to a halt in the middle of the road. The cabin door opened and a swarthy man looked out; he had glittering black eyes, parched skin, broad hands, bony feet, a head held high, a hoarse voice and a ready word.

The women were the first to recognize him. It was José Domingo returning from death, the death that everyone believed had claimed him when he was left alone atop the stamp-mill tower, from where the loads of rock were poured into the devil's jaws and ground to a dust that left only pure gold.

José Domingo jumped down and ran to embrace his brothers, but not one of them recognized him. It couldn't be José Domingo, for he had neither scars nor the marks of the lash.

José Domingo tried to convince them that he had really come back, that he had escaped when he'd seen how the others were being trapped like animals. He had watched to see where the sad-eyed men went, had seen what they do, and done the same, spoken as they speak and learned what they know, and recovered the gold that had left Caruquia. Here he was back again. And he finished by announcing: "I have bought Caruquia!"

They answered him coldly: "You have bought our death. Stay here

185

alone with it."

At that moment José Domingo thought he had the most brilliant idea of his life. He wanted to tell his brothers that he had come back to return the gold to the mountain, that they might once again have the pleasure of mining it for themselves, with the joy of labouring with their own hands and enjoying with friends the fruits of that labour.

But the miners of Caruquia had already gone. José Domingo saw no more of them than their hard backs. The miners of Caruquia had left with backs marked by scars, ears deaf to shouts and insults, eyes oblivious to laughter and tears, hands that were stilled and flesh that was numbed. They were like great rocks that walked of their own accord. At that moment eternity began.

Unborn Things

Patrick Lane

After the dog drowns in the arroyo
and the old people stumble into the jungle
muttering imprecations at the birds
and the child draws circles in the dust
for bits of glass to occupy
like eyes staring out of earth
and the woman lies on her hammock
dreaming of the lover who will save her
from the need to make bread again
I will go into the field
and be buried with the corn.

Folding my hands on my chest
I will see the shadow of myself; the same
who watched a father when he moved
with hands on the dark side of a candle
create the birds and beasts of dreams.

One with unborn things
I will open my body to the earth
and watch worms reach like pink roots
as I turn slowly tongue to stone
and speak of the beginning of seeds
as they struggle in the earth;
pale things moving toward the sun
that feel the feet of men above,
the tread of their marching
thudding into my earth.

The Children of Bogota

The first thing to understand, Manuel says,
is that they're not children. Don't start feeling
sorry for them. There are five thousand
roaming the streets of this city

and just because they look innocent
doesn't make them human. Any one
would kill you for the price of a meal.
Children? See those two in the gutter

behind the stall? I saw them put out
the eyes of a dog with thorns because
it barked at them. Tomorrow it could be you.
No one knows where they come from

but you can be sure they're not going.
In five years they'll be men and tired of killing
dogs. And when that happens you'll be the first
to cheer when the carabineros shoot them down.

from Incas and Other Men

George Woodcock

The next day, Sunday, we caught the early morning bus to the Huancayo market. It took us over a cross-country road that revealed very dramatically the perils of driving in the Andes once one leaves the few main highways. Deceptively, the road began in a mild gravel lane leading out of Tarma into a dark valley where a stream gabbled over its cascades among meagre thickets of willow trees. But soon it narrowed into a dirt track, scooped and gouged by the rains, and barely wide enough for a single vehicle. This mockery of a road began to climb the steep wall of the valley in a series of hairpin bends, so sharp that the bus could not take one of them in a single turn. Each time there had to be a series of complicated backings and creepings forward, during which the outer wheels would churn and manoeuvre within inches of the precipitous verge. A slight miscalculation in steering, a barrow-load of earth crumbling away from the edge that looked so insecure, and nothing could have saved us from crashing far down into the valley.

At such moments we realized that the warnings we had been given about Andean roads by people like Señor Merida had not been all exaggeration. As if to emphasize the lesson, one of the sharpest corners was decorated by a cluster of small wooden crosses, on some of which wreaths of paper flowers were still decaying. 'A truck went over,' the driver explained, grinning. 'Many Indians were killed.' The light way in which he talked of the tragedy did not strike me as callous; rather, it seemed to express a stoical acceptance of danger and a relief that — his own cross had not been among those thrust into the treacherously loose earth beside the road.

Eventually, travelling through serpentine villages of white mud houses and over bushy slopes that were fragrant with a kind of yellow acacia, we climbed to the high, bare grasslands on the top of the range. The long curves of the open pastures were broken, here and there, by gray traces of the Inca roads and by ragged out-crops of rocks from which, as we approached, small mountain birds would burst in twittering clouds. On the other side of the pass the road fell in serpentines into a valley bright with abundant quinoa. Here the villages were more compact and also more dirty than those near Tarma, and their people had a formidable naturalness of manner. Once a magnificently dressed young peasant woman who had got on at one of these villages asked the driver to stop the bus. She stepped down, spreading her crimson skirts about her like the corolla of a gigantic poppy, and squatted unconcernedly in full view of us all; a moment later, rising and lifting her skirts clear of the ground with an adroit twist of the hands, she walked back to the bus, not without dignity. The Indians looked on indifferently, some half-breeds laughed, and the driver, as he released the brake, muttered: '¡Son animales!' with all the contempt that divides the mountain cholo from the Indian.

When we reached Huancayo, the feria was already in full swing; it had transformed the town almost unrecognizably. This was the largest market in the Andes, and possibly the largest in Latin America. Multitudes of Indians had come in from the haciendas of the valleys and from the communities of the mountainsides, travelling by truck and bus, on horse and donkey, and often on foot, driving their slow trains of llamas through the early morning darkness or toiling down the mountain paths with their own backs burdened under the produce they hoped to sell. And they had turned Huancayo, from the cholo town it was on any weekday, into an Indian fairground where one tramped among crowds in homespun for whom the twentieth century existed mainly as a source of wonder.

Many of these Indians were members of villages still organized on the ayllu system which was already old when the Inca dynasty began. Under this system the land belongs to commune (or ayllu), and it is re-divided regularly so that each adult in the village gets his fair portion, while many tasks like house-building for newly-married couples are shared by the group. The ayllus are mostly self-supporting; they grow food primarily for their own consumption, with the potato as the basis of their farming, and they weave their cloth from wool produced by their own sheep. In the markets they sell only the scanty surplus of subsistence farming, and buy such useful or colourful objects as they themselves cannot make. There are nearly five thousand such communities in Peru alone, and many in Bolivia.

Some of the people of the ayllus whom we saw in Huancayo were far more primitive than the valley Indians with whom we were already familiar. Often they were almost unbelievable dirty, and poverty did not seem to be the cause, for some of the most expensively dressed, the most heavily loaded with gold rings and bracelets, were among the least washed. Physically, even, they seemed a different race, leaner, smaller, darker. The women were often bare-footed, the men shod in hairy pieces of llama skin drawn together roughly by leather thongs. With their hair unkempt over their timid, shifting eyes, these people would flit agitatedly from stall to stall, chattering in Quechua among themselves, and occasionally, if they felt courageous, bringing out to some dealer a phrase in a Spanish that sounded outlandish even to our ears. At lunchtime many of them crowded around the hotel to gaze through the dining-room windows at the strange manners of the creoles; under their blank, persistent gaze one felt like a fish in an aquarium on Bank Holiday.

What struck me immediately on looking at the stalls in the market was the enormous quantity of manufactured goods that had found their way into the mountains. The displays of cheap cloth and ready-made garments alone stretched for hundreds of gaudy yards. There were sellers of furniture, of mattresses, of great tin chests painted as gaily as gypsy caravans, and of plaster figures of Santiago valiantly flourishing his sword against the heathen. Only here and there, in this flood of modern shoddiness, did one come across the native craftsmanship for which the feria was once celebrated. The potters, who still contribute so much to Mexican and Guatemalan markets, had almost vanished, routed by the triumphant vendors of enamel ware, who stood shouting by their stalls with chamber-pots on their heads. Even the better handwoven cloth (which is still made in considerable quantities) did not reach the market, and we tried vainly to buy some of the beautiful materials which the Indian women wear. There were, indeed, some gourds carved in relief pictures of the mountain farmer's life which had a stiff Egyptian quality, and some wooden spoons from the jungle with geometrically patterned handles. But these scanty examples only emphasized how far craftsmanship has decayed in Peru since the eighteenth century. During that time there has been no growth of any kind within the Andean Indian culture, but only a slow draining away of the creative impulse in the imitation of set styles, followed, in the end, by the decay of these styles themselves under the impact of modern mass-production.

Yet, if the Indian no longer practises to a great extent the craftsmanship of the Inca days or of the first stimulating period of contact with Christianity, his life is linked with the past in ways which are perhaps just as fundamental, and there are aspects of a market like that of Huancayo which have undoubtedly hardly changed at all over the past four or five centuries.

We saw this, for instance, in the products which the peasants had brought in for sale in the vegetable market. In almost every case they were the fruits of plants already grown in this region when the Sun God shared with his worshippers the crops of the Andean terraces. Maize and beans and potatoes— all native to the Americas—were there in an amazing variety of strains and colours. Of the potato alone five hundred types are said to be grown in the Andes; the most prized in Huancayo was a small yellow variety to which the women would draw our attention, shouting at Inge: '¡Las amarillas, señora! ¡Las amarillas! ¡Son buenas!' But more curious were the tiny dried potatoes that looked like grey, semi-translucent pebbles. These had been subjected to the most ancient of dehydration processes, and, by means of alternate freezings and sun dryings, had been reduced to about a fifth of their normal weight. Potatoes of this kind, which keep indefinitely, are called chuño, and once they were a great staple of the granaries in which the Incas kept supplies of food as a precaution against famine. Another tuber we saw at Huancayo, where it seemed almost as popular as the potato, was shaped like a Jerusalem artichoke, but its ivory skin was blotched and mottled with red and purple. It belonged to a plant called oca, which is peculiar to the Andes, where it has been a popular food for millennia.

If, in health, the Sierra Indian eats and grows almost exactly what his forefathers did, in sickness he remains just as faithful to tradition. A whole section of the market was occupied by native healers, or curanderos, and to look at their stalls was to slip back into the magic-ridden nightmare of medieval medicine. There were, of course, any seeds and leaves which doubtless had some curative value, for the modern European pharmacopoeia is largely indebted to the discoveries of Peruvian Indians. But the curanderos regard herbal medicine as only secondary; sympathetic magic is the real basis of their healing. Their stalls were cluttered with such ingredients of the witches' sabbath as snake-skins and armadillo shells, hides of foxes, paws of porcupines and bodies of freshly killed condors. All of these had a place in the lore of the Inca medicine man; the broth made from a young condor, for example, was strongly recommended for the relief of feeble-mindedness. But some fragments of European magic seemed also to have been adopted, for the curanderos sold spiral gold rings on which written charms had been engraved; these seemed indispensable to both the Indian women and the cholas, and we noticed that even the poorest peasant from the remote hills would wear at least one of them.

The curanderos of the Sierra are a feared and honoured profession—a profession which is almost a cult, with its traditions, its ritual and even its Mecca, for the best healers, feared as sorcerers and valued as counter-sorcerers, come from the village of Collahuayas in the Bolivian altiplano. In the past the Collahuayans would wander over the Sierra from Quito down to the Gran Chaco; stricter frontiers have doubtless restricted their journeys, but still their methods dominate Andean folk medicine. Their secrets are guarded, so far as the Indians are concerned, by terror, and, so far as strangers are concerned, by silence. Usually we found the Indians in the markets quite willing to talk about whatever merchandise they might have for sale, but this was never the case with the curanderos, and to the most elementary queries about the names of plants or seeds they would always reply with a hostile: '¡No sabe! I don't know.'

But heresy creeps even into Indian medicine, and the Collahuayans have their unorthodox rivals in the Sierra markets; these are Jívaro Indians from the Amazonian forests, who have as great a reputation in the jungle as the men of Collahuayas in the mountains. The Jívaros are a venturesome people, and many of them find their way into the Andes and even down to the coast, where they live by selling remedies made from jungle plants. There were two of them at Huancayo, a middle-aged shaman and a youth who acted as his assistant. They had the kind of picturesque oddity which the real curanderos lacked. They wore the striped toga called cushma which is characteristic of their tribe; on their heads were basketwork coronets, and bands of black and white beads were crisscrossed over their chests like ribbons of distinguished orders. They were nimble men, with mobile, knowing faces, and they enticed the duller mountain Indians with a miniature circus which any self-respecting Collahuayan would have despised. Two monkeys played tricks, a coatimundi was pulled out of a sack and put back hurriedly when he refused to perform, and a young boaconstrictor with magnificent orange lozenges was induced to wreathe himself torpidly around the shoulders of the assistant. Finally the shaman himself went through the vivid pantomime of a man, in the extreme agonies of toothache, gaining miraculous relief from applying an infallible mixture which the assistant immediately began to hawk among the crowd, in sealed envelopes bearing the medicine man's photograph. It was one of those occasions when two worlds slip together, for the Jívaro shaman's peculiar antics reminded me vividly of a Negro quack who haunted the Shropshire markets in my boyhood, selling mandrake root as a universal panacea.

The nearest thing to a universal panacea in the Andes is the coca leaf, which is used, not for the exceptional ailments of the flesh, but for the hunger, exhaustion, cold and boredom which are the daily sicknesses of Sierra life. One hardly travels a day from Lima without noticing the Indians chewing ruminatively on their green quids as they hump their burdens through the streets of the Sierra towns, but it is in markets like that of Huancayo, where most of the coca-trading goes on, that one realizes the role this mild narcotic plays in the lives of millions of Peruvians.

Coca is a state monopoly, but the actual selling is done by chola women, whom we saw in Huancayo, sitting as solemnly as Rhadamanthus before the brass scales on which they carefully weighed out the small, dried green leaves. They had many customers, mostly of the poorer class of Indians, who would buy their coca by the double handful and thrust it into woven pouches; afterwards, they would often go on to other merchants who sold the prepared lime which the coca eater carries with him in a bag made from a bull's scrotum. A pinch of the lime, taken with each wad of leaves, helps to release the narcotic quality of the coca.

So far as we could see there is no attempt at a serious control of coca consumption. The state makes a middleman's profit, but the Indian appears to buy as much as he can afford. This is one of the ways in which Andean life has actually changed a great deal since the days of the Incas, who used coca moderately for its pain-killing and euphoric qualities, but supervised its distribution so that the people should not become addicted to its use. The Spaniards, however, found that it was profitable to grow coca and sell it in unlimited quantities; they also found that with coca an Indian will work more, endure worse conditions, and be content with less food. With such manifest advantages to be gained from free distribution, the Spanish authorities never gave serious thought to control, and the present universal coca-eating of the Sierra dates from the elegant age of the Viceroys. No Peruvian government, of any political tinge, has since been prepared either to abandon the profit it can gain from coca or to risk the Indian unrest that might result from restriction; and among educated Peruvians there is still a great deal of disagreement as to whether coca-eating is really harmful.

As we walked on through the feria, observing, comparing, exclaiming and clicking our camera with a diffidence which lost us all the most revealing shots, we moved to the noisy throb of Andean music, blaring crudely from the cheap cantinas, which celebrated the weekly arrival of the Indians by playing records of Sierra music. It was a strange music—quite unlike the Spanish-Negro style of the coast; wild and melancholy, curiously complex in its rhythms and so oriental in its tone that for a moment, when first we heard it, we imagined that some Chinese bar-keeper must be playing nostalgically the songs of his own country.

The music from the loudspeakers was so distorted that we could hardly distinguish the instruments that were being played, but we soon had an opportunity to listen to living Sierra music, for when we entered the main plaza we heard the mountain rhythms once again and saw that one pavement of the square was occupied entirely by makers of musical instruments, the one craft that still flourishes without diminution, since it is in music more than in anything else that the vitality of the Indian past is preserved.

In one group sat the men and women from the hill villages which specialize in drum-making; softly and in curious little rhythms they beat their instruments of llama skin, listening intently and carefully adjusting the strings whose tightness determined the pitch. Beyond them sat the makers of the quenas, the short cane flutes whose shrill notes add the eerie background quality to the Sierra dances. And finally, flourishing their great instruments over the heads of the other musicians, there were the men who had brought from the jungle villages along the Ucayali the larger bassoon-like quenas, at least ten feet long, which need strength to hold and skill to play; we saw many men lay them down with disgust after producing no sound worth the name of music, but in the hands of experts they gave a deep sound like that of a long Tibetan trumpet, so rich and at the same time so dolorous that it seemed to express more effectively than any other music the feeling of melancholy which accompanied one's delight at all the coloured gaiety of the sunlit Andean world.

Gaiety and melancholy: as we walked that afternoon among the thousands of Indians from all the strange inhabited corners of the valleys and mountains, among men and women from the edge of the jungle and the edge of the snowline, we realized how much these qualities were combined in the nature of the Andean people as well as in their music and their country. They strike one at first as a sad race, but the stoney gravity of their faces can change abruptly into laughter, and that night, as we drove back to Tarma, we caught a glimpse of this other aspect of a people for whom the burdens on their backs seemed so often the best of symbols. On the edge of a village which we passed just as the light was failing, the beat of drums and the shrill of quenas was starting up, and we could see the women whirling into the wild and monotonous course of the huayno, that spinning, skipping, skirt-swirling mountaineers' dance which is the favourite of the Andes. In comparison with the people we had seen all day, these seemed transformed into the personifications of freedom from care. And yet there were many who still danced with the burdens on their backs.

Time Falls

Paul-Marie Lapointe

(the earth is our menace

at the corner of the street, each noon,
  the same well-fed face
the assurance of the passing parade
the fanfare
and all the dead that hole in the heart . . .)

time falls
       families showers gusts of sparrows
time falls
       a lost tribe floats up to the surface
       children of the pyramids of the sun
       amphoras of dust corn and furs
       cliffs of dead
       (cliffs like hives from which the gorged
         souls of the death eaters the whites
         take wing)
       stupefied family

time falls
       Abenaki Maya Birmingham Negro
       civil souls of my dead savages
       anger interred in the dung heap
         of horses of prey

       in the knowledge of soldiers and saints
       in the armed frigates
       for the swooning delight of an infanta and
         the pathos of a tribute to the unknown
         soldier

time falls
       in the month of the salmon the villages
         are installed the municipal offices
       the fishermen and anglers
       the capitals polished with death's hand

time falls
        slave galleys
        Atahualpa
        today's savages
        wiped out
        (Cinderella palpitating in silk her three
          square meals her prince
        O peaceful sleep
        round earth where the houses all alike
          hug each other
        the final rest may come from one day to the next)

time falls
        the small men of prehistory eddy
        between the buildings
        in the rain freighted with missiles

time falls
        satisfied species

The Cuzco Leper

Patrick Lane

In the morning madness of lost languages
the blind leper sits and sings of night.
The grey bones of his eyes roll
as rosaries of flies like stuttering nuns
circle the remnants of his fingers.
He thrusts his empty bowl
at the sound of the market knives.

He has sat through the morning
and received nothing. The alms he exacts
from the people no longer come.
The fear of his falling apart has been
explained by the doctors from America
and he is no longer considered holy.

A woman, dressed in crusted skirts,
crawls from beneath a cutting table
and fills his bowl with blood.
He drinks
as the flayed and bloody animal
heads stare at him
great mouths empty of tongues.

Spines of Agave

Gary Geddes

There's no pain now. The Inca child
reclines against a wall, head resting
on knees and forearms, hands pale and expressive
as if they'd just caressed the carved llama
and her issue, or rearranged the nightly retinue
of little friends. A strand of black hair
that never would stay put descends his face.

Five hundred years ago, when coca leaves
had done their work, a father tried to brush it back,
placing, with utmost care, the favoured sun-doll
among the folds of garment, its eyes impious,
its red hair rampant. What else could he do,
there, utterly alone, on the roof of the world,
where clouds take on the form of dreams,
where a grief rose up inside so large it burst forth
as thunder into the slow mist and gathering peaks.

* * * * *

She sits on a small outcrop of rock, where the llama
is tethered, spinning wool from woven saddle-bags,
while he baits traps and wrings the necks of small birds.
Child inside impatient; ten more balls of wool, perhaps.

He keeps the hawk out of sight beneath an outer garment
to surprise her, then presents it belly-first, its pink
breast no larger than the circle of wool in her lap.
She smiles and reaches out, but the hawk lunges forward,

its wings beating furiously the air between them.
The llama rears up. The taut rope tightens and topples her
to the rock below, where she lies twisted and still,
mouth open as if to speak and the wool clutched

in her hand. Her eyes hold no reproach, only a sky
of moving cloud. He takes the knife and opens her belly,
lifting out the male child into the cold morning.
Its bloodied form gasps against the hawk's spiral.

* * * * *

The bird-man plants himself at the door of the Overseer,
a minor official in the employ of the Inca,
and waits for the sun to rise, the child perched
on his shoulder, snores of the sleeper vibrating in the cool
air. The man appears, sour-faced and unkempt,
making a pretence of covering his nakedness.
He removes one knot from the quipu, the rope of census,
and returns to his bed and woman.

The bird-man squints into the sun, nesting overhead
among the peaks, and thinks of the campaigns of Pachacuti
and his son Tupa Inca against the neighbouring states,
how they fell like birds of prey upon the enemy,
but understood the generosity of the clean kill.

* * * * *

This is a mother-doll,
says the bird-man.

Father and son
look at the cloth figure
with long black hair
and white shroud.

What's a mother?

Birds are not their only frame
of reference; there are llamas too.

The child will not be silenced.
He rocks back and forth
in the cave on stick-legs,
flapping his arms
and making bird-sounds.

Aeiii, Aeiii.
I was born from an egg,
I will learn to fly.

* * * * *

The child weeps for each dead bird,
ignoring meals and his father's entreaties.

Let him go, says the shaman,
there is no cure for soul-sickness.
Spirit is tortured in its cage
of bone.

Against this verdict, strict laws,
vast storehouses of grain, are useless.

Swift ministrations.

Some cooling ointment on the forehead,
then the potion of coca leaves.
Smooth stones gathered in a sack,
bird's-claw rattle and drum of llama skin.

He passes the bone-tube over the boy's face
twice, blows gently on closed lids.

* * * * *

Not fit even to make chicha: old women, jaws rotating
like sun-wheels, churning the hard corn to pulp
and spitting it into fermentation jars.

Then the chasquis, the Inca's post-runners,
turning their backs as he approaches,
blue scarves a slash of sky at their waists.

The bird-man surrenders his lease, inventory of traps,
and takes leave of the woman in her lonely cairn,
the boy in peace at last amidst his impish toys.

* * * * *

The only way, not flinging himself headlong,
but layer after layer until the clouds,
no longer intimate, sail between crags and promontories
and the air hangs heavy in his lungs.

The bird-man moves as one drugged towards the Great Sea
the shaman spoke of, where a man could wash clean
his mind and heal all manner of wounds.

Naked now, bereft of mountains and the black-winged condor.

Gone are the terraces, spines of agave, wild geranium.
In their place, the arid foothills. He does not look back
at the profusion of peaks, canyons in a maze.

A separate death for each touch
of the condor's shadow.

* * * * *

After peppers and carob trees with their flat tops,
the dunes. Broad expanse of sand with here and there
a thin trickle of moisture from the mountains,
along which yellow reeds, cane, half-hearted palms.

He reels from the heat and scrambles among rocks
to moisten a cracked and bleeding tongue.
The bloated face of the Overseer. Another knot
removed from the quipu, and the writ of banishment.

Small fingers close upon his wrist like talons,
lifting it upward in a kiss. Breath no more
than a whisper: Bring the mother-doll.

* * * * *

Here angry lava comes to rest
in cooling waters; here, too, the sea
is full of birds. Gulls, terns, brown pelican,
and the long hooked bills of the quemoy.

He takes from his waistband two black feathers
and holds them at arm's length, anticipates
their slow descent to healing surf.
Before his cracked lips form a prayer,
a gust of wind carries the feathers off.

Gulls lift from the twisted slabs and plinths
of lava in pursuit, a feathered escort,
then wheel, like some winged vessel, landward,
casting their dappled shadows on the solitary

Machu Picchu: by the Sacrificial Rock

Eli Mandel

There was a sickness inside me.
Bird of unknown colours.
And I thought, I will go to Peru,
to the high mountains, to the cities
Inca Lords built in impossible places.

There it will fly out of my mouth
this hissing bird. It will sound hot
as if cut from the living breast of one
held toward the sun. The Incas say,
in their bird speech, the sun is god.

And the Inca himself is a bird
who flies toward the sun.
Thousands and thousands of birds
die every day so he may be clothed
in the plumage of the sun itself.

At the stone called the sun's hitching post,
at the altar of sacrifices I waited,
the air thin as a knife blade,
my mouth opening and closing.
But the sun fell into a mist.

What is the sound of oppression
or royalty? In their markets
the Quechuan whisper and listen,
transistors muttering to them
languages ancient and implacable.

Not even in mountains so high
they take your heart out of your mouth,
not even in cities perched like condors
where the sun rides out of the universe,
not even now will you gain or be given
ransom/release. The Quechuan whisper
and listen, the sound of ancient bondage.

Letter to a Cuzco Priest

Earle Birney

Father   whose name
your smalltown paper took in vain

Young father   whose face
blurred in the cheap newsprint
I could not recognize in a street

Father   who will never know me
nor read this   which is written
in your honour
in the terms of my worship

Father   forgive yourself

>   This morning two Quechua
>   tramped on their horny feet
>   down sun-ravaged slopes
>   clutching cardboard banners
>   Thirty more Indians followed
>   sunfaced   silent   ragged
>   and as many boneknobbly goats
>   maybe a hundred sheep
>   gut-swollen   yammering
>   Their dust rose   was carried
>   by thin winds like incense
>   over sculptured rocks
>   that once bore up the Moon's Temple
>
>   Dry wail of the beasts
>   dropping over denuded terraces
>   enchanted the ears of travellers
>   lining up two Cuzco kids
>   (dressed like Inca princelings
>   by the Oficina de Turismo)
>   to be shot by cameras
>   in front of the Bath of the Priestess

Father   worship yourself

>Where stony slopes level
>to unfenced valleys   the sheep
>took over the lead   sniffing grass
>not the boundary stakes

Father you were not with those shepherds
but your Word sent them

>A local watchman for the Lima agent
>for the American banker
>for the Peruvian landowner
>living in Madrid
>phoned the Cuzco cops
>who phoned the army regiment
>quartered locally to handle such jobs

Father   the guilt is not yours
though words that blazed last week
from your pulpit lettered their placards

>The two who bore them are dead

Father   the guilt begins
in the other pulpits and all the places
where no one will say your words

>"The Government is only
>an armed front for Fifty Families"

where no one calls on whatever his country
>"Let the land feed its people"

Father   the guilt is not that you spoke
nor that the poor listened   acted
have come again to defeat

>Twenty of those who followed
>into convenient range of the troops
>tend their own wounds
>in the jail's bullpen

Father   forgive all men if you must
but only in despite of god
and in Man's name

> Their flocks   driven back
> to the spiny heights
> are herded now by the boys and women

Do not forgive your god
who cannot change   being perfect

> Blood dries on the uncropped grass
> The goats eat dust

Father   honour your Man,
though he will not honour you
in whatever priestly purgatory
authority muffles you now

> In Cuzco the paper that quoted the sermon
> and printed your face
> today demands death
> for the Red (Indian?) spies in the Andes

Father   gullible and noble
born to be martyred
and to be the worthy instrument
of the martyrdom of the gullible

> I who am not deceived
> by your cold deity

> believe

> for there is no other belief

> in the wild unquenchable God
> flaming within you

Pray to yourself above all for men like me
that we do not quench
the Man
in each of us

Wetback

Dennis Gruending

Lima is always cloudy in July, a low overcast promising a rain which never falls. The Jorge Chávez airport is sixteen kilometres from downtown, right on the coast in the port suburb of Callao. It takes an hour to get there travelling in a crowded bus through Lima's decay.

It was cold and damp as I struggled into the airport with my suitcase and assorted bags, the accumulation of nine months in Latin America. The passport check was perfunctory, and I climbed the steps of a jet heading north. We climbed quickly through the dull cloud into a vast, sunlit plain of white fluff. I began to write in another of the small notebooks which had been my diary from Canada to southern Chile. I recalled another moment ten years earlier, in a half-filled plane high over the Atlantic. I was a twenty-year-old on my way home from five months in Europe, writing in another diary, trying to explain the inconsistent mixture of fear, homesickness and exhilaration which I had encountered.

Peru's coastal desert stretched below, then the tropical lowland as we approached Guayaquil to change planes. Soon we were in the air again, destined for Bogotá in its mountains. The Colombian mountain ranges spread into the valleys like parched brown fingers. Occasionally there was a plantation, where Indian and mestizo peasants pour their lives into labour, receiving in return a few crumbs for existence. Some of the valleys contain coffee; others conceal crops of coca and marijuana destined for the drowsy pleasure of North Americans. Into these valleys it is dangerous to travel.

Bogotá has a reputation for some of the world's worst slums; and for its thieves, the street children who have no homes. They travel in packs, moving in expertly to separate tourists from their jealously-guarded possessions. That separation occurs most often at the point of a knife. I had seen the scars of these encounters on the faces and arms of gringo men as big and bulky as football players.

After a brief stop in Bogotá to deposit and take on passengers, we climbed again, destined for Mexico City. I sat, as always, against the window. Another man had taken a seat on the aisle, so quietly that I only sensed his presence. He smiled shyly. I nodded slightly in reply. He was a small man, his black hair gleaming, cut in what at home we used to call the shingle.

It wasn't until we were above Costa Rica that he began to talk. Did I know Mexico City? Yes, a little. Did I know of a place where it was cheap to stay? Yes. I gave him the address of a hotel I had used. At five dollars a night I thought it cheap. He took out a notebook and copied the address—69 Calle Uruguay.

Finally we introduced ourselves. His name was Raúl Marca. He said he was a carpenter from Ayacucho, a small colonial city 2,500 metres up in the Andes beside what is called a highway between Lima and Cuzco. He had boarded in Bogotá, not Lima, I said. Quickly he produced his passport, the Peruvian green with gold letters. It indicated he had been to Colombia, to Venezuela, and back to Colombia.

He said he had gone to Venezuela looking for work. He had given up on Peru. There was no work in Ayacucho, so he went to Lima. Millions had preceded him. There was little work there, and what he could find paid only 200 soles a day, less than two dollars.

I knew he was telling the truth. I had met another carpenter when I stayed at the Hotel Colmena in Lima. His name was Celestino Calderón. One morning when I awoke to hammering outside my room, I found him riveting steel ribbons onto a bed frame. We talked several times during the next few days, and once he told me that he was paid only a dollar a day. Many days he found no work at all. He asked if I could get him into Canada.

Another day while we were talking, we heard the sound of crowds in the street below. We ran to peer over the ledge of the roof. The army was invading a square to disperse striking teachers. Celestino said the teachers had struck for eighty-one days the previous year to win a settlement providing a salary of fifteen dollars a week. The contract had never been fulfilled. Now they were out again, supported by whole sectors of the population angered by recent price increases of sixty percent for food and gasoline.

The army converged upon the plaza. First came a grey truck spitting out a column of water. Behind it followed a group of soldiers in green fatigues, wearing helmets and plastic masks, swinging nightsticks at anyone who moved, or didn't.

In an airplane ten thousand metres above Costa Rica, Raúl Marca was telling me that if life was bad for teachers, it was even worse for people like himself and Celestino Calderón. Raúl had a wife and three children in Ayacucho. He had to leave them when he went to Lima. He had gone to Venezuela looking for work . Venezuela did not want him. Venezuela has struck it rich. It belongs to OPEC. It has oil, and the world must pay for oil. But Venezuela does not want the thousands of hopeful immigrants converging upon it.

When he arrived at the border, Raúl was told he needed enough money to last for thirty days before he would be allowed to enter. He had not known that. Even if he had, he could never have collected it. In Peru you are happy to have enough to get through each day. Raúl had a brother in Venezuela working in the Orinoco oil fields; somehow the brother had managed to get in and stay. Raúl wrote asking for money, then waited in a Colombian border town living on bread and Coca-Cola. Fifteen days later the money arrived. He was allowed in, but only for thirty days. When he tried to hide, they came and took him.

His brother had given him money for air fare to Mexico City. Why, I asked, did he want to go to Mexico? From what I had seen it was a country with its own arresting poverty. Each year millions of Mexicans try to wade the Rio Grande or steal across landed border points into the United States.

He had another brother in Virginia, Raúl said. The brother had been in the Peruvian merchant marine and jumped ship. He lived in Arlington. I didn't ask if he lived there legally. Raúl had called his brother before boarding, asking him to send money to Mexico for air fare to Washington, D.C. He had no idea where he would stay, how long he might have to wait, or whether he could get into the U. S. He had forty dollars in his pocket. I recalled my advice about cheap hotels to someone who had spent fifteen nights in the streets of a border town.

I thought of the time an hour or two away when we would clear the Sierra Nevada and drop into the wild sprawl which is Mexico City. That was only the first hurdle. What about the wall of regulations, the systematized exclusion which exists to protect Fortress North America from the have-not hordes south of the Rio Grande?

We said little after the announcement by the captain that we were above Chiapas, a Mexican state a half-hour out of the capital. We agreed that I would stay close to him at the customs gate so I would know if he were stopped. He gave me his brother's telephone number in Arlington. After landing and a delay in getting off the plane, we were confronted by a lounging, leering clerk. He had just rummaged through the pack of a young American woman, then called for another clerk to check it more closely. Colombia is the drug capital of the western hemisphere, and Mexico City is a favourite conduit in the trade.

The clerk was suspicious of Raúl. He looked closely at the passport. Why was Raúl in Mexico? Tourism. Did he have relatives here? Yes. Where did they live? Number 69, Calle Uruguay, Raúl answered without hesitation. That convinced the man, who suddenly appeared to have grown tired of such diligence. He waved Raúl through and barely checked my bags as I followed.

We were in the crowded barn which is Mexico's international airport. We decided to call the American embassy. We located the public telephone and called. No answer. I wanted to try the Peruvian embassy next. Raúl said no. He had called them when he was in Bogotá, and they told him to go away.

Then he suggested that maybe Canada would take him. I had been waiting for him to say that, fearful that he would. I remembered Canada's green paper on immigration in the mid-1970s and the regulations which followed, making it more difficult for Third World people to get in.

We called the embassy and the woman said curtly that it would not be possible to interview anyone from Peru for two or three days. I wasn't surprised by the response or her tone. I had visited the embassy several times during an earlier stay in Mexico. It's located in the wealthy west side of the city. A red and white maple-leaf flag hung somnolently from the fifth floor windows, the only floor in the building sporting air conditioners. I hadn't gone seeking any of the renowned Canadian hospitality; nor did I receive any. I went to read newspapers and Canadian literature. We may not be able to find copies of *Stony Plain, A Winnipeg Childhood* or *rag & boneshop* in most Canadian bookstores, but Canadians abroad can find them in embassies, thanks to the largesse of the Canada Council.

Raúl and I decided to look for a travel agent to ask some questions about visas. There was no agency in the airport. A woman at the information desk told us to try the Holiday Inn nearby. We walked into the rain, Raúl carrying his one small bag and a couple of mine, cheap straw mesh bags bulging with books, magazines and newspaper clippings. I carried one large ugly red suitcase, borrowed from a friend in Lima. We were wet when we reached the hotel. A doorman eyed us with suspicion.

Raúl asked a man seated before a partition plastered with travel posters about buying a ticket for the United States. The man asked if he had a visa. Raúl said no and that he was Peruvian. The man said the U.S. would demand a visa which Raúl had little chance of receiving. He said crowds of Mexicans waited each day at the American embassy for visas, but most were denied. The Americans, he said, knew that Mexicans entering the country could lose themselves and stay, working as illegal aliens. He said they allowed just enough Mexicans in to perform the dirty work in fields and sweatshops.

Raúl asked about running the border; taking a bus to the area and slipping across the line at night. It would be dangerous, the man said. He knew of people who had been beaten, even killed by border police.

Every Mexican knows about the border. Those who cross illegally are called *mojados*, "wetbacks." The term derives from their being wet after crossing the river. The American border guards use mastiffs, infra-red detectors and helicopters with blinding searchlights to locate the illegals. The U. S. doesn't want them; or more accurately, it wants only as many as it needs. There are industries which depend upon wetback labour. Aliens can be paid wages below legal minimums. Employers don't have to deal with unpleasantries of paying health and social security benefits. There's a specialty trade in providing those industries with contraband workers. The trade usually involves the complicity of border guards, for a price.

We hauled the red suitcase and bags back to the airport. Raúl called his brother in Arlington, and the brother promised to send money. I asked Raúl if he would use the money to go home. He turned on me with a vehemence I wouldn't have expected, saying he would prefer to die rather than go home empty-handed.

Both of us were exhausted and irritable. We found a lunch bar in the airport. Raúl insisted upon paying. When we finished our beer, we shook hands and embraced. He stepped out into the rain. I went in search of the Canadian Pacific office to arrange a flight to Canada.

V Brazil, Argentina, Uruguay

from Brazilian Journal

P.K. Page

February 3, 1957

How could I have imagined so surrealist and seductive a world? One does not *like* the heat, yet its constancy, its all-surroundingness, is as fascinating as the smell of musk. Every moment is slow, as if under warm greenish water.

The flavour is beyond my ability to catch. The senses are sharpened by *that* smell—a vegetable polecat called jack-fruit which when fallen looks in size and contour like a black porcupine, and when ripe is picked from trees in our jungle; by *these* sights: Niemeyer's bridges, for instance, built over the canyons of this remarkably mountained city—long, sinuous, low bridges on pylons, white as platinum against the green of the *mato*—with bright glimpses of the sea both above and below; recurring couples—on the street everyone is paired—in love, embracing or half-embracing, whatever the heat; and the solitary figure in the window, usually female, framed by a mat of hot air and gazing off into a kind of languor, as if all time were designed for that purpose.

It is hard to get anything done. It is hard to focus. A thought is barely born before it melts, and in its place so lovely a void one could hardly have guessed emptiness so attractive. We swim now, in the great hot pool—not cooling off, merely drowning our wetness in a greater wetness—while next door the Sisters sing their Aves in the totally dark convent. The other night we heard the giggles of a host of small girls, and leaning on the balustrade in what must surely be the classical Brazilian pose, found—instead of a children's party as we had thought—the Sisters themselves, those whom we have seen at dusk, silently reading their breviaries under the cassia trees, now swinging on the swings, black robes flying. A wonderful subject for Pegi Nicol, had she been alive to momentarily lay aside her bright jujube colours and try the inky ranges of blues and greens.

I think of her now, perhaps, because her joyful, bright oils, bursting with life, somehow parallel all this tropical exuberance. And once reminded of her, I see again her posthumous show at the National Gallery of works painted when she was dying—beautiful, brilliant, large canvases, filled to overflowing. It was as if the lethal, proliferating cancer cells within her had been transformed into a multitude of life-giving images which made dance the grey air of the gallery.

And because our reception rooms are like the shell-white grottoes where mermaids might sober up after a drunken night, a large Nicol of girls gardening and bending in a profusion of colour would shed a warmer light in all this green and white. A Nicol, a Lillian Freiman, and a great Bonnard.

213

The Goodridge Roberts in the small *sala*—and all my life I've wanted to live with a Goodridge—is dark and totally without movement. Its pines against the sky are characteristic as a signature—but it might be forged. Sky, trees, water—his best ingredients—lie locked on the canvas. What would I not give for his large still life from the National Gallery—the fruit, the bottle, the plate, painted as if he had suddenly descried a world in which all objects glow.

A. is spilled on his bed like warm milk, and the frogs, tree toads, cicadas, and whatever else cut, saw, bang, and hit the black tropical night. Around and around the driveway the armed guard in his sand-coloured uniform strolls, like a succession of men. In the darkness between the pools of light shed by the lamps he is totally lost. The frogs sound like dogs, like hens, like drums, like strings, and when they stop—which they do occasionally, as if obeying a conductor—one hears the other drums and the weird singing from the *favela*.

It is from the *favelas* that the sambas come, according to our host of the other evening—a small Brazilian of Italian origin. He is, he claims, a true Carioca (citizen of Rio): loves the heat, the movement, the noise, the Negroes, and he loves the sambas and takes pride in having published many of the best, which he claims to have found when visiting the hills.

April 25

Episode of the goat. Yesterday Morel, the cook—who is slim and rather effeminate with a peroxided streak in his hair, and who looks absurdly young in his white uniform and chef's hat—asked if he might bring his goat. He is, he said, an orphan with no relatives, and Negrinha is his only family. I agreed on one condition: that he obtain the consent of the gardener.

Today the goat arrived. I was taken up the hill at the back of the house to meet her. Negrinha. She is indeed black and female, as her name implies. And she is most comely. She was tied to the little abandoned house up among the wild mango trees, safely beyond the reach of all valuable plants. If she was excited by the sight of me, she was nothing like as excited as Morel was by the introduction. I asked if she was noisy. He assured me she was almost mute.

A great bleating began in the *mato* just as A. returned from work. In the hope that his attention would not be drawn to it, I pretended to hear nothing. He, thinking that it was some kind of wildlife, was intrigued to see how long it would take before I showed some interest. Finally his curiosity overcame him. What, he asked, did I think that noise was? "O that," I said, making it nothing at all, "is our goat." And so we climbed the hill in order that A. too could meet her.

When I suggested to Morel that she was far from the mute animal he had described, he assured me, "It is only because she feels strange here. She will soon get used to it and then you will never hear her." Returning from an ambulatory tour of the garden before dinner we caught a glimpse of a slim dark silhouette by the kitchen door and, catapulting through the same door as if shot from a cannon, José, our *mulato* cleaner, and Morel in his chef's hat. The chase had begun.

But Negrinha was too quick for them. The three nimble-footed, fleet young things leapt flowerbeds, crashed through shrubs, and made an all-out dash around the swimming-pool and across the lawn until they were brought up as if against a brick wall by the stream. Negrinha, wily and fast, made a lightning turn and headed for the driveway leading to the gate. There she was caught by a triumphant armed guard and led away by a flushed and pleased Morel—who told us as he passed that he would like a picture of her by the swimming-pool!

April 26

Episode of the goat continued. This morning I was wakened by unbroken bleating—not from the *mato* at the back of the house, but from somewhere in front. Negrinha, it appeared, had escaped during the night and been caught, this time, by Ricardo the gardener, who had shut her up in his gatehouse. It was reported by Salvador's wife, Mary, who brought our breakfast, that Ricardo liked Negrinha very much—so much, in fact, that he wanted to buy her. But Morel would not sell. Negrinha was no ordinary goat. She had travelled with a circus. She was an artist.

Later this morning, when I went down to the kitchen to talk menus with Morel, he told me, nearly in tears, that Negrinha had escaped from the gatehouse. Had he my permission to go in search of her? Of course he had, and when last seen he was hurrying down the drive, a length of heavy wire in his hand, in search of the wilful circus artist.

His crestfallen and empty-handed return in the afternoon made me so sorry for him that I suggested we search for Negrinha by car. "Have you seen a black goat?" we called to pedestrians as we passed. *"Uma cabra? Uma cabra negra?"*

Occasional leads took us to the tops of hills and down again to the beaches, but nowhere did we see the least flick of her black tail or hear the least whisper of a bleat.

Morel, in a voice filled with emotion, told me, "Madammy, if we find her, I will give her to you. She is yours." And I, protesting his generosity, told him I couldn't dream of accepting the only member of his family. But that afternoon the present was not his to offer nor mine to refuse. Despite the bright day, Negrinha was as invisible as if it were night.

I assured a downcast Morel that we would advertise for her. But before there was time for the ad to appear in the paper, an animated Morel announced that a man had phoned saying he had found a black goat at Ipanema—an enormous distance for her to have travelled. He understood it belonged to the Canadian embassy.

Morel's final announcement: that Negrinha is once again shut up in the gatehouse. And that she is mine!

April 27

Conclusion of the episode of the goat. Wakened again this morning by Negrinha's song to the dawn. Mary, bearer of breakfasts and the latest news, told us that what is now known as the "goat of the *embaixatriz*" had twice escaped during the night to the convent next door, and twice been returned by two unamused Sisters of God.

Too much, too much, I complained to Morel. We wanted no more songs outside our bedrooms at five A.M., no more chases, no more . . . But as we were discussing her, Negrinha escaped again. This time, starved from so much time in the gatehouse, she was on an eating rampage—day-lilies, anthuria, the tenderest buds of the peacock plants and the rose grape. Now the gardener gave chase, and the *mordomo*, Salvador. Ricardo, a tiny Portuguese like one of the Seven Dwarfs, and Salvador, a tall, elegant Italian in a white sharkskin jacket, were a kind of tail to her kite—zigzagging and darting as Negrinha made her split-second turns and sudden leaps. Here a bite, there a bite. Black Negrinha ravaging the garden. Now Manuel with his rake and Morel in his chef's hat joined the breathless trio just as Negrinha made a wild dash for the gate. But this morning there was no guard to stop her, and as I watched Morel and Salvador and José and Ricardo streak after her in their various attires, I vowed that never again would I aid in her search.

After a long time they returned, flushed and goatless. This was the moment for which Ricardo had waited—the moment when Morel, nonplussed, worried, fed-up, would be willing to be rid of Negrinha. It is a point one has seen reached in human relationships—when the scale finally tips, the situation can no longer be borne. Ricardo was now ready with his offer: two hundred *cruzeiros* for a vanished goat. And willingly Morel accepted, as if Ricardo were doing him a favour, and altogether forgetful that Negrinha was mine!

Later I was told that Ricardo, by some alchemy, found and caught Negrinha without delay and led her straight away to his weekend shack on the outskirts of Rio.

Peace reigns once again on Estrada da Gávea.

Thread and Needle

Ricardo da Silveira Lobo Sternberg

Stern, starched, mustachioed,
my great-uncle spent the days
policing the stones in his garden,
the mangoes on his trees.
He spoke to me of the emperor.

Sinhazinha, my aunt, the seamstress
purblind with cataracts at sixty-five,
would hand me the needle and ask:
child, thread this for me.

If I moved my head a certain way
Sinha was inside the aquarium
lost among the ferns,
sewing and muttering prayers
oblivious to bright fish
threading in and out of her hair.

> Silver needle, golden thimble
> I will sew your bride her dress.

Sanctuary of boredom, that house
was a world, a system complete,
self-sufficient as the aquarium.

So who was it that interfered
introducing into the house
a device that could thread needles?

I no longer remember.
But soon after I touched it
the contraption would not work
or would not work as well
and Sinha, suspecting
a demon in those gears,
turned her eyes towards one
lost inside the aquarium
and asks, again and again:
child, thread this for me.

Ana-Louca

Antic-prone and crazy
breast-feeding her dolls
through the streets
or on Sundays marooned
by herself in a pew,
she offered her litany
of curses and profanities
to no one in particular.

Thursdays she would come
demanding that which habit
had made hers by right:
the warmed leftovers
she wolfed down, standing
against the green backdoor.
Finished, she rattled thanks
from the gates and was gone.

A packing crate her bedroom,
she slept by the docks.
Amid rags and broken dolls,
asleep and for once, quiet,
a grizzled girl
lulled by the ocean's rhythm
as if cradled in its blue arm.

from Les voyants

Robert Baillie

The street in Rio has a murderous undertow, like that of the sea. It takes hold of you, carries you along, drowns you. Jeanne, who's suddenly become so thin, and Gino, so unexpectedly white, in the midst of the exuberant dark pack that roils heavily around them. Even Gino seems grey, white blue in this golden crowd. When you're as thin and milk white as Jeanne and Gino, the human swell and the tide of vehicles are transmuted into an aggressive crush. Just when everything seems to flow toward certain evacuation, you're suddenly snatched up, held tight, like a grain of sand in the oily gears of some violent machine that devours you and then spits you out in shreds. The dizziness grabs you by the nerves and leaves you on edge.

Being ashamed of their whiteness, as disgusted as Jeanne with the brittle angle of her hips that won't roll, and with her emaciated, rachitic knees that crack at every step. Her revulsion at Gino's milky body. The worn sweaty hairs between his thighs. That transparent back like blue-veined silk; all those green protruding veins on his hands and neck. He also feels ridiculous in those heavy eyeglasses that keep slipping down his shiny nose. And that odour of white man, of white woman. How can anyone bear that sticky scent of rot that comes oozing out of their bodies' unfathomable depths? Like a suppurating abscess that bursts open fetidly on their skin. Feeling like an unsightly piece of evil-smelling garbage amid the effluvia of a saline crowd that fills the air with the smell of lavender, musk, and paba gel. Jeanne and Gino would have returned to the safety of the hotel if they had dared admit their mutual disgust at the moment they lay down on the sand of the beach at the Copacabana.

Forget yourself. And quickly get inside the skin of a *Carioca* athlete or under the tan of a beautiful Amerindian woman. Forget yourself. And become one of those perfect men who run along the beach in groups to keep in shape. Or even be this tanned old woman with silver grey hair who is training with a team of retirees next to the waves. Or that Greek god of a sports instructor or those young people who make a show of working-out, accomplished gymnasts who pump up their biceps with all the muscle-building equipment that clutters up the beach. Or become that colossal phony black man, nonchalantly lying in the sun. To be one of those deliberately ragged adolescents who let the gold of their pubescent buttocks show through the holes in their washed-out jeans as they play soccer. To be non-plussed by the soccer ball kicked toward you, and especially by that intriguing look as green as the jungle or the sea, a tender, devastating look that gnaws at you and that is less bothered by your starchy ugliness than by why you should be getting flustered over just kicking back the over-heated ball. To be that look itself. Or that other Gino without glasses. Windsurfing over the waves, feeling the sail carry you off toward the same hedonistic pleasures. Whole clusters of muscles that burst through the rigging. To be that minuscule Jeanne, smooth and lascivious in her minute, feline bikini. A young panther gleaming in her fluid *tanga*. The girl from Ipanema, the beautiful mulattress of that sweet song. Tam ta da da da, tam tam ta da da da, tam ta da da da tam. A samba or bossa nova moving to the rhythm of the sea. The dance of that black woman in the market, rolling her hips, her belly, her breasts, hawking the lemonade, fresh tea, cold Cokes, and light foaming beer that you always want so badly but never ask for. Because you're terrorized to the bone by the beauty of others. Jeanne and Gino sink into the white sands of Copacabana like snow-crabs and finally disappear altogether, along with their offensive whiteness, unhealthy, naked, obscene, into the impregnating Rio sunlight.

They certainly have to seek shelter. The noonday sun has quickly found them out. Jeanne and Gino have to face it. The small fortune they paid that health-goods store in Sept-Iles didn't include any guaranteed skin protectors. All those creams and sessions under sun lamps were useless in preparing them for this lethal luminescence. Among the crowds of pallid charter passengers at Dorval, Mirabel, or New York, Jeanne and Gino had seemed like recent arrivals from Florida. But here, in this exuberant light and among this nation of sun-worshippers, they look anaemic. At four o'clock, when the tidal wave of native *Cariocas* surges onto the public beaches, Jeanne and Gino cover up all that remains of their burnt and suffering dehydrated flesh under their yellow ratteen underwear and move to the refuge of their beach umbrella.

Their guilty skin ached for days. They had to resign themselves to wearing masks of zinc oxide just to walk around the city. Farewell to the beach, at least until they returned from their trip to the back-country, which was the main reason they'd undertaken the whole expedition to Brazil in the first place. They would have to wait till some other Saturday before risking further exposure to the Rio sun. Thus, crouched under their shadeless parasol, they became even more appreciative of the slow and harmonious sway of the bodies passing by. The *malevolência*. Jeanne and Gino had to make do with the role of voyeurs amid the refined cruising that raged around them.

They faced the sea, but were cut off from it by a walking theatre. A theatre of intimate and collective seductions. The crowd of passersby asserted its beauty like a single splendid body. Jeanne and Gino felt self-conscious. There was such perfect sensuality in these women and men standing naked and vertical against the horizontality of sea, beach, and sky. It was a perpetual ground-angle shot of well-proportioned curves, roundnesses, motor elasticity, the moving elongation of a dimension of life that became the sole dimension of all life, of all reality. A living museum of breathing forms that touched themselves right there where it hurt, where it made you quiver, where you didn't even know how to look due to the abstraction of all our rational and puritanical prohibitions.

For Jeanne and Gino, lost between one sea and another, sex is no longer just a concept. Sex is a cleft in a blue silk triangle that a man's finger lightly strokes and then traces along the crease. Sex is a bulbous protuberance that a woman's hand surreptitiously caresses just before a raucous burst of laughter. It's a startled, satisfied bird that is just barely able to take flight. Or bathing trunks that are half-way pulled down in teasing and then left like that to flout and arouse. It's a macho *Carioca* ladies' man who hugs another *Carioca* Casanova with all the lazy virility of the rich young race that's shaped them. It's one *mulata* who bends down over another to rub oil caressingly between her friend's breasts that spill out of their bikini top.

And it's especially the *garota*, a girl of twenty, not yet completely a woman, but a thoroughbred, fresh, with a graceful silhouette of formal perfection. She opens her whole hermaphroditic body to the waves and turns, her buttocks as firm as ripening apples, like an image of a virgin from an illustration, her waist thin and diaphanous. It's the cage of her hummingbird breasts, it's her head rising from an alabaster neck, thrown back toward the foam of the sea, and her long arms moving like mad windmills searching for the lanky arches of her legs. Suddenly her limbs streaming with water droplets, her oblong thighs, her fingers, her toes like bunches of purple blackcurrants all explode with laughter and the flash of the enamel of her teeth in their bright vermilion frame. Beneath her cameo nose and the closed shells of her eyes lies an exotic beauty, a purity no one has ever seen.

Death Squads Kill One Child Per Day In Brazil

Paul Chamberland

The article is on the last page of the sports section. When will these incomparable champions of death make it into the Olympics? Most of the page is taken up by an advertisement for Bell Canada: "Come on, Alex, settle my score!" Is Alex, "the most tuned in of the tuned in" now an expert at getting even?

Millions of children, as many as the whole population of Canada, are thrown onto the street in the desolate slums that surround the great Brazilian cities. This "process of rejection" (the polished euphemism of the social sciences) goes so far as to include direct extermination. There are now communities that unabashedly treat their children as vermin.

"Pay up!" order the bankers at the IMF. "Get rid of this scum!" say the retailers of São Paulo, Rio, and Recife.

An ex-killer tells his story. "I made more money than a cop. But I had to be more efficient, too. They'd bring in a kid who stole; you'd give him a beating; they'd bring in another . . . It was endless. And a thief's a thief, whether he's ten years old or forty. If you can't stop them stealing, someone else will. Your job is to liquidate kids."

Extermination is for when everything else has failed: mistreatment in police stations, in reformatories, on the street—"the routine of torture."

"I have to admit that, unfortunately, there are police officers who kill and who protect other killers."

"The time comes when you can no longer tell who's a crook and who's a cop."

"The police are rotten with corruption everywhere in this country."

Declare the Directors of Public Security for the States of Rio, Pernambuco, and Amazonas, respectively.

Sometimes children's bodies are found. Their eyes have been gouged out; their ears, tongues, and genitals have been sliced off; their bodies are covered with cigarette burns or knife cuts.

Such a beautiful country.

"Enormous palm trees rustle in the wind. The perfumes of hibiscus, gardenia, and strelitzia waft on the air. Waterfalls and private lagoons top off the fantasy. Your personal balcony opens out onto a tropical paradise whose beauty, charm, and serenity will fill you with wonder. Tropiques Nord offers you a unique opportunity to live in paradise."

When he gets home, V.N. finds this brochure in his mail. He's invited, urged to accept, to "Come home to paradise." A tanned couple is shown luxuriating next to the falls. They obviously have the minimum $269,000 that it takes, according to the ad, to open the gates of Eden.

Atlântico do Sul

Hugh Hazelton

lighted city and mountains
rise up behind
the beach where candles burn
     in sand altars
     in Imanjá
     the sea goddess

we stand in the night
     water moving over our feet
     my arms around your waist
     lips against your hair
and watch
     smooth, warm, white waves
     break out of nothing

Sons of the Cangaceiros

the highway
is a black river
     that cuts
     across their lives
     without touching

they stare from mud shacks
     crouching at the roadside
     of vast estates

cars, express buses
huge chromed transports
     pass laden with
     bread, meat, fruit
     that they'll never taste
for another nation
within their country

boys hold up small pet monkeys
        for sale
        as drivers go by
they scream and wave their arms
wanting to throw the monkeys
splattering across windshields

Yavari Mirim

wilderness of dense photosynthesis
        breathing foliage breathing
        since the first green fibre formed
trees soar like monumental pillars
distant branches twined
        with lianas
        that hang motionless
        in sombre light

fallen log across the ravine
        a column of army ants
        swarms over it
        dead insects carried
        on a mass of red bodies
soldiers' pincers poised above

the woman
        with bare breasts
        and lines of tattoos on her face
        is taking her child to the river
as I come forward
        they run away screaming
white man and bush ghost
        are the same word
        in their language

Trans-Amazonica

writhing vibrant lime green line

snake
trapped by the banks
of the road

people stopped
        surrounded it
        hurled rocks
        ran their tires over it
        squashed its head with a crowbar

and watched a graceful agony
on a dirt highway through cut-open forest
        long eroded wound of red soil

Boa Vista

        new country
      long-grassed rolling savanna
     blue-forested distant mountains
    fences of fresh steel
   and herds of fat zebu hydrids
  people from every continent
come to buy land

hitch-hiking
   at the side of a mud track
      a jungle Indian turned peon
        his adolescent wife
           carries a withered baby
            who stares
               from a scab-covered face
                with old eyes
                  dying

Iguazú

Jean-Paul Daoust

Iguazú. The falls. The exotic in all its splendour. Its force. Five hundred different species of butterflies frolicking around in the middle of orchids, magnolias, bougainvillea, and cascades of flowers. These waterfalls! One hundred and sixty degrees of vertigo, shattering columns, delirious architecture, and wild fountains. This ochre water that falls in rainbows, that spreads forth beneath a dome of indigo. Walking among the cataracts (yes, in their midst, like on those flowering islands at the centre of the waters' roar), in a storybook luxuriance. This endless show of technical perfection. Neither the eye nor ear can escape. These avalanches of water are troubling. They affirm that time does not exist. Or that it is not what we think it is. And the orchids above them are so calm, so alive, so demented [...] These falls that touch three borders: Argentina, Brazil, and Paraguay. These falls that touch the sky!

The raised pool at the Hotel La Cabana gives a magnificent view. It's a superb afternoon, and I've installed myself in a comfortable spot on a small island in the pool from which I can observe the tropical forest. The sunlight on the wings of butterflies. The water that copies the sky. And I'm thankful to those who have defended this sea of emerald green, more fertile than anything I've ever imagined. I wonder how I can compete with such excess, such exuberance. I stretch out like a garrulous rattlesnake, a golden *jararaca,* an ebony-coloured *naja,* and envy the orchids suspended between earth and sky, clinging to bark, exquisite parasites.

Yesterday there was a torrential rainfall. The rain vied with the drumming of the falls [...] But today the sun is soaking up all these perfumed colours and it will soon be up to the full moon to continue the job. Everything will then turn to a mysterious shade of mauve. I know that I'm smothering every phrase with attributes: it must have something to do with all this flowering, always adding an orchid! A mayfly like one of these, so seductive and delightful, makes me think of infinity. The time it takes a petal to fall. Like these mad falls . . .

I look happily into M.'s eyes and the shimmering reflection of the landscape around us. There is the same harmony in the greens of the jungle as in the yellows of the desert. And I see myself once more in those blond waves of the Sahara, walking on light and then contemplating light as it floats in the air, pulverized into a thousand mirrors and shot through with myriads of particles of shining dust. Here it's the humidity after the rains that assails you. The greenhouse effect. [...] I watch the shifting patterns of greens and browns on the skin of a near-by lizard, signs of its happiness lying in the shades of the setting sun. It's playing an entire symphony and I'm the only audience. I move closer to it, setting aside my glass of white wine that is now a bit lukewarm, and this lizard, I swear, smiles at me. And his smile is greater than all the inflation in Argentina! The beauty of life strikes me right in the face. My eyes, inextricable from those of the lizard (what kind is it, I wonder? How ignorant I am . . .), slip down to its tongue, and I suddenly find myself wanting to run after and hunt the shining green wings and tenacious scents of those outrageous butterflies that splash through the light. I dive into this scene filled with atrocities and marvels. It's twilight, the most beautiful time of day, when the heart stumbles and sways toward the true side of things, when reality finally believes in the mystery.

Argentina

Argentina, "land without hope," as Borges said. The first thing that strikes me, right from the taxi, is the colour of people's eyes. Pale. Like a mixture of green, blue, and grey. The pastel eyes of Buenos Aires, city of refinement. Its European architecture. Its Opera House, an exact copy of that in Paris. And its parks (one of which is entirely devoted to roses), its monuments, and the unnerving beauty of its patrician cemetery. I leave fresh carnations at the gate to Evita Perón's tomb, placing them alongside the other flowers that are slowly drying there. Next to the cemetery is the School of Fine Arts, where I'm happy to find that an exhibit of young people's art is just opening. Immense streamers float above the streets surrounding the museums. Its the Recoleta district. The Restaurante Lola proves to be excellent. And I return by one of the largest avenues in the world: the impressive Nueve de Julio. Then a stroll down the Calle Florida, with its elegant shops of leather goods and its passersby all so dignified and seriously dressed in their sports jackets and ties. Tangos are coming from a record-store doorway. The tango is not as much a part of daily life here as is the samba in Brazil. It hangs in the air like nostalgia. There are tango shows in the tourist restaurants, but it seems absent from daily life. But let me return to these courteous citizens of the beautiful city of Buenos Aires.

And yet this country is collapsing beneath the sheer mass of its problems. The debt, corruption. The writer Marcela Sola says, "This is truly the ass of the world." And Santiago Kovadloff: "Buenos Aires is a fiction." The energy crisis. The city is plunged into darkness. The telephones are a laugh. Nothing works any more. Inflation is permanently out of control. And the poor estuary of the Rió de la Plata! People tell me, "The government's been corrupt for fifty years!" In pleasant cafés they serve you a whole horde of hors-d'oeuvres for a dollar. It's seven in the evening. There are a lot of people out on the street. We'll eat later, like them, at around ten o'clock. I watch them and find myself wondering which ones were the torturers and which were the victims. The military regime is not so far in the past, and it threatens to return.

228

People say, "The three pillars of Argentina; religion, the military, and the unions." "This nation is rich in bankruptcies." "We could be as wealthy as Canada, you know: we've got everything here. And we've wrecked it all!" Yet even so, along one street after another, the city (whose name doesn't mean anything anymore, especially on streets as polluted as Santa Fe) still displays its charms. Sometimes it's a corner that reminds you of Paris, or Madrid, or Vienna. But people's eyes are so sad. Like hunted animals. They look beaten. As if the best were over. There's a moribund dream in their washed-out faces. It's a city in whose heart is open about showing its nostalgia.

And this heat! But don't even think of walking around in shorts! They look at you with a confused expression. "Ah yes, those American tourists, they're so easy to spot!" What a pleasure to sit down in the shade of a *gomero*, (a gigantic tree that's related to the baobab). There are whole avenues of flowering trees: the *palos borrachos* ("the drunken sticks": what a splendid name). The city still seems luxurious. Yet there's that freedom that everybody wants, no matter what. Buenos Aires the majestic, rich in history and adventurers, standing around trying to find itself, seems indecisive at the dawn of the second millennium.

The Tango of Paola Sola

Nicole Brossard

at night thinking is easy
at nightfall we venture out
desire warm within us
we swim upstream against certainties
our arms charged with fervour

* * * * *

I walked slowly down Corrientes
night was in my thoughts
something intimate and shared
a *bombilla* between my lips
the night poured out its sensations

* * * * *

at night our supple imaginations
envision how beauty moves
among paradoxes and music
our whole being remembers, calls for
more scenes without compromise

* * * * *

in the café, the music was just
about to begin
the bandoneon player was setting up
people were already applauding
I watched Paola Sola, the soloist
the night would be the highest art
of silence and rapture

230

at night there is noise
in passions, perfumes
the noises are identical
like multiple secrets
filled with refrains and opinions
at night noises are vertigoes

* * * * *

Paola played, her hand sometimes
her eyes, the tango summoned
her whole being
sometimes the night changed the nape of her neck
sometimes her breast
the night travelled along
vales, valleys, of varying sounds
Rió of rain, Rió to infinity

* * * * *

at night we think closely about things
our hands on well-chosen verbs
we venture out into the improbable
with the surest instinct
we linger in the most daring places
of delirium and words

* * * * *

Paola played. The café filled up with smoke. Melancholy faded, dreams
returned. Life went by. Paola played. Only women were in her eyes. Paola
played. Her whole being, sometimes her hands. Sometimes her eyes, exile and
words cut short.

* * * * *

at night we give in to barrenness
our hearts full of deadlines
we feed while it goes on
we confuse desire and beauty
the great whole
of the method
of living, of sensations

* * * * *

I was walking down Corrientes
inhabited by Paola's words
I was tango, Plaza de Mayo
Thursday
madres.
I was walking down Corrientes
a fresh wind blew in from the sea
between the bodies
the sea would gather the night

* * * * *

at night existence absorbs us
like an obsession
existing imposes acts upon us
that take the wind from our thoughts
I was walking down Corrientes
there were so many resources
so many dawns and nights
in Paola's tango
there was the well-tuned music
of our bodies
the ineluctable form of desire
at night I always write
my hand on the verb to be

The Handkerchiefs of Plaza De Mayo

Mary Di Michele

a thousand mothers dressed in black
white handkerchiefs on their heads
silently circle the perimeters of the plaza

they whisper prayers for invisible sons
they want the earth that has swallowed the boys to cough them back up
they want the sea to return what she has cured in salt

the white handkerchiefs ruffle like pigeon breasts
in the faint breathing of the square
they never fly but they carry messages and the names of young men
the handkerchiefs grow fat feeding on crumbs of hope
and women's hearts
held up like sacramental wafer for all to see
before the unblinking eye of the government
goggled in brick and mortar

the handkerchiefs seem to rise above the dark heads
of the women like clouds over Buenos Aires
and from their billowing folds emerge
the faces of sons and lovers, almost perfect.
a facsimile of their boys, almost perfect,
almost every one of them missing nothing
more than an ear or a nose or an eye
and a life

Prison Report

Phyllis Webb

The eye of Jacobo Timerman looks through the hole and sees
another eye looking through a hole.

These holes are cut into steel doors in prison cells in Argentina.

Both eyes are wary.
They disappear.

Timerman rests his cheek on the icy door,
amazed at the sense of space he feels—the joy.

He looks again: the other's eye is there,
then vanishes like a spider.

Comes back, goes, comes back.

This is a game of hide-and-seek.
This is intelligence with a sense of humour.
Timerman joins the game.

Sometimes two eyes meet at exactly the same moment.

This is music. This is love
playing in the middle of a dark night
in a prison in Argentina.

My name is Jacobo one eye says.
Other eye says something, but Jacobo can't quite catch it.

Now a nose appears in the vision-field
of Timerman. It rubs cold edges of the hole,
a love-rub for Jacobo.

This is a kiss, he decides, a caress,
an emanation of solitude's tenderness.

In this prison everything is powered electrically
for efficiency and pain. But tenderness is also
a light and a shock.

An eye, a nose, a cheek resting against a steel door
in the middle of the dark night.
These are parts of bodies, parts of speech,
saying,
I am with you.

Monologue: Prisoner Without a Name

Lorna Crozier

Blindfolded,
you can't see who beats you.
It could be someone you called friend.
It could be your neighbour, or
the woman you saw buying bread,
the one who returned your smile
as she tapped the crust with her finger.

Sometimes there are voices far below
the pain. You hear about their children,
how one's son is failing school,
how another's daughter is growing beautiful.
You hear about the suppers that await them
in their houses on the other side
of town.

When all you have is pain and darkness
time stretches ahead like a desert
you can't walk out of, a desert
in a dream you cannot touch.
There is no reference point,
in two hours, tomorrow—these are things
you can't say, you don't know them anymore.

The first temptation is suicide,
then madness.

But one day you choose to survive.
You eat your food, the same food,
but you eat it differently.
You listen for rain on the roof, for wind.
You imagine wind in a woman's hair.
You sense when the one who beats you
is nervous
when he doesn't want to kill.

And so when you leave,
if they let you go,
there is something left of you
like a pebble you have hidden
all these months in your pocket,
a pebble you've polished in the darkness
behind the blindfold, bringing out its colours,
its shy designs.

And if you are lucky,
if this a lucky stone, let's say,
you can push away the bitterness
and there is room for something else,
another feeling, perhaps something
close to love.

From El cazador de ilusiones

Pablo Urbanyi

Avenida de Mayo, in Buenos Aires, has got to be one of the most beautiful avenues in the world. It begins in front of the Casa Rosada, the Presidential bungalow, and ends at the Congress, that old mansion full of representatives and senators. Not far from the President's little hut, I'll have to turn in at a doorway with a number I'd rather forget, take a broken-down elevator up to the sixth floor and then a wooden stairway to the seventh, and get back to work putting up with everybody's problems, whether it's a pearl necklace that's been expertly lifted, a child or parent who's disappeared or been kidnapped, a bloodsoaked murder, a ruthless betrayal or swindle by some friend or lover, a slimy case of blackmail or, well, any one of the unpleasant predicaments we're subjected to by the chaos of modern life.

At the end of the stairway there's a corridor with three offices, only one of which is occupied. Written on a piece of cardboard and pinned to the wooden door with thumbtacks is a sign that reads:

Mack Hopkins
Private Detective
Please Knock

And inside is where you'll always find me, whenever I'm not out investigating some case or haven't gone to visit the pigeons in the Plaza de Mayo. I'll be there alone, at the orders of whoever may need me, as alone as only a true loner can be.

On that particular day I had finished an especially hard-fought and exhausting game of checkers with myself: playing with the white ones, I had crushed the blacks. I was tuckered out, without even the strength to make myself a *mate*, and had thrown myself onto the cot in my bedroom, which is separated from the office by a plasterboard partition and a curtain that muffles my steps.

I was toying with an unloaded revolver, a .32, while reading a detective novel, my favourite way of relaxing and learning at the same time. I was rereading a certain passage with amazement and admiration. I've always found my fellow detectives to be unbelievably busy, either driving at enormous speeds in convertible sports cars on mountainsides covered with thousand-year-old pines overlooking the sea, or sipping scotch on a patio, or waiting for a contact in an airport, or in the arms of a beautiful blond or reliable redhead, or with the blond or redhead in their arms, at least according to them. They bemoan their miserable working conditions, but they always seem to have plenty of jobs and clients that sweat pure gold dust. If not, how are they able to pay for all those scotches and airline tickets? I didn't use to have enough cash for a shot of rotgut wine or the bus. Sometimes I even had to dry out my *mate* in order to use it over again. In one thing, however, I always managed to stay ahead of my colleagues: they systematically ruined their days off by working, while I never lost a single one. In fact, I was always able to enjoy my free time to the fullest, as I was doing at the moment, and simultaneously recharge my batteries while not wasting energy eating. I was, all told, a free and private detective.

The phone rang.

I threw the book to the floor and jumped off the bed, almost tearing down the curtain, tossed the gun to my other hand, and lifted the receiver.

"Mack Hopkins speaking."

"Mister Mack? I have a call for you," said the receptionist.

"If it's from the landlord, I don't want to hear about it: 'You still owe me for both the rent and the phone bill.' I know that tune by heart. Anything else?"

"I'll put you through. Go ahead now."

"Is that you Romero? I mean Hopkins. Mack? It's Alfonso."

Alfonso, a retired police officer and colleague, was the head of the Global Detective Agency. He was also trying to make it as an independent. A great guy and sharp dresser. He'd gotten me out of a jam more than once. A few months before he'd also thrown a few clients my way: elderly cuckolds from good families, jealous and frustrated, who recommended me to their friends and ended up lining up outside my door in unbearable droves. I'd finally had to throw all of them out.

"At your orders," I told him.

"Are you busy?"

My day off had just been shot to hell!

* * * * *

"The subject that you have to track down is named Storch, but you know that that doesn't mean much: today he's called Storch, tomorrow Pérez."

"Describe him to me."

"He's of normal height and build, but naturally he could be using elevator shoes or loafers with recessed heels. He could also have gained weight or gotten thinner or fatter or have a pillow attached to his stomach."

"Of course."

"He used to sport a thick moustache like a guerrilla; however, he might have trimmed it, grown it larger, shaved it off, or started to use any number of false ones. He has dark brown hair which he wears rather long, but he could have had it cut or dyed, or might have donned a toupée. His eyes are also dark brown, though he might now be using contact lenses of a different colour, or have started wearing glasses. He has thick, bushy eyebrows, unless of course he's plucked them, and he's got a hooked nose, though there again, he could have had it changed with a little plastic surgery. His ears stick out a bit, but of course we know all the ways there are of disguising that. He likes wearing bright-coloured clothes, but if he knows we're looking for him, he might possibly start using dark ones. He also swings his arms about as he walks, but he may have changed his stride. Are you following me, Mack?"

* * * * *

The sun was setting behind the buildings. It would soon be dark. I felt myself walking straighter. My good looks had proved as successful as ever. That woman, so close to the boss, had to be conquered. Two birds with one stone. Too bad my suit was a little worn, especially with a trip in view. Anyway, I'd taken an important step forward. I only had to find out exactly toward what and for how long.

I'd never had an offer as good as this: a long-term proposition with good pay. Before then there'd been nothing but routine jobs with pathetic rewards: I'd worked as a guard at mills and factories where the workers were on strike, as a night watchman, as a night watchman's replacement, and as a bodyguard for bill collectors, without of course getting involved in the whole business of shaking people down for money or becoming violent about anything. I know from experience what it's like to be broke. I hadn't followed many people: other detectives told me I was too tall and that I used to stick so close to my mark that it looked like I was running after a gold coin rolling down the street. If I worked with women, they'd usually end up getting it on with me, like those baggy old girls that Alfonso used to send over. It was all monotonous work that was over fast or bored me stiff or ended up turning into something else that I didn't want to get involved in. Various stories circulated as to my abilities, and I gradually found myself running out of both work and friends. The only one who really still remembered me was Alfonso.

People have called me a Don Quixote, a dreamer, gullible, unrealistic, a jerk. But I've always held my head up high and told them that I'm honest and optimistic, and that my guiding motto has been, "Be patient and wait your chance." This seemed to be my chance, a reward for my honesty.

It was beginning to get dark. I walked along the Avenida Santa Fe. The sky was fading to dusk, and lights were coming on in the windows of the larger stores. I pressed my nose against the shop windows and looked at the goods inside; they seemed to be right there next to my heart, as if the glass had become cellophane. I remembered the words of the philosopher who used to tell me, "Gerardo, the human heart and the heart of the world beat to the rhythm of merchandise." Now I understood what he'd meant. I felt happy; the world wasn't such an alien place...

* * * * *

I never mentioned that I'd been a police officer: people have funny ideas about cops. In those days I didn't have all the problems that I have now, like not enough work, for example. I wore my uniform with pride and honour. I was very happy, and my father was too: whenever he'd get drunk, tears would come to his eyes and he would stroke my uniform, brush it, iron it, and polish the nameplate. He used to tell me, "Gerardo, my son, you've no idea how much I envy you: if I could wear this uniform, I'd be saved. I'd be able to kill your mother in self-defence." My mother was the daughter of German immigrants to the province of Misiones and was over six-foot-six, while my old man was only about five-one. She used to hit him a lot when I wasn't home.

I still remember the joy of leaving for work every day. The neighbours would start waving to me as soon as I came into view. They were always respectful toward me; if you consider my size and throw in the uniform and the .45 at my belt, it's not surprising that they treated me with esteem. On the train, bus, or subway, people always made plenty of room for me, and I used to travel quite comfortably. Nobody squeezed up too close or got in my way. They either feared me, respected me, kept their distance, or became panicky when they saw me, "depending on the situation," as the philosopher would say. "Or according to their point of view," I might add.

The only one who wasn't afraid of me and didn't show me any respect was my mother. "Ass-licking cop! Bribe-taker!" she'd yell at me. It hurt then and still does now.

We're not all equal. I didn't take bribes. I even got into arguments about it with my fellow officers. They'd slap my back and tell me, "You'll learn." But I never did. They even accused me of corrupting shopkeepers and bar-owners by always paying for what I bought or drank or ate. They made me a driver so I wouldn't ruin all their favourite places to stop.

I never gave up hope. I read a lot. From the time I was a kid, Superman, Batman, and Captain America were my favourites. Following the advice of the philosopher and the astrologer, to "take it easy and not blow my stack," I began to read Salgari, Verne, Dumas, and I don't know who all else. Then I started in on detective stories. My reading bore out my feelings and my belief that justice did exist in this world and that there were other ways of imposing it. I dreamed of being an authentic Argentine private detective.

from Apenas un caballo

Maeve López

until I remember your name
I'll go on reciting your face
which has fallen to pieces
your neighbourhood your pampas grass
your head like a water-tank
your beaches and the rings under your eyes
your old waters without new sand
your songbirds your dark irises
seeing you on a map
I discover my own geography
looking at myself in the mirror
I see your unrecognizable face
badly sewn together blood-covered degraded
on the operating table
of international politics

*****

I squeeze out your juice
so that later you won't say
that you're fertile and undulating
with fields of blue clover
yellow broom
that your flag has the sun on it
in this endless winter I put you in the juicer
wizened juiceless orange
milk without a moon
emaciated cow guilty
unwed mother
of so many militarists
forever in the unhealing abscess
of a forever suppurating
wound

*****

242

give me a razor blade to cut down the obelisk
so that no poor gentleman
will ever be so unfortunate
as to fall out of an airplane
and get it stuck up his ass

*****

the last to have died
were already dead
and amid the dust and gunpowder
men and women assembled in the plaza
with rifles slung over their shoulders
not just to
celebrate their victory
but to organize a new life
the men built transparent worlds with their voices
the men carefully chose
presidents
ministers
generals
builders of bridges and roads
captains of ships
school officials
railway inspectors
soldiers to defend the borders
the men chose and chose men
until there wasn't any cake left to share
then they realized that the plaza was still filled
with shining-eyed women with rifles slung over their shoulders
and they sent them back to their homes with speeches
to wash to iron to give baby bottles
to future men of the new nation
the men sent them home with speeches that said
how deeply they loved them
that they were saints and martyrs
that they were indispensable
for lighting lamps
for bandaging wounds
for cooking meals
for taking care of pigs and chickens and children
and for patiently waiting for tired husbands coming home from work

and the men declared that they were sending the women back to their homes
because women were like tender ears of sweet corn
and were different from men
because although women were brave and generous
they were different from men
and although they were capable of great sacrifice
they were different from men
and although they had fought at the side of men
they were different from them
and the women were finally convinced and laid down their guns
and returned to their homes with lustreless eyes
to wait for the men to build the new transparent world

VI   Chile

The Loyal Order of the Time-Clock

Marilú Mallet

I know I'm fat and boring. I realize it when I get to the office and, without even thinking about it, start tapping with my shoe at the loose piece in the parquet flooring. I've had this little habit for ten years now, ever since we moved here to the central building on the Alameda. I never know what to do all day long. Not that I lack imagination; but there's a certain absence of desire to be up and about. There are times when I'd like to move my desk, or stop saying hello to the others. I don't dare. Something could happen! What I admire most about Don Julián is the way he keeps busy. Don Julián is my boss. This is the timekeeper's office. My job is to wait until everybody has punched in, pick up the cards and calculate the late arrivals.

In the mornings I check the previous day's overtime. But the Ministry doesn't pay for overtime. My boss is very hardworking. He's always fitting glass into little metal tubes, very strange, though of course I know by now that he's making telescopes. Because he gradually brought in his emery wheel and other tools. He has a big brown table covered with pliers, tweezers and screws, and nobody bats an eye at the fact that he assembles telescopes in the office. Or that he only uses the phone for his private business. Or that people come to see him, and the little sofa is always full of customers, what with the acrylic sign outside that says: "Telescopes made here." I watch him for hours on end, the patient way he manages to place a tiny screw with his tweezers. One of my tasks is answering the phone and it's almost always for him, about his work, for he makes new telescopes as people order them. Or else it's the dwarfs calling. Don Julián is a skinny, nervous man. His wife is like him, very skinny. They've been married twenty years. The first son they had was a dwarf. The second son they had was a dwarf. The third one was normal. The fourth child turned out to be yet another dwarf. Sometimes I wonder if they adopted them. I admire his patience. When I watch him I get the urge to marry or move my desk, but the only thing that happens is that I've reached the second section of the paper and my leg is moving, making my foot tap on the loose piece of flooring. I read the paper from beginning to end, I don't even skip the obituaries. It's entertaining, but not very. The truth is, I'm always bored, it must be from living alone. Though I was lucky to find this boarding-house, not far from here. They don't serve breakfast, but what do you want for the price? And the house is quake-proof, after all. That's the main thing: quake-proof and hot running water.

"Azucenas! How's the old fatso?"

Guzmán and I always trade newspapers. He buys El Clarín, I buy El Mercurio, and we make the first trade at ten in the morning, then again at eleven with other colleagues. Of course, it's always the same news. At one o'clock we leave for lunch, and walk all together down Bandera Street to the Mapocho River district. I always go back to the office early. Don Julián doesn't go out. He brings a box lunch or one of the dwarfs comes with a hot dish. He's always fiddling with some little bolt that he can't screw in. In the afternoons his customers arrive and fill the office.

Today I came across a surprising news item. I talked about it over lunch with Guzmán in the Frying Fish: incredible that such a thing can happen in Chile in the twentieth century. Those poor people! And so far away! Perhaps near C—. A little later I bought a map and we realized it was near Serena in the interior. Even farther inland than where Doña Gabriela Mistral was born, much farther, right in the mountains. I tried to show it to Don Julián, but he was quite taken up toying with a minuscule nut. Guzmán called me on the intercom saying bring the map, and there we were looking, with the people from room seven fourteen, seeing where the flood was. Everybody talked a lot, especially Lucy Varela and the other secretary. Those two are always organizing meetings or demonstrations or God knows what. They say we mustn't just sit on our thumbs. I was rather impetuous. That's what I think now. Then I had the urge to do something different, something that . . . something just to show them. So I offered to get a collection going, though I'm not a great talker, I did the seventh floor and then the sixth, with my newspaper, explaining. And you should have seen what they brought! I can't even cram the stuff into my closet! I collected ten kilos of lentils, five kilos of string beans and twenty bags of powdered milk. And three cartons of old clothes. The boss was giving me dirty looks, but I went collecting on the lower floors just the same. A colleague said I should go to another Ministry to rustle up help.

Now we're into the third day of this affair and we've had to evacuate the office to make room for parcels.

"But what can I do, Don Julián!"

He doesn't know what to do with his customers. The smallest dwarfs take up position in the doorway to serve them. But what a disaster! Twenty days with nothing to eat and flooded out of house and home! It's enough to make you feel a little solidarity with others, eh?

"Can't you see we have to do something to emerge from our underdevelopment, Don Julián?" The demagogue was coming out in me.

Guzmán and I went to the Ministry of Education. They're going to send along a ballet troupe and a film when we deliver the packets. Now that's what I call assistance!

"Good old Fatso Azucenas! He's given up clock-watching!" people say to me. I never noticed before that people didn't like punching in.

The Defence Department is giving blankets, and we'll travel in their trucks. Who'd have thought it? And all I did was go around with the newspaper story. Sure, sure, I did a bit of talking, too. I know my sales pitch by heart now. And I've lost weight, that's worthwhile in itself. We're going to end the collection on Friday the 13th, not because we want to but because the

Undersecretary came along and said our motivation was good but everything was piling up in the offices. It's true, government employees are hanging around in the corridors, doing nothing but talk. Others take off downtown on personal errands. There are cardboard boxes everywhere, clothing, shoes, food, in the rooms, the toilets, the corridors, on the chairs, the desks, in the closets. I don't know why they all ask my permission, as if I were the boss. Oh, yes, I'm still in charge of the timekeeping records. But I've almost forgotten that; I seem to be in another world. We're leaving Saturday for the village of C—, in three trucks, plus a bus for the ballet troupe.

"Very well, Don Julián. I'm asking for my days off, but you should understand that I'm not going to leave a task like this to just anybody, it's a great responsibility, and letting them go by themselves is no solution, either! It's as if you handed out unassembled telescopes to your customers!"

At last he began to understand. And off I went with Guzmán for C—. Luckily I ended up in the truck with the nurses. Liliana and Gladys. And Corporal Fuenzalidas at the wheel. I'm crammed against the right-hand door, you'd have to see it to believe it: they're like me, plump as pudding, those two girls! Just my type! They work in the National Health Service and are coming along to care for the sick. The newspaper said there were people injured, and quite a few. The time goes by quickly what with talking, and anyway we had an early start at seven. The place is near Serena, in the interior. The truck follows the curves, this way and that way, and there's always a leg against mine. Gladys, she said I could call her. She gives me lots of little smiles. Is this me, Guzmán? I never had any luck with women, now I have to make a pass. The fact is, I'm shy. We had to tank up on gas and the Corporal got out with Liliana. Gladys and I, we stayed in the cab alone. She sort of snuggled up to me and I had to put my arm around her shoulders, very affectionate, as they tell it in the Ministry, and without intending to I touched one of her breasts. It's soft, I thought. And she looked at me with her little smile. Just then the others arrived. They asked:

"What's going on?"

"Funny business," said Gladys.

"Don't get any ideas," I warned them.

She told me she lived in Santa Rosa near Matta Avenue. She's separated and has a little boy. They talked about the Health Service, how hard they work, and . . . there we were in Los Vilos, time for lunch. We had seafood and white wine and got pretty happy. I started telling jokes, a thing I never do. I hear lots of them, of course, at work. We talked about my job, and about the luck of the road, for we saw a man in a loose black overcoat, with a black cat, and I'm superstitious. It happened again somewhere near Tongoi. Seeing him twice gave me the creeps. Shortly after we stopped for a Pilsener and everybody had something to say about the incident. So we were getting close to Serena, then going by the place where the famous Gabriela Mistral had lived. You should have seen me . . . I wasn't shy anymore, and I sat between the two of them, my arms around their shoulders, and giving them a pinch from time to time. What tremendous legs, Guzmán! (But where did you get to? There wasn't a sign of you anywhere!) And this was me, who'd always felt fat and boring!

We were approaching C—, up in the mountains already. What a surprise! There wasn't a soul in the place. And no flood! After some effort we did find an old man. He said they all went out in the fields, and came back just before dark.

"All of them?"

"Well . . . the people . . ." he replied.

It was a strange place. There was no village square, there were no trees, just a general store on one corner, and the main street. We got out, and so did the ballet and movie people. Liliana said it was all the fault of the black cat and the man in the loose overcoat. That evening the villagers came back from the fields and stared at us, astounded. The little old guy we'd spoken to played the trumpet. And—what a scare!—there was the man in the loose overcoat, parading in front of the public with his cat on his shoulders and a violin. It's like a tale of the possessed, I thought. I started out by making a speech about the flood and the disasters that take place in Chile. I had it all ready, and even though there was no flood I had to say something. The people watched us suspiciously. The worst thing was when we showed the movie— it was a nice film, for my taste—the people left and the children ran away crying. The ballet troupe danced to pacify them. Then the people barbecued some young llamas, fit to make you lick your fingers. And we handed out the relief packages, the blankets, the food, everything. The old clothes, too. The keeper of the general store got angry. He said we were going to put him out of business. But the village people were ever so pleased. They came, and they kept coming, you had no idea where they came from, maybe from up on the mountain. Or maybe I just imagined them all, we drank so much pisco, even Corporal Fuenzalida, who fell asleep. I went off for a chat with Gladys near a gateway where there were some bushes. . . . Did we have a nice time! Wow! We were almost caught by an old woman who came poking around there. Guzmán was chatting with Liliana. Somebody allotted a ballerina for Corporal Fuenzalida to chase. The people started singing and dancing the cueca. Gladys and I, by the gate in the bushes, went on with what we were doing and so forth. Suddenly the man in the overcoat appeared, playing the violin as he came.

"Gladys, we'd better stop!" I whispered, and jumped to my feet.

I walked over to where everybody was and started talking about the quality of the meat. I have no idea why I got to talking about white flesh . . . I'm so shy! Then a group of peasants told me they had a present for us. A thank-you gift for the Ministry. How original, eh Guzmán? Nothing more nor less than a llama! A llama with a leash just like a dog.

We spent the night in the village. I stayed at Peyuco's house, the owner of the llama. So nothing doing with Gladys. But nothing. The girls slept in the school. Next day, for lunch:

"Hey! Chicken stew with dried corn!"

We drove back. I don't know what was up with Gladys, she was playing hard to get. I rubbed my leg on hers and she moved it away. I tried it out on Liliana. Mind you, the animal didn't make things any easier. Lying with his four legs tied up at our feet. But he could move! He was a real agitator, Lord knows! He made as much fuss as two hens. I took this as my excuse to calm the girls with gentle pats, incidentally stroking Gladys' knees, but nothing doing. I slid my hand up a little further. Then she laughed the way she had before. She gave me her phone number. We agreed to get together in Santiago. I'll call her up at the Health Service. The return trip was fast. The Corporal didn't say a word all the way. Except for grumbling about a waste of time, as he called it, adding that more important things were cooking in the capital. On Tuesday at the Ministry they nearly died, they were so impressed when I walked in with the llama. Don Julián was mad because I put it in the office. Later when it filled up with his customers they all wanted to see the animal up close. One of the dwarfs began charging admission. He explained that it was to buy sweets. These kids! My boss's boss called me up:

"You can't keep that critter in the office!"

"I can't take it to my boarding-house," I said.

I went off to the zoo, intending to donate it. They liked the idea.

"But you'll have to get a gift certification from the owner."

"The owner presented it to the Ministry and the Ministry doesn't want it," I said.

I went back to the office and brought my boss's boss up to date. He wrote the certificate for me. What with all this fuss I couldn't even call Gladys, especially because the llama chewed my pocket and ate her number. . . . And imagine my surprise when the Inspector General's people brought me a summons because I had donated an object before it was entered on inventory.

"That's not my fault!" I shouted.

One sure thing is, I don't eat lunch at the Frying Fish with Guzmán any more. A poor guy just trying to do something for his country . . . no lunch for me. They say I'm still losing weight. It's ten days now since the animal arrived. The office is filthy. I clean it with loving care. The poor creature spits occasionally. "Don't worry, you'll be going to the zoo," I console him softly.

Maybe I should listen to them. They said I was summoned. It was the people in Seven Fourteen:

"Go to the Inspector General's office and ask for Don Crispín, in 'Disciplinary Measures.'"

I went, and there was no charge against me at all. It was a joke. I came back to the office about two in the afternoon and found no one there. Suddenly I heard noise and singing coming from the reception hall. I went to have a look at what was going on. There was a big laugh when I walked in. They were eating the llama. It's the old story: they resent me because of the time-cards. One man tripped me up in the doorway:

"Just wait, you son of a whore, now you're going to get my docked time right up the ass."

I left for home. On the way I met Pepe Lazo. After all these years! He comes from Chillán, just like me. He wants us to go into business together. Paper Christmas trees. We had a coffee and a chat and afterwards we went to his room. He showed me the little trees. There's nothing to it! You wrap some cellophane around the sticks and that's it! This is a good deal!

So now I'm doing the same as Don Julián. I stamp the cards and then get down to manufacturing the merchandise. A little money on the side. I bought a new suit at Falabella's. Living is so expensive. Lucy Varela and the other secretary are going around collecting gold rings for the reconstruction of the nation.

"Those two switched sides fast, eh Don Julián?"

He doesn't even answer. He's all wrapped up trying to get some little screw in its hole. People are telling all kinds of stories. Employees being arrested. Others getting fired. Many talk about torture. . . . Me, I don't pick a fight with anybody. I just look after the customers who phone. I don't even think about Gladys, or the llama, or things like helping people. I don't even read the paper. I drift with the times, that's all. Yes, I drift, and I spend the whole day making little Christmas trees to sell in December.

Morning

Lake Sagaris

Morning, red as a cigarette butt
dropped by night and forgotten
igniting grass and clouds

Morning, chased through hills
running up and down stairs
after the birds' cries

Morning, rain and sudden a clear knock
against the darkest doors

Morning, shouting to free
the light imprisoned
in an exhausted bulb

The City

Streets teem
Parks are overwhelmed by truant
children, their blue school uniforms
an inky spill on grassy pages
kicking balls around trees
hugging on park benches   men hidden
in women's kisses seen only by
the envious   a child leaps from a
bus in flight   and stumbles   the box
balanced on his palm   almost topples
the peugeot behind   almost hits him
condemns him with a sharp blow to the
horn and races on   Undaunted
the tattered boy flags the next bus
full of clients   Singing
"¡chocolate-eh! ¡chocolat-eh! ¡chocolat-eh!
¡uno en diez! ¡tres en veinti cinco pesos!"

In school our children's voices
goose-step around the national anthem
On that corner four machine gun men

push the park, the twisted river and the
children, the tattered boy, his clients and
the chocolates
into a sunset car

Santiago shudders at the noticias
pounding like blood in four million
pairs of ears

The businessmen chatter anxiously over the expresso
with creamy strudel, the pobladores
can hardly swallow their tea with bread
Children forget, their parents don't remind them
Lawyers rush to file recursos in the courtrooms
Nuns sit down on the streets, priests raise their hands
Compañeros make urgent phonecalls, the government makes
announcements, the police make denials, a helicopter
        carrying God
leaves for hell

Curfew drops its load of darkness on the city
Santiago stares blindly into nightmares
A cry explodes in an empty field   Songs lie
dismembered on the grass
Sunrise lifts the curtains and shines boldly
into the funeral parlour, shirtsleeves up and
wrinkled, dry palms rub together

Saturday struggles into existence but
nobody pays attention, radios bleat and
sigh, but lovers take their leave, the
sky is a deep endless blue, but no one
wants eternity today

At 7:15 the twilight stained city holds its
children a little more tightly, mothers become
widows, fathers wave see you later and
sink into memory, children start up
frightened by their own deaths

Santiago has entered the morgue
labelled "NN"

two men were kidnapped
three deaths have been announced

from Coming to Jakarta

Peter Dale Scott

IV.xv

But when you control
       most of the world
      you cannot stop

it has been managed before
         so you are expected
      to manage it again

the cunning plan
         becomes in the streets of Santiago
      a biblical whirlwind

Jakarta is coming
         in *Tribuna* a photograph
      of General Baeza

who led the assault
         on the presidential palace
        when they machine-gunned Allende

holding up in his hand
         the justifying card
      Djakarta se acerca

mailed to military officers
         to make them believe
        they were scheduled to be liquidated

just as officers in Jakarta
         had been made to believe
        they were scheduled to be liquidated

after the CIA
         in Santiago was instructed
      to author conclusive evidence

Allende government
        planned to take country by force
    while the same card

Djakarta se acerca
        had been mailed to leftists
        and published in *El Siglo*

the aim the CIA
        had explained in '61
        was to polarize Laos

where Hecksher had been Station Chief
        before presiding in Santiago
    over the so-called *abduction*

of the constitutionalist General Schneider
        and so three years later
    Z

the alleged secret plan
        to murder the chiefs
        of the armed forces

and the formal excuse for the coup
        Jakarta Jakarta
        there was no truth wrote David Phillips

to the belief of Mrs. Allende
        whom I know to be a fine person
        that CIA was behind the coup

but when we talked
        before the Susskind show
        your right eye twitching

in its efforts to disrupt
        your attempt at a guiltless
    television smile

I could still not bring myself
        to be its accomplice and proclaim
    you murderer liar or even

256

Chief of WH Division
　　When *CIA agents*
　　in Santiago assisted

in drafting bogus Z-plan
　　documents alleging
　　the Allende and his supporters

were planning to behead
　　Chilean military commanders
　　and delle Chiaie's Aginter contacts

appear to have been active
　　in the bombings and riots
　　of *Patria y Libertad*

supported by Kissinger
　　and the 40 Committee
　　Djakarta se acerca

before *P y L*
　　joined with the military
　　in the mop-up brigades

many of whose
　　maybe 30,000 victims
　　were *tortured to death*

the bodies sometimes
　　disfigured beyond recognition
　　headless corpses like logs

clogging the Nuble River

Waiting for Godot

Leandro Urbina

for R. Parada

The gunfire downtown has intensified in the last half hour. The radio has started to broadcast threatening statements. Two airplanes have passed overhead on their way to the north end of the city, and now they cross the sky in the opposite direction, roaring over our heads. The skinny shopkeeper shouts out, "They're going to bomb the son of a bitch." Some workmen from the brewery watch him in silence. I'm waiting for my brother who has a job at the Ministry of Public Works. My mother sent me. She says Chito is a bit crazy and might stay outside and not obey the curfew. That's what I'm doing when, to my right, my English teacher appears around the corner, walking with difficulty. I haven't shown up at school for the last couple of days. He recognizes me, brings his myopic eyes and pale face close to me and says, sternly, "What are you doing standing here, Fernández?" "Waiting for Godot, sir," I say to him jokingly, knowing that is his favourite play. Just then, with an infernal noise, the first bombs explode over government house. Before us we see two great columns of smoke rising toward the sky. My teacher clutches my arm with his large hand and says to me, trembling, "Don't wait any longer, Fernández. Godot's not coming today, you'd better go home."

Our Father Who Art In Heaven

While the sergeant was interrogating his mother and sister, the captain took the child by the hand to the other room.

—Where is your father? he asked.

—He's in heaven, whispered the boy.

—What's that? Is he dead? asked the captain, surprised.

—No, said the child. Every night he comes down from heaven to eat with us.

The captain raised his eyes and discovered the little door in the ceiling.

Portrait of a Lady

for Valentina

In the light of dawn that filtered timidly through the window, she smoothed her dress carefully. One of her fingernails cleaned the others. She moistened her fingertips with saliva and smoothed her eyebrows. As she finished arranging her hair, she heard the jailers coming along the passageway.

In front of the interrogation room, remembering the pain, her legs trembled. Then they put a hood on her and she crossed the threshold. Inside was the same voice as the day before. The same footsteps as the day before came over to her chair, bringing the damp voice right up her ear.

—Where were we yesterday, Miss Jiménez?

—We were saying that you should remember you're dealing with a lady, she said.

A blow smashed into her face. She felt her jawbone crack.

—Where were we, Miss Jiménez?

—We were saying that you should remember you're dealing with a lady, she said.

The Fence

Jorge Etcheverry

When he went out
they would only stare at his back,
avert their faces in some false distraction,
like a barren plain suddenly opening up in the middle of the street
in the thick of the crowd.

Leaving a place, a group of people,
he would hear a foreboding like the wind whispering
as it blows across vast grasslands, wheatfields.

Like an ceaseless murmur.
Then he would make his boots heard
and would walk around slowly
with his cartridge case open.

The Torturer

It's as if the meat weren't meat
Nor humans, human
As if the girl
Or the fruit vendor on the corner
Or the newsboy, say,
Were masks ready to fall
As if they hadn't any flesh, or bones, or tongues
As if death weren't death
Being alone
Trying to knead mute bloody
Clay
Knowing that outside there are still so many, so many others.

Embers

The embers smouldered beneath the ashes
The fire had to be put out completely
But after throwing water on it over and over again
it was obvious that a subterranean heat could still be felt
if the open hand were held close
about a foot away
"You can't ever be totally sure. Things happen."
That, and the singing of crickets
and the possibility of sudden fire in the night.

Recommendations

Don't smoke at night
Consider every civilian your enemy
Make the uniform respected wherever you go
More than anything else
Uphold the prestige of your weapons
The school tradition
The name of the homeland
Remember especially
Not to speak to anyone on the street
Not to take your finger off the trigger
Don't accept cigarettes from strangers
Walk in pairs
Mentally repeating the current password to yourself
Don't keep anything from a raid
And above all
Show no weakness
Never forget the password

from Homage to Victor Jara

Patrick White

IV

Prison-commandant at the bottle-neck
   spotted you in the stadium
      Estadio Chile
where the new prisoners came in
   miming the guitar
       you Victor Jara
snake-killer
   are you here
      with your songs and ideals
your clever hands
   the talented popular man
      I struggled into uniform
to be recognized
   my true abilities
      walking the line
while you philandered

   and you were
      of flesh and blood
fear and bolstered courage
   long nights with your wife
      the anaesthetic horror
of your last poem
   the death of friends
      days on earth
flying against the windowpane
   and at night
      listening for the serpent
unsteeled memories
   plunging into your blood
      they shall end all this
testing the air with their tongues
   swollen and gorged on hearts
      killing poets and philosophers
murdering the peasant who wanted a window
   the man who asked for bread
      here in the locker-rooms of death

on the playing -field of murder
    bleachers of horror
        the new Olympics
the audience gathered
    the commandant nervous
        before his first gig
recasting the discipline of his hatred
    moulting his humanity
        aching to come in the mouth
of the world in
    the mouth of everything
        the axe
striking twice
    the fingers of both your hands
        falling before you
the blinding white light of pain
    coating your eyelids
        the black soporific orchid
screaming in a shower of shattered glass
    from the greenhouse
        deep in you brain
death washing you downstream from Joan
    invisible arms about you
        the commandant beating
your body
    falling upon you with his fists as if
        he couldn't kill you enough
the boy from southern Chile
    working beside his father
        playing out parts
singing lightly
    the young poet
        NOW SING YOU MOTHERFUCKER
SING
    getting up raising
        your truncated candelabra
leading the stadium in a chorus of
    the Unidad Popular before
        the pre-emptory chatter of
stupefied machine-guns breaks like
    involuntary applause

To Someone Listening

Elias Letelier-Ruz

When they've been found—
        in a black trunk
        in a dark room—
who will position the stars?

And when we cut new paths
where will our steps lead us?

When will the search end:
when the sun is taken for the moon?

Now, our people,
disguised as fireflies,
begin to shine.

Barefoot Funeral

And the living were turning into steam,
red coming out of the earth,
and from the sky,
hanging like icicles of rusted metal,
the scream,
the sigh
and the calm of the human eye.

And there were the fox,
the hyena
and the frightened bird
that stopped in mid-flight
and opted for walking, testing out the space.

And the old men,
seated in front of their graves,
looked at the walls for the forgotten portrait;
and with a cosmic roar
that, with blood, mourned all the stars,
they made the dead speak,

to fight with their broken bones,
to awaken the people in the middle of the war.

And the servants by mandate.

The women of my country,
so forgotten,
conceived to give birth
like the cows give birth;
then were themselves left without stables,
were themselves alone;
and from grave to grave they went,
marching to rearm the country.
And they became guerrillas,
and they were called terrorists,
and they reclaimed justice,
organizing the resistance.

And the children, with their limitlessness,
with the profound power of their smiles,
with their children's strength and hands,
paid with their lives, battling
the egoism of capital,
the egoism of the very few.
It means,
finally,
that the children were dying
the way rats die;
and they continue dying in my country,
like a dream hunted by a shotgun
within the same dream.

Sorrow arrived like this in my country
when everyone was waiting for spring.

And when the young,
in the street,
poised their warm pollen on top of the scream,
there simply flourished a death.
And then,
then, each death was a complaint,
then every complaint another death;
until the sabres
interrupted their rusting
and, from the walls, grew wings,
and, imitating the thunderbolts,
left for the war without a farewell.

I

Jorge Cancino

my shoes don't know anything about the seasons of the year if it's winter or summer fall or spring they only know how to walk and walk night and day with rain and heat taking me from one place to another without knowing where to find the cordonnerie parisienne and the palace canary was found to be out of tune this morning the canary national investigation unit detained it on suspicion the wall is whiter every day it looks like aspirin I get out of my chair before an electric storm descends on me and the darkness discharges the knife is a dangerous weapon especially for steak and on the other side of the sheet there is no one they must have gone out to buy a pencil to write something on this side and the breasts cannot get into the senate because it is prohibited under the constitution morale and other unoralities recently the day that I changed myself into a bird I realized that liberty was a myth they downed me with a slingshot and there are erasers for rubbing out sins the only thing that opens the way to beauty is reality it was the spring and the trees were bare the leaves had disappeared because of the political social and moral crisis of the forest in the factory they are giving pink slips to the workers it's all right as long as they're not death certificates a nuclear explosion destroyed the word people were left more dumb than dead I am now twenty-one years old I think that the earth is square like the people of my long and narrow country and that soccer balls are round the channels of the city filled up with shit those on television too and the fly took off backwards just when the cops arrived and they broke the flyswatter and the narrowness of the long corridor in the lock kept me from preventing the violation of my sisters and of human rights and also from cutting off the executioner's testicles god entered the paradise discotheque and got lost between the salsas and meringues two plus two four god plus god nothing two plus one triangle of lovers life is a great stage where men and women must act every day at whatever cost and without a contract the woman who is most loved is the other man's the word travels from mouth to mouth in all languages where men and birds have a similar independence of flight it all depends on the hunter of words of birds and on the calibre of the firearm the abandoned bottle in the attic longs for the taste of wine smashed to bits on the floor they took all my books all my papers my notebooks my penthouses my playboys my selected works and others not so much my condoms my song books my free time the identity card from the university the one from the party the portrait of my grandfather the photo of my mother and the one of louis armstrong the records of bix and brel a song by marlene dietrich that said that flowers dance in gardens of spring to the lullaby of the warm wind soft the sun stripped of clouds lights up the fiesta with colour and the aroma of our love the only things saved were in a desk drawer a sheet of paper an eraser and a pencil in the end it's never late to begin again and along with inventing liberty humans created laws that prohibit alcoholic speeding being poor pissing in dark harmony with the wall writing with the left hand making love in parks in hotels in automobiles on the beach against trees in someone else's bed in your own bed in the alleys in the country in the hall because it's a sin it is forbidden to be a homosexual communist dissident be an atheist be ugly be black be a dwarf be a person be indian be human be a suicide it is forbidden to live freely you're not allowed to scream I shit absolutely on all the powerful and their fucking laws! I would be antisocial a subversive and all I want to say is that I shit absolutely on all the powerful and their fucking laws!

Poem No. 66, from La ciudad

Gonzalo Millán

Were the streets wet?

No. They were dry.

Was it cold?

No. It was hot.

Was it winter?

No, summer.

What time was it?

Late.

Was the house dark?

No. The lights were on.

What colour was the automobile?

Grey.

How many automobiles were there?

Two.

What colour was the other automobile?

Grey.

Was anybody on the street?

No.

Had the curfew begun?

Yes.

Were the streets being patrolled?

Yes.
The city was quiet.
The streets were empty.

Were the children awake?

The children were sleeping.
The children play all day.
The children were tired.
The children were sleeping.

Did you hear the automobiles pull up outside?
No.

What were you doing when the automobiles arrived?

There were dishes in the dishwasher.
I was washing the plates.
The man was tired.
The man was sitting in the armchair.
The armchair is comfortable.
Several men entered the house.
Basketball players are tall.

Bodyguards are hefty.
A woman opened the door.
She's thin.
Our house is the first on that block.
It's white.
The bakery is around the corner.
The man got up from the armchair.

How were the men dressed?

Normally.

Were they wearing uniforms?

No. They were dressed as civilians.

What were they like?

Basketball players are tall.
Bodyguards are hefty.

Afterwords

Lorna Crozier

A man is nothing.
A snake even less.
They put a hollow tube
like a drinking straw
between his lips.
In this, they force a snake,
stuff the opening with cloth
soaked in gasoline,
set the cloth on fire.
The snake explodes
down the man's windpipe.
It goes crazy in his lungs,
the man goes crazy.

A snake is not a life,
a woman even less.
Inside a woman's mouth
they saw a rat.

You ask me about Chile.
This is why it's so hard
to tell you.

There are sounds
we don't want to know
the meaning of animals
that live inside us.
We must learn their language—
words to calm a snake
churning in our lungs,
words to make a rat
lie still.

Chacabuco

Tito Alvarado

Barbed wire
A town fenced in
Chacabuco
A town forgotten
Ghost or skeleton wandering through dark dust
moaning in a corner of hated sand,
crouched watching the street from rachitic houses.
Wind or memory opening doors
or windows onto the barren horizon
in the quiet hours of the mind.
Friend or fear, watching the prisoners,
guarding, because of an error on the calendar, living heroes
who wait on a corner spattered with portraits.
Revulsion or shit master of a gun
decreeing total war
on the poem saved in an imaginary pocket.
Chacabuco
camp concentrated by barbed wire
lightning condemned to explode.

Bong

Daniel Inostrosa

I walk about peacefully in this cell on the tenth floor of Parthenais Prison. Sometimes I look out the window at the Jacques Cartier Bridge that crosses the St. Lawrence River and joins Montreal to the South Shore.

I'm in a placid state of mind. The guards view me with distrust: maybe all the other murderers break down, pace their cells obsessively, or try to explain their innocence to whomever is at hand. Not me.

In 1973, during the coup d'état in Chile, I was arrested by troops from the Navy. They took me to a barracks where they beat me savagely for no apparent reason, perhaps simply because I happened to work for the bureau of revenue and taxation, as I had done for years under various administrations. Politically speaking, I had become a teetotaller: that is, I completely abstained from consuming or imbibing any form of what is known as political militancy. My grey and reserved persona had enabled me to survive in the civil service, and my wide knowledge of the fiscal archives, coupled with my good character, had always allowed me to act as advisor to new employees whenever there was a change of government.

I was in my early thirties at the time, and my sole responsibility was to my widowed mother, whom I visited every other Sunday. She lived in Talagante, a delightful town fifty kilometres outside of Santiago.

Due to my shyness with the opposite sex, I had never married. This doesn't mean, though, that a few of my girlfriends hadn't tried to trap me by inviting me over for dinner and introducing me to the whole family, including the cat. I was sometimes tempted to declare myself officially engaged to one of them just to avoid the loneliness of my bachelor apartment and to flee forever from suppers of canned soup; but solitude also has its charms. As for other necessities, I would visit a discreet house on the outskirts of the city, where I was always respectfully received and where the same young woman from the provinces always took care of my needs. This enabled me to get through the week without undue irritability.

When the troops at the barracks finished beating me, they dragged me out to a patio where I was left for hours with my feet and hands tied. This physical position, along with the mental anguish and uncertainty that I felt, made the minutes seem like centuries. The soldiers finally decided to move me to a small cell originally built to hold six prisoners, but now containing fifteen. I spent a day there, after which I was again taken to the patio and tied up.

That evening a group of hooded men, accompanied by a lieutenant with his face uncovered, appeared on the patio and told me that they had invented a game in order to keep themselves amused. From now on, I was to be a bell. They hoisted me up by my feet and hung me upside-down from the branch of a tree. Then they pulled me back and let me swing forward, and I was supposed to say "Bong!" at the exact moment that my head hit the tree trunk. Every time they let go of me, I tried to chime as I had been told to do, but I was so scared of the impending blow of my head against the tree that there was always an interval between the blow itself and my cry of "Bong!" At one point the lieutenant grabbed me by the front of my shirt and said, "Do you know why you'll never make a decent bell? Because you Reds don't believe in God. You can't hear the call of holiness."

His blue eyes and curly blond hair have remained engraved on my retinas forever. I don't want to bore you, but after my head had struck the tree many more times, during which my "Bong" never coincided with the impact, they threw me back half-dead into the cell. Ever since then I've suffered from terrible headaches that haven't diminished at all over the years.

Later I went into exile, first in Argentina and then in Canada. I've tried as best I could to forget the whole experience, but I've never been able to. So when I was passing by an Italian restaurant on the corner of St. Urban Street and Laurier Avenue here in Montreal a few days ago and happened to glance inside, I immediately recognized the same lieutenant, smiling and well-dressed, though perhaps a little fatter. There was no doubt about it: it was him.

I skipped work and waited on the corner, and when he left the restaurant I followed him to his hotel on Park Avenue, where he disappeared into the lobby. I waited a few minutes and then went in myself and told the woman at the reception desk that I found myself in a rather ridiculous situation: I was looking for a Latin American friend who was staying in the hotel, but I couldn't remember his last name, and if she would only be so kind as to let me look over the guest registry, I was sure that I would recognize my friend's name as soon as I saw it written out completely. The only Spanish name I found was Juan Ponce, Room 32. I smiled regretfully at the receptionist, shaking my head as if I hadn't seen anything encouraging. Then I thanked her and went out into the street.

I sat down at the window of a café across the street, from where I had a clear view of the entrance to the hotel. I ordered a beer and settled down to wait.

Two hours later, just as I was getting ready to leave and look for someplace else to watch from, the lieutenant reappeared, fresh as a lettuce, and began walking down the street, slowly reading the menus on the doors of the various cafés and restaurants that abound in that part of town. I followed him until he finally entered a Greek place and found a table.

I also went in, took a table on the other side of the room, and asked for a menu. My torturer finished making his choice and got up to go to the washroom. I waited a few seconds and then followed him in. When I entered, he was washing his hands. I stared straight at him, almost smiling. He looked at me out of the corner of his eye; he must have thought that I was a deviant of some kind. I stood staring at him without moving. This time he turned toward me and frowning slightly he slowly asked me in laboured English, "Do I know you?" I lifted my left hand and grabbed him by the hair, while with my right I stabbed him directly in the heart, and looking straight into his eyes I told him "Bong!"

Remember Me

Nelly Davis Vallejos

for Laura Allende

When you see my comrades
gathered in the shadows,
remember me.

When you hear a tortured scream
in the middle of the night,
remember me.

When you see the crowds
surging forward with anger in their eyes,
remember me.

When you smell the explosives
that liberate my people from the tyrant,
remember me.

When you hold a clandestine diary
secretly in your hands,
remember me.

When you think you hear the footsteps
of your murdered brother at the door,
remember me.

When the sun rises
on the night of our dead,
remember me.

When the hour of our triumph
over the paralysis of hate draws near,
remember me.

When the waters of the rivers of Latin America
flow together into one,
remember me.

When the voice of our peoples

rises up to the stars,
remember me.

When we sing in peace and work,
remember me, remember me,
for I have never forgotten
what I learned from your blood.

Ritual

for Francisco

On rainy nights,
while celebrating the rite of love,
we have travelled
with the storm,
the wind
and the ocean's swell.

We are like small animals
naked
playing,
searching for the vital oxygen of life,
like fish,
birds
and deer.

On rainy nights,
my heart is a delicate vial
that the warmth of your mouth
awakens.

And my being bends forward
like a vessel
of clay
trembling
at the wisdom of your hands
of a knowing potter
of a patient
and tormented architect.

Regard to Neruda

Pat Lowther

When I heard that
the world's greatest poet
was running for president:
being north american
I would have laughed, until
I thought of the campaign trek
over country that was
his blood and bed,
the persistent human song
for which he became
rivers, harps of forests,
metallic skies of cities.
and I thought also
of the tenderness implied
in his handshake.

Could I see with his high vision
(man with thick hands and belly
full of good things)
the naked feet of beginnings,
the sons of rare minerals
transforming the earth,
could I wash my country
with songs that settle
like haloes on the constituents,
I'd campaign
to be prime minister
without kisses.

Often now I forget
how to make love
but I think I am ready
to learn politics.

The Return

Tom Wayman

The poet comes back.
After the agony in the great stadiums
suddenly converted into prisons:
the torture of the young woman
in the corridors under the bleachers,
the rape and beating of the journalist's wife
while he is watching, the daily executions,
the electrode making contact again and again
on the body of the student strapped face-up on the table:
its black point darting in like the tongue of a snake
now searing the scrotum with terrible pain, now the tip
of the penis, now the inside of the lower lip,
the nipples, the tongue, now the eye is forced open
and the electrode brought down toward the pupil . . .

After his body is stilled, the poet returns.
He knows that on one jailed the former Ministers of Health
when the new government began for the first time
to distribute milk to the poor.
But the hands of a woman who worked in that program
now never stop shaking.
No one wished to interrogate the local executives
of a foreign mining company
about the long years of sorrow and sweat wrung out of Chile.
But there is a miner who lay on the concrete and bled inside
from the kicks of the police, until he died.
And no one sent for a squad of torturers from America
to investigate those Americans found living in Santiago
after the election. But a certain unit of the Brazilian military
instructed in the American school in Panama, and in their own country
flew in to begin processing their countrymen
discovered after the coup to have previously fled into Chile.

And there is a woman who heard so much screaming
she can no longer utter a sound.
There is a body dropped from an Air Force truck
into the street of a slum, that only on close examination
can be seen to have been a woman.

But the poet comes back.

His breath, his voice, his book
once again begin journeying.
His country goes down again
into the horrible night of its continent
but the poet continues to move.
Everywhere he comes to the poor like a man in trouble
and is taken in or not depending on their nature.
Those who receive him risk everything
just as though they hid again the living fugitive
but, as before, when he leaves he departs as their friend.
Those of the poor who are fearful, and turn him away
go on being poor, being frightened, still waiting
for the miraculous knock on the door that they know
will one day arrive to show them a better life.

The poet goes on. His words
are specks of light gleaming out of the darkness.
Death surrounds us all, but his words
go on speaking out of the blackness.
Hunger still sits in the stomach
like an egg soured into a chemical burning in the guts.
The muzzle of a gun is still pressed against the head of a man
who is shot before he can say a single syllable.
The voice of the poet is powerless to stop this.
The man who is beaten, his front teeth
snapped off under the sticks of the police
—he, too, loved the sound of the fresh salt wind
pouring in continuously over the waves of the sea beach . . .

But to everyone left numb
in the silence between these cries of agony and despair
the poet's voice goes on talking, calmly, persistently.
Also through the long drudgery of a lifetime
it keeps offering to those who have lost them
the words that mean a gift of the earth.

The poet says: "They burned my house in Madrid,
the house of flowers, geraniums, and a green horse.
They pulled down my house at Isla Negra,
brought down its great ceiling beams carved with the names
of dead companions, lowered my flag: sea-blue, with a fish on it
held in and let free by two chains.
And when I saw the house of poetry was destroyed again

I knew that poetry now would be most needed elsewhere.

"So I began travelling. When I was alive
I took my place in the struggle. Now I am dead
my voice still speaks, ringing like a vast silence
which is really a mouth, filled up one by one
by those who take up my cry, which is their cry,
sounding our words together, drowning out torture
and the police, louder, drowning out hunger and fear,
louder, drowning out sickness and want, louder and louder,
speaking our life on this planet as loud as we can
until at last we drown out death."

Santiago Under the Sun

Hernán Barrios

The city received him with the whispers of a cover-girl, showering his fingernails and forehead with its contact of asphalt spattered with petunias, beggars, and women oiling their buttocks in cotton that was sanforized, non-perishable, unsugared, impervious to the rhythm of nipples and hips. The sun came pouring through the corners of his glasses, like a yellow weasel biting at his eyelids, his lumbar vertebrae, where droplets of sweat were suddenly incarcerated like filibusters in a foreign frigate. He walked unhurriedly, digging his feet firmly into the surface of the sidewalk, at times caught up in the howling of the traffic or in the purring of the automatic sprinklers that scattered their freshness into the heated air. Here he was, home again, *en casa, chez lui*, with hands a bit moist, eyes dilated, and his most important muscle inflating and deflating like the breathing of a leopard in ambush. He walked in the shadow of houses, lined up mutely along the edges of his eyes that tried to remember a gesture left motionless so many years before. It was as if those objects had never disappeared, had never left this apparition that stood out against the light at the ankle of the mountain, because this was a city of mountains, of truck exhausts that lashed out at space, like brambles rearing up in fear; the city held onto the cosmos like a hunchbacked nova ashamed of its hump before the splendour of the stars. He had come here to invent a new heartbeat, a zero with suspension marks, with transverse rays that would be suffused with light. Tired of living in the penumbra, he was returning to a place where actions were struck from the soul, where time flowed backwards contrary to the movement of his Seiko with its chromed watchband that was fastened to his wrist with the determination of a Japanese battleship on watch in Nagasaki. Under pincers of light glistening in the early afternoon, his soles pecked at the pavement, going along streets peppered with shadow, where walls as white as frameless mirrors thundered in their isolation the absence of birds. He had returned, perhaps to be snared again in the stickiness of guns, potatoes in mayonnaise, and philodendrons, to the brilliance of a childhood afternoon in the foam at the beach in Cachagua, to the ceremonious parade of ants the colour of chocolate dividing the sidewalk tiles into two parallel universes, black, white, evil, good, right, left, northern hemisphere, southern hemisphere, paradise and hell. How he would have liked to have been a Victorian explorer, Mungo Park *por ejemplo*, cutting through lianas without doubting himself, his faith, his loud moustache, or the amber whisky riding tightly in the back pocket of his pants. It was difficult enough to come back without a rôle, but even worse to watch the stage without being able to change the libretto, because this country's script had been written in pencil, obviating the advances of modern typography that call for the publisher's imprint and double spacing. The producers were inventing the rules from Miami; they were still confusing Guatemala with Peru and Uruguay with Ecuador: *those Hispanics are all alike, you know.* This country, that country, was after all his by right of his father, mother, grandparents, and great-great-grandparents who had put their helmets, breastplates, and shields into the belly of the willows and brambles with all the carelessness of people who are unaware of the virginity of wilderness or the luminescence of what is untouched by iron, religion, and scurvy. They had taken over a world of wizards, lapis lazuli, animal blood, and the smell of jasmine that now reached him iridescent from exposure to the centuries, the computers, the Bostonian executives, the hunger, the discovery of the atom, of hertzian waves, and of toilet paper. He walked along breathing in the drowsiness of the Saturday afternoon streets when everything is living inside, within garden courtyards, as if reciting a childhood prayer learned without knowing why or for what reason the words were being said, words that are nevertheless so much like repose, like a way of slowing down one's stride, any stride. It was on afternoons like these that Eduardo used to talk to him about Benares, about the boils of Karl Marx, that old German-Jewish grandfather who invented the favourite metaphysical aerodynamics of our time, about *the social thing* and so many other diverse topics that dwarfed the police news and all the articles about Hemingway's massacres of antelopes, train platform love affairs, and deaths beneath bulls' horns.

Options and circumstances in a country where children sometimes played with scabies while the military amused themselves with electric shocks and Belgian divas in gigantic operas written by a deaf musician and directed by a little blond cripple with a silk tie and a flashy sports car. He was walking along and sliding back in time with an outboard motor into the Amazon, scanning the transfigured shore of trees as black as monks, shrinking space, the interstellar universe, the Milky Way *au complet*. This lair attracted him like the honest perfume of Estela's apron, which used to frighten him as a child, along with fears of thunder, of earthquakes, and of all the world's other cataclysms. That usually happened when the cataclysms occurred on the outside; now that they gestated from within, *dentro del cuerpo*, in the interior of the soul, there weren't any thighs to hide between, no fresh smell of carrots or garlic and pepper to calm life lived live, *en direct*, like a sharp pain in the heart, without the right to chloroform or to a peppermint to distract his fear. "A peppermint," she told him that afternoon after making love, her rumpled skirt lying under a wall of portraits of a retinue with shotguns hunting on the shores of the Adriatic, which framed them like set of a detective movie: Balkan princesses and buffoons in knickers, with hunting horns and misty eyes. A peppermint to freeze our breaths that use up this air, this country, this continent, this world which he and she once owned. Maybe that was the difference: now he wasn't the landlord anymore, but instead the tenant of a space that didn't fit him, even in fahrenheit, in the usual northern temperature. He lit a cigarette at a street corner without changing pace, his mouth dry, inhaling the smoke suddenly, a cloud of memories emerging from the myriad circumvallations of his medula cortex like vampires in a full moon, breathing him in to the last drop of blood, to that instant which was so well sustained by the grace of two percent homogenized milk, one pound steaks, and strawberries from California.

We people of an earlier time, he told himself, were no longer the same; or rather we ourselves were no longer of former times, and never had been; we were always people of the moment, of now, of the time with which we were never able to merge, which we could never keep in a little music box next to a porcelain ballerina called Tamara, Isadora, or Scheherazade. But perhaps it was too late for questions or answers, and all that was left was the counting-up: one, two, three, that's it, and he entered the water suddenly feeling the cold of the river on his face, chest, and ribs, swallowing water while dodging away from José Luis, who came at him with his impeccable Australian crawl; he choked on more water, at last feeling the other bank, and his father lifted him out, shouting "you're my son, you're like a tiger," and he emerged and collapsed panting with his cheek stuck to the stones where butterflies with orange and black crosses spiralled upwards, setting the afternoon on fire. Counting up this and that, more *boleros*, more kisses, more bullets, more tunes by Manzanero, the Mexican dwarf who made a fortune singing because kids have so many complexes that they're sentimental, as his Aunt Mary used to say while putting a red cross-stitch into her emerald green fabric. "Esmeralda, Daughter of the River," was the name of the soap opera on the radio that his mother would listen closely to on those childhood afternoons when everyone felt so much like the son or daughter of a particular place, that they were formed by it, belonged to it, to a country, to a certain party, team, class, love, to a certain kind of orgasm, of the singing variety, or to a specific religion, lodge, parliament, neighbourhood or wine: Santa Carolina Three Star, buddy, better than a Frenchwoman reeking of Chanel after three hundred days without it, man. So much of something, though of course it was now rather a question of being without anything, that the words sounded like the name of a Chinese emperor from the Third Dynasty; so much being without or not being of any particular thing wasn't very important now at this point in life, a life badly led down the pathways of the imagination, of the infinite moment, which, like all infinite moments, was actually very finite, in spite of certain indications that time might itself be round, and eternity an instant in this somersault of mirrors called memory. "Forever," she had said, moist with kisses, without spikenard or seashells, to the tapping of an old Venetian blind and the lash of bougainvilleas tearing at their noses.

His cigarette was already dying out between his fingers as he began walking along an avenue bordered with trees that stood in Indian file like motionless ocean liners. He was back once again at the first square on the chessboard, trying out poses that might help him adapt to the landscape, poses that his blind body immediately recognized. Things adjusted themselves to his hands, whether they were light switches, glasses, forks, bottles, belts; or to his height, like chairs, bar counters, sandals, buses, as if he had never left this Andean universe of jasmine, shoe-shine boys and itinerant knife-sharpeners, all of it wrapped up in smog, neon, and pisco with lemon. Sweet and bitter mixed together into a cohesive paste of unexpected arabesques, in an art of birds splashing about in the water. "The arabesques on this tablecloth, son," his father used to tell him many years before, as he took another spoonful of soup, "are remarkable not only for the great skill of their crochet-work, but because they are the veils of a soul hidden within their threads, the soul that holds in place the wine glasses, the plates, the place settings, the bottles, bread, salt, pepper, mustard, and wine in the midst of this world's tumult. This world into which he was once again entering, exploring, with the senses and intuition of an impala wounded by hyenas, recognizing the high pastures, the freshness of the acacias when the sun began itching at the edges of the sore. Searching in the land's irregularities for the nerves' button, for the genetic maps, for the neuroblasts, squeezing reality from the senses, until death do you part, divide, and reunite in the high sierra, the secular towers of Osiris, Zoroaster, or the Prophet Mohammed. He had returned again, to face those bald crags, unbelievably sharp, dark, and metallic like Knights Templar guarding the Holy Sepulchre. He was right here with a sweaty spine and the electron of memory jumping around like a doped-up Irish setter. Here, *il était ici*, in this city, *en esta ciudad*, without the stage lights, for better, for worse, to defend the beach against the beating of the sea.

For My Father

Claudio Durán

There we were, among sand, water
and seaweed—he, speaking humorously
and always thinking,
his abandoned height and
white mane over the waves,
under the waves, between
heaven and earth, salt
in a face made moorish
by the shadow of birds
and perfumed algae.
Under that burnt sky, with hundreds of molluscs
clinging to his stomach—
the water green, transparent;
the sand a white, temporal infinity;
the sea, behind, like a ship
of white smokestacks
and, on the waves, our longing locks,
the setting sun

The Thief

Rosemary Sullivan

Our bus careens over the backs of cars,
belches its innards. This is rush hour
any time of day. The rush is to sell.
Each furtive stop someone leaps up—
six bandaids, a safety belt,
ice trays offered in ransom
to the heat. A basket
comes down the aisle on legs.

At Alemeda we pick up an old man
in a T-shirt. He lurches in his bones
like a passenger, the smile sliding
off the side of his face.
He begs for our ears like Antony.

"Citizens, I'm a thief," he says.
"Freedom is hunger. At least in jail
we ate. I don't want to steal your purses.
Help me rehabilitate.
In our country
only the big thief eats."

We grin. The pesos drop
in his hat.

Domestic Apocalypse

Gonzalo Millán

The sheets given as wedding presents
are worn out and full of holes.
The plates have all been broken
in domestic battles.
The cups are cracked and their handles have snapped off.
Forks have been lost and the stainless
steel knives are rusting.
The blender doesn't work.
And the diamond ring's been pawned.
The dates on the wall calendar
have all been crossed out.
The clock's unwound.
There's no more tea, coffee, bread,
butter.
Only a few drops of oil are left.
The eggshells are empty.
In the refrigerator there's only
half a mealy onion
and a baby bottle with sour milk.
A mouse in its hole
is gnawing on the remains of a sugarcube.
The stove went out last night
after the fuel was gone.
The telephone's been cut off and soon
the electricity will be too.
Two or three lightbulbs in the house
still work.
The candles have burned to stubs.
The toilet paper's finished,
and the toilet itself is blocked
with pieces of newspaper.
The soap will disappear next time
someone washes his hands.
Her comb is missing another tooth.
The crack in the mirror is another wrinkle.
There are no more clean clothes left.
The washtub is full of dirty diapers.
The last button on the shirt
has fallen off.
On the table top

marks from small hands
bibs, dirty plates
with crumbs and fishbones.
Glasses with dried purple residue at the bottom.
In the empty fruit bowl, curled up,
the cat is sleeping.
The old car parked outside
hasn't started in months, years.
Its axles rest on
piles of stones and bricks.
The tires and headlights were stolen
and more parts get stripped every day,
like a huge dead insect
devoured by invisible ants.
The garden is wild, luxuriant,
invaded by weeds that have choked off everything else.
The coils of the watering hose are invisible.
The canary has escaped from its cage.
And the goldfish has drowned
and is floating belly-up
in the dirty water in its bowl.
The dog chewed through its rope
and ran away after a bitch.
The milkman doesn't come by the house anymore,
and the paperboy has stopped delivering the news.
The mailman only brings unpaid bills.
Envelopes with windows that no one opens.
The bill collectors bang harder and harder on the door,
but no one answers.
The garbageman comes twice a week
but always too early.
The garbage cans on the patio are overflowing
and stink.
The television is on, but the sound's off.
It casts flickering shadows
on the floor covered with plaster dust
drifting down from the ceiling.
A child in a playpen,
surrounded by toys
is crying and screaming its head off,
hungry, its pants wet,
humid mouth open,
eyes glazed with tears,
it is watching
the beast with two backs
snarling convulse writhe on the floor
trying to devour itself.

Soccer Love

Daniel Inostrosa

I catch your feelings in the air
with the soul of a goalkeeper
And though at times
you shoot me
an affectionate kiss
from your lover's corner
I fend it off with one hand
and kick it halfway
down the field of indifference
Sometimes
with a blind and domineering
"I love you!"
you boot in a penalty kick
from twelve yards away
It misses my face
by two inches
but I fly
from post to post
covering the net
of the heart
I can't believe that
one of these days
you'll really score a goal on me
and I'll lose the championship
forever
as well as my shirt
with a "Let's get married,
my love"

The Circus

Rodrigo González

Over a weekend, without street orchestras or sound-trucks, it burst upon the school. There were no explanations: a circus simply turns up on its own. The whole adult zoo immediately leaped into motion: "Shine his shoes with wax, straighten up his hair; if his overalls haven't been washed, get rid of the biggest stains; wipe his face before he goes out, at least with a washcloth and a lick of grandmother's saliva; give me a kiss; try to—Don't lose your ticket!" And there we are, getting ready for what could turn out to be anything, without books, but with huge question marks between our eyebrows. A circus? "A circus is just a circus! Sometimes there's animals—turn around—with acrobats, trapeze artists—lift your head up—I love circuses—stop fidgeting! Make sure your ticket's in your right-hand pocket. You'll see, and stop putting your hands in your pockets! Where'd you put the handkerchief? The ticket! I told you, the ticket goes in your right-hand pocket. Like I was saying: trapeze artists, animals—lift your head up!" But, what exactly is a circus?

Once we're out in the street there isn't any time for greengrocers' wagons, horses that make sparks fly from the cobblestones, or evangelists announcing the end of the world. Accidents, people who fall off of buses: it can all wait. Today the circus takes up all our thoughts. Circus, circus, circus, trapee-, trapee-, and animals. I wonder if they have a Sputnik? The ticket! In the right-hand pocket! Whew! The tick-et! We'd better run. Running to school? Just running! Anyway, if we're already trotting and galloping, why not run? What's more, we're not carrying any books and we've got the circus in our heads. Where's that ticket?

Everyone in the whole school has his hair combed, shoes shined, and overalls ironed—or at least pressed under the mattress. Eyes are sparkling, faces are red from having run so much; out of breath, we form a line outside the auditorium and sing the national anthem.

"*¡Puro Chileeee!*" We look around everywhere for something that might be a circus. "*¡Y ese marrr!*" An object, maybe a bit of smoke, who-knows-what machines or animals, a balloon in the sky, any clue would do. "*¡Dulce patriaaaa!*" Rokambol assures us that the circus is full of merry-go-rounds and caterpillar rides. But on the patio there are only papers and puddles of frozen water. "*¡Es la cooopia feliz del Edénnnn!*" Others contend that there are lions, bears, orang-outangs, men that fly, human cannonballs, knife-throwers. The national anthem is finally over. "Students will enter in order with their tickets in their hands! One at a time, please!"

The circus is presented with chairs lined up in front of an old discoloured curtain. Not a single roar, elephant's foot, or caterpillar ride. In silence and shivering with cold we sit down and suck on our fingers, waiting for the show to begin. We're read a list of recommendations, "Things Not To Do," that we immediately forget. The circus is gnawing at our curiosity.

Someone yells, "Curtain up!" and the rags begin to rise in little jerks until you can see the dome lit by a pair of ancient spotlights that go off and on again for no visible reason. The stage is full of shadows. There isn't any music and then suddenly, it's starting: the circus is here at last.

A child with a very large head and his face covered with rouge suddenly appears on stage and begins performing something strange with a tie. A girl who's a little taller and stronger-looking enters and folds herself over backwards; her mother and father run on stage and begin to fight. The mother walks on her hands. Another man enters and spits fire. The child with the big head comes rolling back out, and the girl and her mother start doing things that hurt, like putting pins through their throats and climbing on top of the kid with the big head and then throwing him up in the air. We sink down in our chairs. The younger students look around for their teachers.

A man in a big hat announces the clowns, and two people with white paint around their eyes, mouths stained red, and enormous gloves on their hands come jumping out across the floor. Much whistling from the man with the hat, who dons boxing gloves and begins noisily kicking and hitting the clowns, who fall to the floor, stand up, fall down, and get up again. The smallest clown staggers, falters, turns on his heels, and then finally collapses with a great crash. A cry goes up from the audience. The circus stops so that the front row of children, completely overwhelmed by their first encounter with the circus, can be evacuated. Fake coughs and sneezes arise from the spectators.

Turning up the lights calms our anxieties. The audience becomes restless; our teachers demand that we sit still. Why couldn't the circus have a Sputnik, a locomotive, one of those streetcars with soft seats, a cart full of fruit with an oil lamp and horses that whinny? Or a truck full of firemen, or preachers with accordions, guitars, and mandolins singing about the walls of Jericho? Any one of these things would have been a circus. But why does a circus have to abide by anybody's recommendations? "We're not allowed to go to the bathroom." An uncontrollable desire to take a pee invades the amphitheatre. "Don't drink any water!" and we all immediately begin dying of thirst. Is this what we were all waiting for? Nobody's concentrating on what's happening on stage now, and laughter breaks out as the teachers give us threatening looks. They make us laugh more than the clowns.

The second part of the show consists of the girl reciting a poem called "Laughing on the Outside, Crying on the Inside," after which the circus is over for good.

The porter opens the theatre door as indifferently as if it were a morgue and we stampede out to the courtyard to warm up our numb bodies. The bathrooms fill up, somebody starts up a soccer game, and we begin getting ready to go home without further comment. All the while of course we're thinking about the *churros*, chocolates, toffee, gum, and ice cream that we'll be able to buy with the money we have for the circus. The porter locks up the school and it's time to leave.

The circus itself has left us with a mixed impression of cheap clothes and children with hoarse voices who talk like adults and a terror of something indescribable that smells of very strange people.

But the worst is waiting for us outside. In the middle of the street, a no-man's-land, the "little boy" from the circus is standing there watching us with his gigantic face, while the "father," still in his circus clothes, is harnessing the horses. The "young girl," who we now see has a hairy chest and a moustache above her green-coloured lips, is selling photos of herself sitting on top of a wire clothesline, with an umbrella in her hands and lace around her waist.

Next to the cart, in a wooden crate, an enormous cat covered with sores and patches of moth-eaten fur is absent-mindedly licking its paws. "It's a lion," the girl with the moustache says. "Also known as a puma," she adds inexpressively and stares at us.

A little farther on, a gigantic bald-headed bird, suspiciously like a turkey but about twice the size, with black feathers and a curved beak, is dozing in a portable chicken-coop. "A condor," says the boy with the large head, who now invites us to follow him and terrifies us with his hoarse voice, the smell of wine on his breath, and his over-sized hands.

We stop to look at the circus wagon, investigating its axles, smelling its horses up close, watching the skin twitch on their backs as flies land on them. Sixty eyes on thirty heads feed on everything the cart contains, while the woman seated on it, who played the mother in the show, looks down at us blankly. The members of the circus are unhurriedly getting their things together to leave.

A horse with a bag over its eyes is grazing on the grass by the side of the road. Another is drinking water from a pail. Both are tirelessly switching their tails from side to side. A peanut vendor sells us cones of hard candy. The cat and the turkey, or the supposed lion and condor, start getting restless. The sun is stronger now and the day is growing warmer. A clown sitting on the curb with a face full of colours is watching us and begins making faces. He looks friendly now in the sunlight. We burst out laughing at every move he makes. Rokambol smiles and tells us that this is a real circus after all.

The circus boy has overheard us. "A circus with monkeys and little people!" he adds. "It's a dwarf!" whispers somebody in our group. "A dwarf is a grown-up who stayed small," explains another. In the midst of all the clothes and boxes being carted about, a wooden trunk suddenly appears before us. The dwarf reaches inside and takes out a light, colourful doll that he tosses onto his shoulder like a pile of rags, drags along the floor, and then throws back into the trunk, which he locks but which immediately pops open again by itself. We can't figure out what's going on, but our natural reaction is to laugh. The game is repeated; then each of us takes a try at softly closing the trunk in order to watch intently as the top springs open as if someone inside were pushing up on it. This goes on over and over again until we're doubled up with laughter.

Suddenly we freeze in surprise. The doll has jumped out and is walking down the street. Music comes out of the trunk, and the doll follows the rhythm as she spins round and round with her arms extended. It's all done with harmony and agility. Applause bursts out so loudly it seems to have come from the cement. The circus performers smile from ear to ear and throw their arms around the doll, who is, they tell us, the dwarf's son. The child waves to us gracefully, does a backward somersault, and ends up freeing the lion and playing with him as if he were a purring kitten.

Nobody wants to go near the animal, even though the performers assure us that it won't bite or scratch and that it doesn't have ringworm.

The dwarf prophesies that his son will have a radiant future; we've already adopted him as our greatest hero. We go back to the deserted school with him, boost him up to a window, and then crawl through ourselves and begin running through the halls and filling our pockets with chalk. In a burst of madness we even charge through the principal's office and go up into the long-abandoned third floor. On tiptoe and scarcely daring to breathe we follow along a safe distance behind the child acrobat and rediscover an unused laboratory and the printing room, where we pause to stock up on paper.

We want to take the adventure as far as it will go, so we return over corrugated iron roofs, garden walls and gutters. We've shown our new friend the school, and he rewards us by again offering to let us pet the lion, which we again prefer to watch from a distance.

Our friend's mother gets down from the cart to welcome us back. We're surprised to find that she is actually married to the dwarf, and that the father on stage was another performer. Her red hair and freckled skin are as amazing to us as everything else. Her son shows her the presents we've given him: chalk, paper, printed sheets, and some marbles. She tells us she appreciates the chalk, the dwarf father carries off the paper, and we all stand around looking at one another for a few minutes. The dwarf informs us of his alias, "The Pork-Rind Dwarf," and offers to show us the treasures of the circus, its tricks and props. We're fascinated by the boxing gloves, and he gives us a complete lesson on circus boxing.

Smoothness of movement, legs supple as wool, head held out, arms hanging loosely at your sides or waving about, you have to half-jump and then suddenly start thrusting your hand as near as possible to your opponent's face. The key is simply for the person who receives the blows to slap his gloves together and the sound gives the impression of a perfect punch.

We laugh until our stomachs ache as we practise at becoming experts at boxing. Then the dwarf brings out more gloves, towels, and even a bucket of water, and proposes a match pitting "The Indomitable Rokambol" against "That Ferocious Defender, The Pork-Rind Dwarf." Rokambol disappears into the circus wagon and comes out wearing red boxing gloves and shorts and begins wildly hitting out at everything except the dwarf. All of us get into the game, slapping our hands together every time "The Indomitable" pretends to land a punch against one of us. Finally it's the dwarf's turn for a whack, and

Rokambol slips up and actually lets him have it right in the face.

We all stop dead and stare at each other in horror.

But "The Ferocious Pork-Rind," a veteran clown to the end, reacts by looking stunned, spinning around a couple of times, and then falling to the ground as if it were a total knock-out.

There are screams. The girl with the moustache gives a photo to Rokambol and mimes a tightrope number with her umbrella, ending up with her foot on top of the loser of the match. The circus people laugh with us. The girl, who everyone has now realized is a man, puts his arms around Rokambol's neck and hangs on half-seriously. Our laughter is sending us into cramps.

The mother of the company surveys us from the circus wagon as she minces onions and cuts up tomatoes and red peppers to prepare the Chilean national sandwich. They're about to have lunch: "Please excuse us: tea is served," says the dwarf, as they get ready to eat before they leave.

The boxing match is now over, and we're all friends once more, so we climb up on the wagon, pet the horses again, and watch as the performers eat, wipe off their make-up, pack their bags, and divide up the take. When they've hitched up the horses and are ready to go, the dwarf ceremoniously pulls out a few wrinkled banknotes and offers them to us in exchange for a spelling-book.

"A spelling-book?" The question runs through our ranks. Even though they're hated and full of doodles, with pages ripped out and sometimes even shredded, spelling-books are one of the few things that the school has always insisted that we take care of. Nothing is more impossible than getting rid of a speller, because like it or not, a speller means learning how to read.

Suddenly somebody has an idea: whoever already knows how to read doesn't need his spelling-book anymore. Wings immediately grow on our feet and we run back into the auditorium and return with a speller that we offer the performers as a gift.

Something changes inside us as we see the dwarf, the mother, their acrobat son, the "girl," the clowns, the mountain lion, condor, and horses begin to roll forward on the circus wagon.

We run alongside them over the cobblestones for blocks and blocks, keeping up with them till they get to the cemetery. There, winded and so exhausted that we're ready to drop, we finally have to let them go.

That was the first circus that ever came to our primary school.

And of course the last.

The Follower

Renato Trujillo

A gust of wind swept the veranda. The few Indians passing by in the distance walked in silent resignation, their backs curved down, their heads covered by dusk. To Costa's eye they were only a black line against the horizon, a slow procession of ants or dark thoughts. He opened the window.

A sharp smell of damp wood hit his senses. He felt the wind against his face and closed his eyes for a second. Then he leaned his elbow on the window-sill and pointed his rifle towards the line of vanishing men. He leaned his cheek on the cold wooden butt and pressed it against his shoulder. Closing one eye, he carefully looked through the rifle-sight and aimed. In his mind, the Indians fell to the ground one by one. He could hear the wind carrying away the echo of the detonations like the lamentations of spirits doomed to oblivion.

Costa rubbed his eyes with the back of his hand. Little particles of dust had made their way into them, making them water. He retreated from the window, closed it, and propped his rifle against the wall. He turned around and a shadow like an enormous tentacle appeared before him, sweeping the cabin as if seeking him as its prey. Outside, eucalyptus and poplars swayed, drab ghosts pointing their dry, thin fingers at the dark, round sky.

Duarte came in. Without looking at Costa, he said under his breath "It's time to go," and began to gather a few belongings from the cot on the far side of the room. Costa went to the door and scanned the sky. "Rain is coming," he thought to himself. Then, as if suddenly pushed forward by a strong hand, he rushed out to get the horses, leaving the door open behind him. The sun sank like a ship in the distance where the sea lapped incessantly at the coast.

Duarte rode a few metres ahead of Costa. His long black poncho undulated a split-second behind the rhythm of his horse's gallop. There was nothing but the cold wind and a certain stabbing anxiety in Costa's spirit as he followed his partner on the long, winding short-cut through the forest. The smell of wet pine and cypress was intoxicating. At their left, the river hummed unintelligible messages which crept into their hearts, increasing their urge to reach their destination. Thunder exploded far ahead. The sun vanished and the slowly advancing evening engulfed the riders like the mouth of a tomb.

There had been times when Costa pondered the strange twists of his life, when he found himself doing what he wanted to avoid, experiencing joy and sadness at the same time. At such times, an unexpected movement, one unanticipated gesture of the spirit, could dispel his malaise in an instant. Now, propelled by a power beyond his will or understanding, he found himself galloping on a horse that shone in the dark forest as a knife's edge glitters in the night before it strikes. But now nothing came to his rescue. He urged his horse onward mercilessly, no longer wondering. Their fate was painted on

294

every leaf, at every turning of the thin road which led to Costa's cabin, first stopping-place in their race, where night would cover their eyes and sleep would come, as mysterious and restless as ever.

* * *

Costa did not regret his ordinary existence, but disregarded it. His senses became blurred, his steps hesitant. When in town, he did not go drinking in his usual places. Instead, he sat with his own bottle on an abandoned freight-car and gulped his liquor, his eyes lost in the distance. And he waited for his partner. Hours and hours of vigil passed while Duarte carried out his illicit ritual of love at the house at the edge of town, where a tiny and sinuous thread of smoke tried to reach the skies.

There are silent dialogues which defy understanding and yet can leave deep marks on people's thoughts. What mysterious lace is spun around the lives of these two men? The young man, Costa, serves an unknown purpose in Duarte's life. He is taciturn, silent as he follows the older man's path. Or is it Duarte, despite all appearances, who unknowingly plays his part in the life of Costa? The obscure designs of the southern night dim the stars. Nothing illuminates the doubts and obsessions: they stay dark, nebulous and intangible, like the moon raising itself up into the deep black sky.

* * *

Mercedes is small and agile, standing near the train-tracks washing clothes. She twists and turns the wet sheets dropping their transparent tears onto the earth, her body arching back as she throws the linen into the air. Like a flapping dove, the white sheet suspends itself in mid-air, and she sees that no wrinkle survives as it drapes itself onto the clothesline. Then she turns and, reaching into the basket at her feet, she produces another wet serpent, another sheet she and Duarte had lain on until Costa had come in whistling by the window with horses ready to depart as the lone train could be heard approaching the town.

Sometimes Mercedes and her lover take the horse and go into the woods, defying the few eyes that might see them in their make-believe nuptial procession. Costa follows at a distance, his rifle protruding from under his brown poncho. Nobody seems to notice their silent passage. Later, Costa hears Mercedes' laughter under the heavy pine trees and stops his horse, becoming as motionless as a statue of a shadow.

* * *

Mercedes' husband travels through the forest with a blue cap upon his head, unable to hear his wife's laughter. Pascual's eyes are small but piercing and he knows like no one else when to reach for the locomotive's whistle.

Anyone who has lived in these southern towns can testify that the lonely laments of the train are not in vain. Sometimes a slow cow does not hear Pascual's warnings; sometimes, it is a drunken forest-worker who fails to hear and the train crosses his body like a metallic centipede crossing a line on the ground. On such occasions, the train's cries as it groans under its load of timber and dozing workers awaken the desolate areas of people's hearts. With Pascual's help, they gather the remains from the track with the charcoal shovel and dump them into the coal-wagon. The smells of metal and death become one. It seems as if only Pascual can make men aware of the closeness of day and night, life and death.

Like all men who work amid trees and water, Pascual is not talkative. He closes the door behind him, dusting his cap against his hip. Mechanically, Mercedes stands on her toes to brush his face with her lips. The smoke billowing from the pot she had been stirring with a long wooden spoon says what their lips will not utter. A kerosene lamp throws their silhouettes against the wall. Soon there are two heads leaning over steaming bowls of soup. Feet apart under the table, they sit close enough to touch one another if only they stretched their legs. The silence outside the house increases the silence inside.

Their heads are now lying on the pillow, eyes tightly shut as they invite the night to quiet their fears. Pascual's eyes are not afraid to remain closed. They have been swallowing distance for a long time, they have plunged his machine into the future day after day, and now his hands are free from the locomotive's whistle-cord. But Mercedes' eyes flicker open many times, as if she were not sure she should welcome sleep. Her hands press her breasts as if she were afraid they would fly away to where her lover is. She waits there in the darkness for the silent, insubstantial steps of his spirit to come and kiss her goodnight.

On winter nights, she can hear the distant lament of the sea across the hills invoking his name. In the summer, it is the crickets who share her confidences, but she knows they cannot comfort her. She yearns for what is missing, and her heart is not content.

* * *

Costa's eyes were mesmerized by the running waters of the river as he sat on a putrid tree-stump damp with dismal green moss. Above his head, low hovering rainclouds were reflected by puddles scattered around his feet. Anguish and fear assaulted his indolent spirit. He looked down at his legs, his hat tilted to one side and wondered what lay at the very bottom of the water. Was there any hope? What prize would reward his efforts to find a clear path for his stride? Who was lurking there in the nearby forest?

There was no one but the image of his partner, Duarte, with a broken heart under his heavy poncho. Duarte, who didn't have to say a word: what he had found was written on his face in violent pain. His position told Costa that Mercedes lay motionless near the door, a pool of blood near her body.

There was a chill in the air which would not go away.

A cart loaded with timber passed. Only the creaking of its big wooden wheels broke the silence of the day. An Indian walked ahead holding his long driving-stick on his shoulder, the oxen following him in quiet submission. Costa took his eyes away from the water and looked at them as if he had never before seen such a sight, as if he could not understand what they represented. Sombre drums played in his chest, each beat announcing the fate his steps had reached. Tongues were meant to talk, lips to move, voices to speak. Mercedes was dead and Duarte held a sharp dagger in each of his black eyes. He moved like a shadow from town to town, village to village, his horse racing with the metal horse of Mercedes' murderer.

There was a cry from a lone bird. Costa raised his head, and Duarte's horse appeared on the other side of the water. Costa saw only a black hat which jerked to indicate that he should get up, fetch his saddle and follow. He was the follower and he nodded mournfully. A new storm was in the offing.

Anyone who knows this region will declare that when rain falls here, it falls for days and days without respite. Sometimes a whole month goes by under the gale. Wet men and humid houses welcome the sun when at last it comes, indolently, as if it were a loan to be paid back later with interest. But now someone had taken the lid off the kettle of the earth and the mist rose like steam.

* * *

And now they had left the forest and galloped along the river. The rain pierced their eyes like bullets, striking hard against their faces. The smell of the air had changed: there was no longer the acid fragrance of trees. The river gave its damp, rotten smell as a gift to the travellers' senses.

They rode in haste, racing against the night. Their horses' hooves drummed on the wet soil, and sometimes a nervous spark would glitter when a stone was touched. A simple adobe house came into view. Its poorly lit interior showed through the window. Nearby, the metal tracks lay under the weight of darkness. The locomotive was like a torn and lacerated monster awaiting some chilling command to kill or be killed.

Duarte stopped his horse and silently dismounted. Without a word, he handed Costa the reins dampened by rain and sweat and began walking toward the lonely train depot. His knife glowed for an instant, then vanished under his black cape.

Costa remained motionless in the saddle, paying no attention to the downpour, still as an effigy while his spirit sank into a mire of disastrous premonitions. He could hear the shuffling of feet, the heavy breathing, and see the force, the sweat, the fearful movements. Unfortunate is the man far from home when terror shines in his closed eyes. Unfortunate is the soul unprepared for the lament of the seas. Unfortunate are they whose hands tremble when these hours fall like an axe upon their thoughts. The lonely night and its ghosts are implacable. Every minute becomes awesome.

Costa's eyes are shut. Rain slithers down his face like tears. A subtle tremor invades the desolation. One of the horses neighs, its muscles taut. A disembodied red glow emerges as if from the centre of the earth, bathing the fields and striking the lone horseman. What is this smell of metal in the air? A slow and merciless ticking like foreign clocks rises to a crescendo in the stillness of the long night.

A horseman can be seen then, dropping the reins of a riderless horse, leaning forward in his saddle, urging his own horse to turn and run. They run towards nowhere, while a silent cry rises in the throat of the vigilant statue left behind. Then man and beast are swallowed by the other rain, the rain that pours inside a man's heart when it is late and birds no longer fly against the distant blue hills and the sea receives the rainy night with open arms and tightly shut fists.

Antimyth

Naín Nómez

This history begins with albert einstein and josé martí
this history begins with ernesto che guevara and tupac amaru

He would be a flash in the uniform night of all time
he would write the first speech with tact and good humour
    crumbling the shadows to pieces
no one would know anything and then from the unknowable void
    would emerge heaven and earth
and after scratching his head perhaps perhaps He would write
    in heaven
(in the vast and still heavens)
and would think let there be light with a magnanimous gesture
and would say day night sea star and upon saying man would
    already be drunk with colours

It is no longer a question of names—you tell me—
no longer a question of my eyes or your metaphysical realizations
no longer a question of the moon or any other unexplored planet

It was necessary to throw aside the barrier anyhow it was
    necessary to try to be a man
He would write beneath the newly emerged suns
a tear a glance The Sea The Sky

and a silhouette would grow like a presentiment about his
annoyance and a long stormy silhouette would begin to project itself
knowingly and gucumatz would be terrified and speechless

When you arrived the clocks stopped all at the same minute and
the centuries began to fall from the divine forge
when you arrived there were no trees to hang his shadows from
no mirrors to record his terror no swords no screams no snakes

He would keep silent as always awaiting the tenuous fall of the
stars beating his silver wings while the wind sprang up and he
would speak of the sand decanting itself in the rivers of forms
moving upon the earth of the new awakening amid torrential rains
    and opaque mists
et je poursuivais d'autres songes vers le reveil

(the eyes of Sleep kept watch)
He would go with other gods to guard the sacred ovens where
the black man was born the red man the white man the yellow man
    chou ku tien and altamira
where the golden man was born who would try to replace him
the regions strangely diaphanous the oceans withdrawing
    fertilization advancing
They the silent ones would meditate sadly upon the future
would meditate without days without nights shaping the fight
among the ovens
and the birds would go to and from until they were devoured
and He would write man without much conviction now with some
misgivings and something soft would emerge from the earth
    rising and falling fatigued from the sun and the stones
(without wings but with a certain grace it has since lost)
and something soft would begin to reign dividing into light
and shadow swelling the weeping among the people of the village

This story begins on other continents where other gods died
in chains for men without being able to wonder what for
    what for
and the usurpers the imperialist foreigners would arrive from
the sea side with beasts and red arms and a toad-like appearance
    and large testicles to rape maidens
in other cycles the eagle tortures prometheus the sun rends
the night the gods are fed from the created form and become
    beggars
for the foreigners arrived the earth upside down the sky
turning over the destroyers against father against mother
order must be maintained the dove of peace and other lies
paying no attention to the combatants who cannot help but go on
appearing in history without weeping or suffering or enjoying
    or being happy
He did not want to keep on rolling down the slopes he did not
want to duck his head under the desk littered with papers he did
    not want to wait for the daily alms nor the gesture of contempt

then came the eagle to tear the rags from his body and devour
his liver and the usurpers like gigantic spiders would suck
    his bones tear apart his ideas pour venom upon his language
and he would go out and preach throughout the streets in the
squares the museums the stadiums in the newspapers and the
television channels in the comics and the films of animated
cartoons he would go out and preach the divine virtues of the
    exploiters

then sadness would travel through the dust sadness would travel
through the stars would eat up the trees and the rocks would
travel on the wind through hunger through death the peoples
would be destroyed by the opossum-rats the covetous
in the government would destroy the fire that burned within
    man

for a great space of time the peoples would be destroyed
 men confused floating like beings in a daydream
for a great space of time nobody wanted to descend to the deep
    abysses of Hell

"this is the dead land"
everything was confused everything mixed up

But it is enough to take each other by the hand open the windows
while someone with a cross on his forehead and a hundred bullets
    in his chest crosses america with yataghans and omens
and not in vain his statue of twisted steel
and not in vain the bonfires of human flesh

He would be a flash in the bloody dawn of the peoples and they
    will devour each other
it could be or it could not be
fury would descend upon the jaguar of the people the red tiger
the mountain lion and the clans would be dispersed the throats
would be cut and the cities would be dispersed the summers
    would be dispersed

and sadness will travel through the dust and the stars will
shine out their goodness

He did not want to do it—The Sea The Sky—nor suns nor bullets
nor battles
He would be a flash in the uniform night of the skies and the
usurpers would arrive the imperialist foreigners and they would
    put him in chains in spite of his power to make men smile
Then would come the sinking of the waters and of the skies

This history begins right here at this instant with feet gnawed by
leprosy choosing the words for which they will shoot me agitating
the mangy hands of ho chi minh spitting our false news that
    the newspapers tell like occidental fairyjokes
this history begins with words and ends with a howitzer in the
belly of a child begins with the sons of the first god dead

in ñancahuazú or greenland or in middle east or in saigon
at my back all the days as I raise an eyelid or lower an eyebrow
    as I walk along the promenade or write my doctoral theses
as the beasts hide the fangs beneath the prostituted sun of the
great cities and slink off to their steel lairs

Multiply the gods and the terror
multiply the lives and the guns
multiply the skins that desire to come together the wounds that
desire to open the minutes that desire to give themselves up
    to the new titans

He would write in the sky and would shoot with eyes blinded
by anger no longer god

it was necessary to try to be a man
I will go out and seek you for I have waited too long

It must be done now.

from Las memorias de doña Alma Errante

Francisco Viñuela

She, Doña Alma Errante, widow of a Hapsburg, was able to declare herself in full possession of her faculties, and affirm that her slow decrepitude was in no way due to lack of funds, but rather to a feeling of interior humiliation and the wilting of the desire to live. And as if the mockery of those who ruled the country at that time were not already enough, there was now also the flood of climbing honeysuckle that imprisoned her like a convict behind the walls of her personal colours and dreams, locked into her own mental obstinacy. Then, in what had to be the absolute height of misfortune, in a moment of inattention, some municipal bureaucrat had erased her house number from the inscriptions in the official registers. And on top of that, the sewers had overflowed with the April rains that always shower and had flooded the basement passageways of city hall and wiped out the records that were stored down there, erasing the very last proofs that her mysterious property actually existed. It was thus that she had ended up abandoned to her fate in a ship slowly sinking into flowers, and no one dared come to visit her. The little needles that measured the electricity in that small dark metal machine behind glass as thick as a diver's helmet had burst one quiet morning in a light muffled explosion, and had thereafter been slowly entrapped by the passionate flowers of *Monsieur* de Bougainville, and if perhaps they understood the metaphor, there it was. So neither the kilos of electric hours nor much less, my girl, the cubic metres of water, had ever been counted by anyone. And from there on in, as Papa used to say, everything had entered a state of lethargy like that of a banana republic, though she was sure that the Republic itself had never had either bananas or banana trees, just as it had never had coffee plants or plantations, because the Republic had never been a tropical one, a fact that struck her as perfectly evident. Although it was also clear to her that everything turned out quite differently when the season for corruption came round. All the Republic's platonic ritual had turned into the same old shit. But in spite of everything, she was still sure that this overpowering torpor was due above all to the bees that sucked and buzzed around like crazy in her hanging gardens of Babylon and not to politics nor to that horde of ignoble louts that had come to ruin everything. To make matters worse, she couldn't get to sleep at night either now that those famous spiders that her nephew had brought back from Equatorial Africa had finally gotten loose. She had known it was bound to happen when she'd first seen the damned things. They'd gone straight back to weaving those immense webs of white cotton, making a noise like the clicking of lace-makers' spindles with their abominable little legs. It was enough to give her goose-bumps, and as they worked the spiders probably went off into nostalgic reveries about the Ivory Coast, which they must have missed quite terribly. The encyclopedia had said that their lives were pure sweat and that the fine dust they left was aphrodisiac.

It looked like the saffron rice that Uncle Julio used to wolf down every Saturday night. The problem, my girl, was that the little beasts threw tremendous parties for themselves all night long, eating up the vitamins that they got from the amazing array of fat beetles that they trapped before sundown. But the spiders were hardly her major problem and never had been. Wait till she wrote her History of the Republic and they'd see who was who. Then one day, early on a winter morning long before sunrise and the cold humid fog that later rose up from the seashore, she had pulled open the rusty iron door and slid outside, solitary and furtive, wrapped up in some dresses that had been hidden at the bottom of her tin-plated wardrobe and had thus survived the great fire. She stepped unsteadily over the cobblestones, her legs barely able to support her, not due to illness and of course not to age, as people were surely going to think, my children. She'd been hungry like that for years and with the passing of time had become completely rachitic. Yet in spite of everything, she always went to mass in the morning, albeit to the sunrise service, so that no one would recognize her. And often she didn't even change clothes but just threw one dress over the other, and after mass she'd remain in the darkest corner of the church under the false doric columns next to the basin of holy water. She would stand there holding out her open purse, the same one lined with white antelope that Papa had given her for her first communion, and as people walked out of the gloom they would fill it up with coins that at that time, my girl, were worth as much as gold. She walked like a saint practising levitation, and it was always a great effort for her to struggle up the narrow road that wound up to the smugglers' fort at the top of the hill. Though all that was really left of the smugglers was the name, since they had become antique dealers of great prestige and had had branches of their stores in the great capitals of the continent for years now, as she had been assured by excellent sources with eternally evil tongues. Beneath her dresses she would carry different pieces of rolled-up cloth which were really nothing more than moth-eaten sacking that had at one time been used to cover the saloon cars parked in the old coach houses. The venerable figure of Edmundo Dantés, the king of the smugglers, would wait for her under the arch of the steel door fitted into the stone wall, of which it was said that no one had ever, even in the midst of an armed attack, succeeded in getting over its famous parapet alive. And Don Edmundo had taken her arm, as befitted a gentleman, for he must surely have been the son of a nobleman rather than of a bitch like others in the so-called Platonic Republic whom she already knew too well. And with the help of that strange huge servant boy whom Don Edmundo himself had trained to look like an orang-outang, so that he had even become covered with fur and always made people afraid, Don Edmundo had helped her walk, supporting and guiding her through the darkness of the gardens to the house that rose up above the forest of palm trees at the top of the hill and was protected by a pack of fierce mastiffs made up of over a hundred puma hounds raised on raw meat and trained to hunt mountain lions in the foothills of the cordillera. There they had cloistered themselves to talk about the secrets of the past, in particular about how inhuman her life had been since the death of Felipe, her handsome husband Felipe who she was sure was resting in peace. And it seemed to her that Don Edmundo had clearly understood her personal misery and that he knew about the secret dirty tricks played upon her by the indifferent neighbours who lived in the port in those memorable times. A few days later they had gone down to the city together to legalize the arrangement that Don Edmundo had proposed to her, and that she, Alma Errante, widow of a Hapsburg, had officially accepted before witnesses and in full possession of her mental faculties, although she knew full well that people were certainly going to question the whole thing. And in full possession of a few physical faculties too, for she had been able to recuperate her strength in the space of a few hours due to a vitamin supplement that the orang-outang had put in her food. And what the hell, it had been over thirty years since she had eaten any solid food, not because she couldn't distinguish between *chateaubriand* and *faux filet*, but because she didn't have enough money to pay for them, so much so that it didn't surprise her when even the angora cat took off one day. Don Edmond Dantés, if they preferred it in French, turned over the following assets to Doña Alma Errante, widow, domiciled in Calle de los Libertadores de la República, no number: a five-story rental apartment building, located on Avenida de los Héroes de la Batalla, together with the assurance of its usufruct until three days following her death, valid for her and her inheritors. And she, for her part, ceded complete rights to some old manuscripts found in the carriage house of Rocinante, the family horse, at the bottom of a manure pile that they knew was no longer needed. She also surrendered ownership to him of a cloth scroll that was nothing more than a bit of old jute with pyrographs, a work made in some foreign country with inscriptions in the Gothic language and on one side of which you could see a painting, most certainly done in oils, and not lacklustre ones either, but in actual artist's oils, and she repeated this so that it would be quite clear, in which you could see a city in the background, with a sky of black ink and some gentlemen with capes and swords that always impressed her on account of the clear colour of their porcelain faces underneath the grime covering the painting itself. Now under that peeling varnish you could barely read the signatures and one of them was that of someone named Vermeer. And Don Edmundo had taken it with white gloves, as if it were made of crystal. In any case, all these goings-on had kept her from paying attention to her appearance, though nobody recognized her two weeks later as she came down from the heights of Valparaíso, which weren't exactly those of Machu Picchu, but simply those of the hills surrounding the port. Good listeners need few words, my girl. She had descended wrapped in an otter stole, swaying like Veronica Lake beneath a lovely blond wig. Fresh and cool, with all kinds of unguents and balms from the Salon Madame Bovary and dressed in the latest European style that had come over with the fashion magazines that year, which, if she weren't mistaken, had been the last of the thirties. Then she had lived surrounded by the respect that everyone said they had never really lost for her, and when she needed anything she would simply ask Edmundo by sending him a note via the mastodon, who, though he never spoke a word, was nevertheless a specialist in delivering messages and performing heavy tasks, so that one could say that he and Don Edmundo had indeed helped the needy, like in the Bible, and had soothed her sharpest pains. And if one day she were to die unexpectedly, which was perfectly possible, it had already been worked out with the parish that from that day on there would be piles of flowers in the Chapel of the Virgin and pre-paid masses *ad aeternam* and without a thought to the cost, as she had specifically requested, until they were sure that her soul had succeeded in entering Paradise and had met Papa's and that the two of them had fused together into one. She was sure that things were done differently up there in the immensity of the cosmos, and she was clearly obliged to specify the word "cosmos" now that thanks to this mania for changing the names of things they had altered the name of heaven itself, which heavens knew she had known ever since she was a child.

Wanderers in the Mandala

Ludwig Zeller

Days prolong themselves upon a well's stone mouth of ants
Lightning accumulates in the downfall of the mastiff and you finally remember
That no one can return and you sharpen knives under the tents
When the day stretches in strips of skin
Conceal yourself to laugh to swallow within your lips
That ferocious gesture the striking of irons upon the sea
Now that the tomb and the wilted cracking of echoes
Seems to be the final season the rain of pebbles roaring
And falling towards that hungry and devouring river from beat
To beat the distant splendour of bonfires and the barking of dogs
On the gallows the day dangles in its cage of horror

Is it this they call wheel? Pestilence! Call it
Visitation of crows and the sleepers come
As if surging from carnivorous furniture at the time of the night hunt
Carrying behind them the enormous black tail of the dead fish
The whale that the sea brought to my life's beach
And we burned it day after day like fleas under the rancid stench of the oil
And in our insanity and wickedness we blasted it with dynamite and the stench
Spread over the cliffs finally its heavy stumps exploded
And like sour fruits the pieces fell upon us
What did we get from it all? Only wretchedness under the face smeared
With shame in a long infinite waiting for the wind to change
And sweep away at last so much carrion so much rotten blubber
And the remainders vomited by the sea we dragged inland
The animals resisted it but the engine knows neither asphalt
Nor fear and its soul answers only to exact emptiness

And so like someone hunting by night protected by darkness
We went dragging the rotten bones but our nights
Were blacker still under the tarred canvas because we had
Seen chance and we knew its eyes were on us
And hastily like criminals we tried to bury evil
Under the soil removed by the tempest there where drunkards
Sing against their fate we left the great vertebrae and returned

But the noise of the water kept breaking in the gully of the eye
Within the ear. This I said and now I repeat it
In a game of dice: Here are we prisoners of Chance?

Small children we cry in darkness moving our rags
In the dust my God, what atrocious loneliness! what bitterness
To live with that memory with all memory of love embalmed
If we cannot cross the canal the boundary and finally see
Eye to eye the dreamed presence the blue hilt holding
The leaves of reality and the thousand simultaneous realities
Unison like a howl or an interminable blaze
That noise of needles whistling of boilers at the point of bursting

But they who were mine turned their horses back not for grass or forage
But for anxiety scrutinizing the heavens advancing in the open folds
Of the south where the wall of mist rises
Cascade of tears running surrounding us in desperation
Among the linden branches the invisible wind

Thirst throbs and panting seaweed of dream covers us
Blue images on the altar of felt the bodies reaped
Abandoned in the night lunar stones forgotten
In another life another conjugation when the line of verse
Is read from above downwards like a knife-edge through sacrificial bodies
Or is repeated ceremonially in ropes knotted under the earth

Then the boatman chews the dry morsel and whistles
On the jetty where the final waters break
Because we are only images painted on paper
Smudged dirty and carried by the wind to the bonfire
And someone takes the oars then in the night
Cursing spitting into his palms because ours is
This fate and not other different dreams
And we must cross the water the darkness and the fog
When the passengers huddle to embark like frightened animals
Whirled by hoarse bugles against barbed wire
And someone who still wants to come aboard is thrust into the waters
And shouts in the stillness and with his hands clutches the bleeding oar
That strikes him.

Go back! Go back!
Another world is superimposed on yours other images
On the present ones and we are rocking in the water
Our memory is pared the earth is worn away by salt
(Land of the howling wind they called it) but our minds
Are closed and our life is the door of a tomb
Through which we go down forward into the unknown
Black flow where we hear the gadfly's noise
And time passes over our bones creases the skin

Changes the sheen of the eye

You pulsing guitar stop time
Tell me of those who dream under the dust
Of syllables that double and the echoes that migrate from this world to the other
Describe for me the interior of the forehead where fever
Kindles its red crest and climbs like a sparkling rocket
Ready to fall in the dead of night we cross a lake
Which is her eyes the black lignite of the stream her thoughts
The thundering call of cascades her heart leather
Bellows that throb like a strange invisible clock of eternities
Let me only remember now to be that flower
Of silence between two great hecatombs

Why do you laugh sphinx why does the echo break on the stairs
And the glass on the harpoon of your gaze not allow man to see
How in the great scab the scar is braided with burnt blood?
White and black and purple we go forward
Another step and already we are in the bonfire kindled
For so many centuries because I know that you are and I am nothing
But the smoke of tinder with which we are blinded in torment
Dogs worse than dogs under the bishop's staff
The sentence flutters. Burn them! and the tar
That now goes by another name or the hospital for sickening
The mind of the dispossessed and the State that is God
Beyond a doubt and if you don't believe the cobra's poison will make you believe

How long will we remain on the same rack
On the same edges of pain growing perforating
The heart's tissues because man is so fragile
That he does not resist scattering his bones etching
The sentence on his back as with Kafka's old
Machine where the eternal prisoner vomits the acrid pap
Of torment the portentous machine multiplied
To the third degree and the blood drying on the waterfalls of thirst
First only form of love broken
With eyes turning towards the cracks of the moon
With razor thrusts we go cane-cutters we strike with the edge
Have mercy have mercy my head aches aches
The interior of the cranial form a bomb ready to explode
To be fire once and for all whirlpool of flames
Scattering the Word in a new religion of fierce automatic love
Knives of poetry in the spiral of lava when the rain
Stealthy serpent of heat rises in a shudder
Of green light and falls on the rope tied to the cudgel that strikes it

Not by water by fire we are consumed and we bury
Our Fathers under the embers inscription in sunspots
The feet stumble among idols and bones but the mind does not rest
When beneath the royal blue rainbow the rain lodges
Beginning and end of all hollow centres the blood intermingles
With flour that falls from the side of the *huaco-lady*

Mistress of a hundred rivers they call her lady of a hundred rivers is her name
You the giver of tears listen to us six feet under
The earth we call you we come singing we come
Clamouring from forever the seeds of the poem beneath our tongue
Make the verse grow macerated by the teeth chewed
By injustice the grinding spider in that centre
From which the light springs. We listen for you in the dark
We have waited for you a thousand years, where are we now?
                                        Our heart grows
Like rivers flung downhill giving birth to the phantom
That you call life but in the immense spiral we are only
Wanderers passing through the signs the glaciation of memories
Where your images are superimposed on the papyrus of solitude

Bewitchment of the falcon a bird of metal pecking in vertigo
Rust of the downfall when the bones split from top to bottom
That bristling edge of lamps in the vital delta of illusion
The cold and total peace of that new waiting where the wheat
Starts to gush again breaking the thousand cubes covered with stamens
And the being of a thousand eyes the one that gives birth to images rehearses again
The forgotten song of a sun warm body heaved up in ridges
By the foam that even beneath the shadow will go on dreaming us.

Notes on the Authors

Alison Acker taught at Ryerson in Toronto and has worked and travelled extensively in Central America. She has published *Children of the Volcano* and is at work on her first novel, *Gringa*. She lives in Victoria, B.C.

Tito Alvarado is a Chilean poet who has lived both in Winnipeg and Montreal, where he is editor of the Latin American cultural review, *Sur*. His fourth book, *Poema de Santiago*, was published in 1990. Translator, Hugh Hazelton.

Margaret Atwood has published widely as a poet, novelist, and critic. Her works include *Selected Poems*, *Bodily Harm*, and *The Handmaid's Tale*, recently made into a film. She lives in Toronto and is active in P.E.N.

Robert Baillie is a *québécois* poet and prose writer who lives outside Montreal. He has published five novels, including *Les Voyants*, which is set largely in Brazil. His latest novel, *La Nuit de la Saint-Basile*, appeared in 1990. Translator, Hugh Hazelton.

Rafael Barreto-Rivera is a Toronto poet and performer and one of the founding members of *The Four Horsemen*. The work included here is from *Voices*.

Hernán Barrios is a Chilean fiction writer who won first prize in the University of Alberta Competition of 1987. A collection of his stories, *Landed Immigrant*, was published in Chile in 1990. Translator, Hugh Hazelton.

Claude Beausoleil, poet, songwriter, editor and critic, lives in Montreal. His twenty published works reflect his continuing interest in the world of Quebec letters and in Latin America. He has recently edited an anthology of Mexican poetry, the first of its kind to appear in Quebec. Translator, Hugh Hazelton.

Henry Beissel, well-known as a poet, playwright, and translator, teaches at Concordia University and lives in Eastern Ontario. His works include *Under Coyote's Eye*, *Season of Blood*, and *The Noose and Improvisations for Mr. X*.

Earle Birney, the first Canadian poet to write extensively about Latin America, is the author of many books of poetry, fiction, and criticism, including *Turvey*, *The Collected Poems of Earle Birney*, and *The Creative Writer*. He resides in Toronto.

Hédi Bouraoui was born in Tunisia, but now lives in Toronto, where he teaches French and English literature at York University. He has written extensively on Third World francophone literature and has also published ten volumes of poetry and edited an anthology of Franco-Ontarian writing. Translator, Hugh Hazelton.

Nicole Brossard is a novelist, poet, playwright, and essayist who has had a great impact on feminist and intertextual writing both in Quebec and English Canada. Author of over twenty books and winner of numerous awards, she is now preparing a new anthology of poetry by women in Quebec. Translator, Hugh Hazelton.

Colin Browne is a Vancouver poet, film-maker, and teacher at Simon Fraser University. He founded *Writing* magazine and is the author of *Abraham* and the producer-director of *White Lake*.

Jorge Cancino is a Chilean film-maker and writer who lived for many years in Argentina and now resides in Montreal. He has published two bilingual volumes of poetry and is editor of the literary review *La botella verde*. Translator, Hugh Hazelton.

Paul Chamberland has been writing poetry and essays since the early '60s. As a founding member of *Parti Pris*, political commitment has always been a cornerstone of his work. Many of his twenty published works also deal with aspects of the erotic and metaphysics. Translator, Hugh Hazelton.

Leonard Cohen is a poet and novelist who is internationally known as a folk-singer. He lives in Montreal and New York. His works include *Beautiful Losers*, *Death of A Lady's Man*, and *Book of Mercy*.

Jan Conn is a poet and entomologist who has lived and worked in South and Central America. Her books include *Red Shoes*, *The Fabulous Disguise of Ourselves*, and *South of the Tudo Bem Café*.

Lorna Crozier, a well-known Saskatchewan poet, has travelled widely and published several volumes of poetry, including *Crow's Black Joy*, *The Garden Going On Without Us*, and *Angels of Flesh, Angels of Silence*. She lives in Saskatoon.

Cyril Dabydeen is an Ottawa poet and civil servant, whose work includes *Distances*, *Islands Lovelier Than A Vision*, and *Coastland: New and Selected Poems*.

Antonio d'Alfonso lives in Montreal, where he is the publisher of Guernica Editions. His books include *La chanson du shaman à Sedna*, *Queror*, and *Black Tongue*.

Jean-Paul Daoust is a *québécois* poet and essayist who has published eleven books of poetry, including *Black Diva* and *Poèmes de Babylone*. He is an editor of the literary review *Estuaire* and travelled extensively in Latin America in 1989-90. Translator, Hugh Hazelton.

Nelly Davis Vallejo came to Canada from Santiago, Chile, in 1973. She has published five collections of poetry in Spanish and one in French. She returned to Chile in 1990 to take part in the reconstruction of the country. Translator, Hugh Hazelton.

Mary di Michele lives in Montreal and teaches at Concordia University. She has published several volumes of poetry, including *Necessary Sugar*, *Mimosa and Other Poems*, and *Immune to Gravity*.

Louis Dudek has had a distinguished career as a teacher at McGill University and as a poet and essayist. He was a founding editor of DC Books and has published numerous books, including *The Collected Poems of Louis Dudek*, *Zembla's Rocks*, and *Continuations I & II*.

Claudio Durán is a Chilean writer who teaches philosophy and social sciences at York University. His books include *Homenaje* and *Mas tarde que los clientes habituales/ After the Usual Clients Have Gone Home*. Translator, Rafael Barreto-Rivera.

Jorge Etcheverry came to Canada from Chile in the 1970s and settled in Ottawa, where he was one of the founders of Cordillera Editions. A painter and illustrator as well as a prolific writer, he works in both Spanish and English. He co-edited *Enjambres: Poesía latinoamericana en Quebec* with Daniel Inostrosa. Translator, Hugh Hazelton.

Gilberto Flores Patiño was born in Celaya, near Guanajuato, Mexico, and now lives in Montreal. He has published five novels in Spanish, one of which also appeared in French. His latest book, *Le Pégase de cristal*, is a collection of short stories for young people published in French by Les Editions Boréal. Translator, Hugh Hazelton.

Hugh Garner was born in England and raised in Toronto's Cabbagetown, which is the title of one of his novels. His works include an autobiography, *One Damn Thing After Another*, several novels, and a host of stories, gathered in *Hugh Garner's Best Stories*.

Gary Geddes, born in Vancouver, is a poet, editor, and anthologist who lives in Eastern Ontario and teaches at Concordia University. His works include *No Easy Exit / Salida difícil*, *Letters from Managua: Meditations on Politics and Art*, and *Light of Burning Towers: Poems New & Selected*.

Susan Glickman is a poet, critic, and teacher who lives in Toronto. Her works include *Complicity*, *The Power to Move*, and *Henry Moore's Sheep and Other Poems*.

Rodrigo González is a Chilean playwright who grew up in Puerto Aysén, Patagonia. He has written and produced over ten plays in French and Spanish in Canada. A bilingual book of his Zen stories for children will be published in 1991. Translator, Hugh Hazelton.

Dennis Gruending, a Regina writer and journalist who co-hosted The Morning Show on C.B.C. radio, is the author of *Gringo,* a book about travels in Latin America, *Emmett Hall (Establishment Radical)* and a biography of Alan Blakeney called *Promises to Keep*. He is currently living in Ottawa.

Claire Harris is a poet and linguist, who lives and teaches in Calgary. She is the author of *Fables from the Women's Quarters, Conception of Winter*, and *Gathering to Parturition*.

Hugh Hazelton is a writer and translator who moved from Chicago to Montreal in 1969. He has published three books of poetry, including *Crossing the Chaco,* a poetic diary of two years' travels in Latin America, and has co-edited several anthologies of Latin American writers of Quebec, both in Spanish and French.

Daniel Inostrosa is a Chilean writer and editor who spent many years as a merchant seaman in Europe and the Americas. He has published a volume of poetry and recently edited *Poemas tras las rejas,* a collection of poetry by women political prisoners in Chile. He is currently at work on a novel. Translator, Hugh Hazelton.

Eucilda Jorge Morelos was born in the Dominican Republic. She went to Cuba to teach in the 1950s and lived there during the Cuban Revolution and the reconstruction of the '60s and '70s. Two volumes of her short stories have been published in Santo Domingo. She now lives in Montreal. Translation, Hugh Hazelton.

Lionel Kearns is a poet and linguist who lives in Vancouver. His works include *Pointing, By the Light of the Silvery McLuhan,* and *Ignoring the Bomb: New & Selected Poems.*

Lesley Kruger is a fiction writer who has lived and travelled extensively in Central and South America. Her first book, *Hard Travels,* was published in 1990.

Jacques Lanctôt is a *québécois* poet whose participation in the FLQ led to his subsequent exile to Cuba and France after the October Crisis of 1970. He is now literary editor of the publishing house VLB Editeur in Montreal. Translator, Hugh Hazelton.

Patrick Lane grew up in the interior of British Columbia, but now lives in Saskatoon. His numerous works include *Unborn Things, Poems New and Selected,* and *Old Mother.*

Paul-Marie Lapointe is a Montreal poet who worked for years for Radio-Canada. His works include *Le Vierge Incendie* and *Tableaux de l'amoureuse.* Translation, D.G. Jones (from *The Terror of the Snows*).

Alfredo Lavergne came to Quebec from Valparaíso, Chile, in 1974, and has published eight volumes of poetry. His latest work, *Las manos en la velocidad,* is made up of poetic meditations as he worked on the General Motors assembly line in Ste. Thérèse, Quebec. Translator, Hugh Hazelton.

David Lawson has published poetry, fiction, and criticism. He was born in the U.S., is a long-time resident of Montreal, and is currently teaching in Xian, China.

Elias Letelier-Ruz came to Montreal from Chile via Halifax. His first publication in English is *Symphony.*

Micheline Lévesque is a *québécoise* short story writer and poet who also works in collage and multi-media performance, often blending different artistic genres. She is currently writing a novel, *Punzante,* set in Central America. Translator, Hugh Hazelton.

Maeve López was born in Uruguay, but travelled extensively throughout Latin America in the 1970s, after which she settled in Montreal. She has published two books of poetry, *Grito con espejo* and *Apenas un caballo,* and is presently spending a year in Venezuela. Translator, Hugh Hazelton.

Malcolm Lowry was born in England and lived for several years in Mexico before settling near Vancouver to write. His published works include *Ultramarine, Under the Volcano,* and *October Ferry to Gabriola.*

Pat Lowther lived and wrote in Vancouver. Her publications include *This Difficult Flowering*, *Milkstone* and *A Stone Diary*.

Joan MacNeil lives and writes in Toronto.

Marilú Mallet is a writer and film-maker from Santiago whose works include *Voyage to the Other Extreme* (short fiction) and *Il n'y a pas d'oublie* (film). She teaches in the Department of Cinema at Laval University. Translation by Alan Brown.

Eli Mandel is a poet, critic, and Professor of English at York University in Toronto. His influential works include *Stony Plain*, *Life Sentence*, and *Dreaming Backwards: The Selected Poetry of Eli Mandel*.

Daphne Marlatt is a Vancouver poet, fiction writer, and journalist who teaches at Capilano College. Her works include *Vancouver Poems*, *Zócalo*, and *Net Work / Selected Writing*.

George McWhirter was born in Northern Ireland, but has spent most of his professional life in Vancouver, where he teaches at University of British Columbia. His published works include *Catalan Poems*, *Cage*, and a translation of *The Selected Works of José Amilio Pacheco*.

Gonzalo Millán is a Chilean poet and recipient of the Pablo Neruda Prize. He lived in the Maritimes and Ottawa and was active in the Cordillera publishing collective. His works include *Vida*, *Virus*, and *La Cuidad*. He currently resides in Rotterdam.

Erin Mouré lives in Montreal. She is the author of numerous books, including *Wanted Alive*, *Empire*, *York Street*, and *Furious*.

Naín Nómez is a Chilean poet and critic who spent several years of exile in Canada, but now resides in Santiago. His works include *Burning Bridges* and *Historias del reino vigilado / Stories of A Guarded Kingdom*. Translator, Christina Shantz.

Emile Ollivier was born in Haiti and emigrated to Canada in 1966. *La Mère solitude*, the third of his five novels, was published in France by Albin Michel and received wide acclaim. It was published in English as *Mother Solitude* in 1989. Translation by David Lobdell.

P.K. Page is the author of numerous works of poetry, fiction, and memoirs, including *The Glass Air: Selected Poems*, *The Sun and the Moon and Other Fictions*, and *Brazilian Journal*. Page, who lives in Victoria, is also an accomplished visual artist.

Luis Pérez Botero was born in Colombia in 1922 and is Professor Emeritus at the University of Saskatchewan. His novel, *Ulises in Sabanilla*, and his short stories have been well-received in the Hispanic world, particularly in Spain. Translation, Dale P. Kirk.

Anthony Phelps is a Haitian poet, novelist, playwright and essayist who immigrated to Canada in 1964. He has worked in theatre and film and has also published twelve books, eight of them poetry. His *La Bélière caraïbe* won the poetry prize of the Casa de las Americas in Cuba in 1980. Translator, Hugh Hazelton.

Joel Pourbaix is a Montreal poet with a deep interest in comparative mythology and archeology who has travelled extensively in Mexico and Europe. He has published four books of poetry and is currently at work on a text set in Quebec, Ireland and Portugal that blends poetry and the novel. Translator, Hugh Hazelton.

Al Purdy, who lives in Ameliasburg, Ontario, is a well-known poet, anthologist, and traveller, whose many works include *The Cariboo Horses, The Poems of Al Purdy,* and *Piling Blood.*

Alfonso Quijada Urías grew up in El Salvador and now lives in Vancouver, B.C. Several books of his short stories and poems have been published in El Salvador and Honduras, and his work has appeared widely in magazines and anthologies in Mexico and the United States. A collection of his poetry, *And They Knocked the Door Down,* will be published by Curbstone Press of New York in 1991. Translator, Hugh Hazelton.

Luc Racine is a *québécois* poet and anthropologist whose long poem about the Americas, *Le Pays saint,* combines his studies of ancient Mexican civilizations with his own personal political commitment. An early co-editor of *Parti pris,* he has published four other collections of poetry and three volumes of essays.

Lake Sagaris was born in Toronto and lives in Santiago, Chile, where she works as a journalist for *The Times, The Globe & Mail,* and C.B.C. Radio. Her publications include poetry, *Exile Home / exilio en la patria,* and *Circus Love,* as well as translations of Canadian poetry and fiction.

Peter Dale Scott grew up in Montreal and now teaches at the University of California at Berkeley. He is the author of numerous works, including *The Politics of Escalation in Vietnam, The Assassinations: Dallas and Beyond,* and *Coming to Jakarta.*

Jim Smith is a Toronto poet and activist who spent considerable time in Nicaragua. His published works include *Virus, One Hundred Most Frightening Things,* and *Convincing Americans.*

Ricardo de Silveira Lobo Sternberg is a Professor of Brazilian Literature in the Centre for Comparative Literature at the University of Toronto.

Rosemary Sullivan lives in Toronto and teaches at Erindale College of the University of Toronto. Her publications include a book on Theodore Roethke, the anthology *Stories by Canadian Women,* and *The Space A Name Makes.*

Fraser Sutherland, a freelance writer from Nova Scotia, was a founding editor of *Northern Journey.* His works include *Whitefaces, Madwoman,* and *The Style of Innocence,* a study of Hemingway.

George Szanto lives in Montreal and is a Professor of Comparative Literature and Communications at McGill University. His publications include *Not Working, Duets,* and *The Underside of Stones.* The story included here won the National Magazine Award.

Naomi Thiers' work has appeared in *The Colorado Review, The Pacific Review,* and *The Dry Wells of India.* She lives in Washington, D.C.

Salvador Torres left his native El Salvador in the early 1980s and has since lived in Mexico and Canada. His first bilingual book of poetry, *Dieuseries et odieuseries* won the Prix Humanitas in 1989 and his short stories and poetry have appeared in many anthologies in Quebec and El Salvador. Translator, Hugh Hazelton.

Larry Towell is a poet and photo journalist who has worked and travelled extensively in India and Central America. His publications include *Burning Cadillacs, Gifts of War,* and *Somoza's Last Stand.*

Renato Trujillo is a Chilean writer and musician (Los Quincha Malas) who came to Montreal in the early '70s. He writes in English and his books include *Behind the Orchestra* and *Milongas for Prince Arthur Street.*

Yvonne América Truque grew up in Bogotá, Colombia, where her father was a well-known writer and literary critic. She has lived in Quebec for the past ten years and has published several collections of poetry. She won the poetry prize of *Humanitas* magazine in 1987. Translator, Hugh Hazelton.

Pablo Urbanyi is an Argentinian of Hungarian descent who has lived in Ottawa for the past twenty years. His satirical novel *En ninguna parte* appeared in Buenos Aires in 1981 and was subsequently published by Williams-Wallace in Canada as *The Nowhere Idea.* Translator, Hugh Hazelton.

José Leandro Urbina is a Chilean writer and film-maker who makes his permanent home in Ottawa, where he was active as a founding editor of Cordillera Editions. He has published works, including *Las malas juntas,* which was published in English as *Lost Causes.* Translator, Christina Shantz.

Edith Velásquez Prado grew up in Venezuela and has lived in Miami and Montreal. She has written numerous short stories, poems, and filmscripts in both Spanish and English. *Una comedia no muy divina* is her first novel. Translator, Hugh Hazelton.

Yolande Villemaire is the author of five novels, eight books of poetry, and a play. Though she is from Montreal, she has also travelled extensively in South America and Asia and is presently living outside of Bombay, India. Her latest book of poems, *Quartz et mica* has been translated into English by Judith Cowan Translator, Hugh Hazelton.

Francisco Viñuela is a Chilean who has lived in Montreal since the mid-1970s, where he has published two bilingual collections of poems. *Las memorias de doña Alma Errante,* his second novel, was published by Ediciones Documentas in Chile in 1990. Translator, Hugh Hazelton.

Tom Wayman lives in Vancouver, where he works as a writer and labour activist. His works include *Waiting for Wayman, Money and Rain,* and *In A Small House on the Outskirts of Heaven.*

Phyllis Webb lives on Saltspring Island, British Columbia, from which she makes occasional forays to teach and travel. Her works include *Talking*, *Wilson's Bowl*, and *The Vision Tree: Selected Poems*.

Patrick White was raised on Vancouver Island, but lives and works in the Ottawa Valley, where he runs Anthos Books and hosts an arts programme for radio. His works include *Homage to Victor Jara*, *Orpheus on Highbeam*, and *Habitable Planets: Poems New and Selected*.

Paul Wilson lives in Regina, where he is programme Director for the Saskatchewan Writers' Guild. His first published book is *The Fire Garden*.

George Woodcock is one of Canada's foremost men of letters, whose works range from the classic study, *Anarchism*, and the award-winning biography of George Orwell, *The Crystal Spirit*, to numerous collections of poetry, criticism, social history, and travel. He lives in Vancouver.

Ronald Wright is a writer and broadcaster, who was born in England and lives in Port Hope, Ontario. His works include *Cut Stones and Crossroads*, *On Fiji Islands*, and *Time Among the Maya*.

Ludwig Zeller, born in the Atacama desert of Chile, is a surrealist poet and visual artist who moved to Toronto in the early 1970s. He has published over a dozen books of poetry, often illustrated by himself or others, and has cooperated on a variety of projects with artists from Europe and Latin America.

Acknowledgements

ACKER, Alison, from Children *of the Volcano*: copyright, the author and Lawrence Hill & Co.

ALVARADO,Tito, from *Geografía heroica*: copyright, the author, translator, and Editorial La Alborada.

ATWOOD, Margaret, from The Collected Poems of Margaret Atwood: copyright, the author and Oxford University Press.

BAILLIE, Robert, *Les voyants*: copyright, the author and Editions de l'Hexagone.

BARRETO-RIVERA, Rafael, from *Voices:* copyright, the author and Coach House Press.

BARRIOS, Hernán: copyright, the author and translator.

BEAUSOLEIL,Claude, from *Extase et déchire*: copyright, the author, translator, and Ecrits de Forges.

BEISSEL, Henry, from *Season of Blood*: copyright, the author and Mosaic Press.

BIRNEY, Earle, all poems copyright the author and McClelland & Stewart.

BOURAOUI, Hédi, from *Haïtois, suivi de Antillades*: copyright, the author and Editions Nouvelles Optique.

BROSSARD, Nicole, from *Estuaire*: copyright, the author.

BROWNE, Colin: copyright, the author.

CANCINO, Jorge, from *Juglario*: copyright, the author and Les éditions Omelic.

CHAMBERLAND, Paul: copyright, the author.

COHEN, Leonard: copyright, the author and McClelland & Stewart.

CONN, Jan: copyright, the author and Véhicule Press.

CROZIER, Lorna: copyright, the author and McClelland & Stewart.

DABYDEEN, Cyril: copyright, the author.

D'ALFONSO, Antonio, from *Black Tongue*: copyright, the author and Guernica Editions.

DAOUST, Jean-Paul: copyright, the author.

DAVIS VALLEJO, Nelly, from *La forastera*: copyright, the author. "For Francisco", from Ediciones Océano.

DI MICHELE, Mary: copyright, the author and Oberon Press.

DUDEK, Louis, from *En México*: copyright, the author.

DURAN, Claudio: copyright, the author.

ETCHEVERRY, Jorge: copyright, the author.

FLORES PATINO, Gilberto, from *El último descendiente*: copyright, the author and Editions Gernika.

GARNER, Hugh, from "Violation of the Virgins": copyright, McGraw-Hill Ryerson and the Hugh Garner Estate.

GEDDES, Gary, from *No Easy Exit / Salida difícil* and *Light of Burning Towers*: copyright, the author and Oolichan Books.

GLICKMAN, Susan: copyright, the author and Véhicule Press.

GONZALEZ, Rodrigo: copyright, the author.

GRUENDING, Dennis, from *Gringo*: copyright, the author and Coteau Books.

HARRIS, Claire, from *Fables from the Women's Quarters*: copyright, the author and Williams-Wallace Publishers.

HAZELTON, Hugh: copyright, the author, and White Dwarf.

INOSTROSA, Daniel, from *De Ausencias y retornos*: copyright, the author.